Praise for
Rethinking Retention in Good Times and Bad
and Dick Finnegan

"Worried about talent walking out the door? Finnegan offers fresh thinking for solving the turnover problem in any economy."

—*Patricia O'Connell, Management Editor,* BusinessWeek

"The Zappos culture is based on the dedication of our employees to our core values. Finnegan's book provides straightforward tactics and best practices that can be useful for companies looking to hold on to the dedication and enthusiasm of their employees."

—*Tony Hsieh, CEO, Zappos.com*

"Dick Finnegan is a true expert on turnover. I have worked with Dick for over twenty years and turnover has been his passion. He understands what causes it, and, more importantly, what individual effective steps a company can take based on its culture to reduce it."

—*Mary Steele, Director of Executive Compensation, Delta Airlines*

"Dick Finnegan definitely has his finger on the pulse of what it takes to retain top talent. Even in today's declining economy, top performers can and will walk out the door if their job isn't meeting their career expectations. Dick is insightful in his assessment of why people leave and what it takes to retain them. The seven retention strategies he has developed have true merit and are right on the money."

—*Dennis P. Gilhooley Sr., CPIM, Associate Partner Public Sector Supply Chain, IBM Global Business Services*

"Dick Finnegan's new book **Rethinking Retention in Good Times and Bad** is a timely publication. While retaining your best employees is always important for every business enterprise, today's difficult economy makes this book a must-read. Full of practical, useful advice, this book can put you to work today to improve retention of your most valued employees. It not only shows you where to look to identify retention problems in your organization, it guides you through the steps for developing the strategies and tactics tailored to meet your company's specific needs. This is not a book just for HR professionals—anyone who manages people will benefit from the insights presented here."

—John E. Sutton, Senior Vice President, Mercury Insurance Group

"Keeping and engaging your best employees—and avoiding the debilitating costs of turnover—are imperatives in today's challenging and ever-changing economy. This book will show you how. Dick Finnegan writes like he speaks—with insight, focus, and clarity—and he will leave you with the understanding and tools you need to systemically tackle this important topic in your own organization."

—Brad Cleveland, Senior Advisor and Former President /
CEO, International Customer Management Institute (ICMI)

"In the quick service restaurant industry, retention is a key metric. **Rethinking Retention in Good Times and Bad** provides real insight, and most importantly, processes that are proven to work across industries. This work clearly moves what was once the realm of well-intentioned HR programs into business-level strategies that rank right up there with the other top-down processes that drive our businesses—like sales, service, and profit."

—John Kelley, Vice President Team Member Services, White Castle

"If you're serious about reducing employee turnover, read this book. Dick Finnegan has written an eminently practical book based on his deep experience and hard-won wisdom. He knows that a top-down, management-owned process is what works, and he has provided the road map."

—Leigh Branham, author of The 7 Hidden Reasons Employees Leave

"This book makes a fresh and compelling case for a beefier talent retention model that is built on the very foundation of *any* business—process, strategy, and outcomes. It is relevant and timely in the healthcare industry, as opportunities and threats today converge to create a powerful opening for HR leaders to impact core business drivers. With all due respect to t-shirts, coffee mugs, and pizza parties as "retention strategies," Finnegan's work is a rare example of sound theory meeting pragmatic, easily implemented tactics."

—*Doug Dean, CCP, SPHR, Chief Human Resource Officer, Children's Health System, Birmingham, AL*

"***Rethinking Retention in Good Times and Bad*** is very practical, thought-provoking and, I have to admit, occasionally aggravating...as in, 'Why didn't I think of that?!' Dick Finnegan has blended solid research with his extensive personal experience and an entertaining writing style to produce a terrific resource full of ideas we can use TODAY to start improving retention. If we'd had this book earlier, maybe Dick would still be with our company!"

—*Mimi Breeden, Director of Human Resources, SunTrust Banks, Inc.*

"Dick Finnegan has expanded and deepened the thought process for leaders in the quest to develop employee retention strategies. His book ventures beyond the traditional first-response approaches and with sound data, presents a true value proposition for retention. ***Rethinking Retention in Good Times and Bad*** is a thought-provoking yet practical guide that leaders in all types of organizations and in all industries can use."

—*Evelyn J. Pulliam, Vice President, Employment, Compensation, & Benefits, SYSCO*

"Retention is keeping the CEO up at night, and the insomnia is about to get worse. Dick Finnegan's new book is just the prescription."

—*RD Whitney, CEO of Tarsus Online Media and ONREC*

Rethinking Retention

in Good Times and Bad

Breakthrough Ideas for
Keeping Your Best Workers

RICHARD P. FINNEGAN

SOCIETY FOR HUMAN
RESOURCE MANAGEMENT

DAVIES-BLACK
AN IMPRINT OF NICHOLAS BREALEY PUBLISHING
BOSTON • LONDON

First published by Davies-Black, an imprint of Nicholas Brealey Publishing, in 2010.

20 Park Plaza, Suite 1115A

3-5 Spafield Street, Clerkenwell

Boston, MA 02116, USA

London, EC1R 4QB, UK

Tel: + 617-523-3801

Tel: +44-(0)-207-239-0360

Fax: + 617-523-3708

Fax: +44-(0)-207-239-0370

www.nicholasbrealey.com

Special discounts on bulk quantities of Davies-Black books are available to corporations, professional associations, and other organizations. For details, contact us at 888-273-2539.

Printed in the United States of America

14 13 12 11 10   10 9 8 7 6 5 4 3 2 1

ISBN: 978-0-89106-238-7

Library of Congress Cataloging-in-Publication Data

Finnegan, Richard P.
   Rethinking retention : in good times and bad breakthrough ideas for keeping your best workers / Richard P. Finnegan.
      p. cm.
   Includes bibliographical references and index.
   ISBN 978-0-89106-238-7
   1. Employee retention.   2. Personnel management.   3. Labor turnover.   I. Title.
   HF5549.5.R58F56 2010
   658.3'14—dc22

2009033109

*For human resources professionals and managers I've known
who've struggled with high employee turnover.
All of your good ideas are here.*

*To my life-long best buddies who coached me for a decade to write
this book. Thanks for making my life better, in good times and bad.*

*And special thanks to my family who share love and support for
their guy who loves his work.*

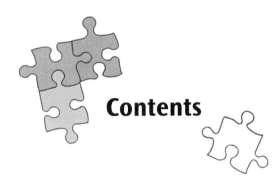

Contents

Appendix C
2007 vs 2008 Voluntary Quits and Job Openings
by Private Industry 263

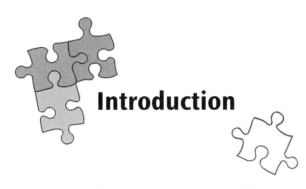

Introduction

The Lesson of
the Three Ps

A few years ago I was invited by a major global consulting firm to facilitate training for a new initiative. The sessions took place in New York, London, and Paris, and included top managers for all locations across the earth.

The opening exercise addressed "the three Ps" by asking this question: As you work with clients to reengineer their organizations, which is most important—people, products, or processes? The managers were assigned to groups of six and given forty-five minutes to construct their winning arguments.

My role during this exercise was "observer," and for the first session we as observers had not been told the correct answer in advance. The New York session was my first exposure to this exercise. There I saw people rushing to flip charts, talking over each other, and presenting snap-thinking, logical cases for their positions. Healthy dissension heated the debates in each group, with few participants remaining quiet or on the fence. Each brought accents from their native languages, which thickened the chaos. Those who got to the flip charts first scribbled words that morphed into multiple-page flow charts. These were best-in-class, super-smart, competitive professionals who saw the prize as winning their team debate and then convincing the entire group their position was correct.

1

As I listened to the instructions and the ensuing discussions, my HR instincts kicked in. As a "recovering human resources manager," my orientation was toward *people*. I immediately developed my own silent argument that mirrored clichés I had heard throughout my career: "people are our business"; "pleased employees lead to pleased customers"; and so on. I fought the urge to allow my bias to interfere with my role as an observer—sort of.

After 45 minutes of constructive noise, the facilitator for this exercise invited one representative from each group to present its response. After all groups had made their case, the facilitator announced the correct answer: process.

The facilitator's argument for process was sound. All aspects of organizations, he said, stem from processes. These might be formal or informal, written or handed down, but they drive every action in every organization. Products, he said, grow from the processes in place to develop them. And people, he said, are hired, trained, coached, and rewarded from processes their organizations develop for them.

This book is about the processes your organization builds and applies to retain your best employees. Throughout the growth of organizational development and the invention of tools to help businesses succeed, employee retention has remained on the sidelines. For decades, companies have aggressively solved sales, service, quality, and safety concerns by implementing organization-wide processes that require high-priority participation from both operations and staff personnel. Retention, though, has traditionally been the job of the HR department alone.

For more than a decade, I, through Finnegan Mackenzie, The Retention Firm, have focused exclusively on employee retention, working with scores of organizations across six continents that were initially searching for that magic retention potion. Like others, they first proclaimed to build a "retention culture" and might have told HR to put retention initiatives into their strategic plans. HR, in turn, reported results of exit surveys and searched for solutions to the commonly reported reasons that employees leave. Some managers continued to believe that workers leave or stay for pay and felt that retention was beyond their control. Others compared turnover to the hopelessness of rush-hour traffic.

Until now, employee retention strategies have been based on instincts rather than research. Organizations have a plethora of tactics, such as tuition reimbursement, CEO breakfasts, and dress-down Fridays, but no firm body of knowledge has been available to tell precisely what to do to cut employee turnover. Missing are the sequential steps and roles that answer who should do what and when. Whereas there are established practices for selling, accounting, and even purchasing, there has been no research-based, comprehensive solution for cutting employee turnover.

Intuitively, we all understand that no goals for sales or service can be achieved without retaining our best people. *So now is the time to move employee retention initiatives from programs to processes that require full management participation and become ongoing staples of performance.* Think of it as moving retention from the side of the organization to the top. Rather than call on HR to establish programs and report results, it's time to elevate retention to top-down status so it joins sales, service, and other essentials by gaining company-wide processes and executive attention.

It's time to Rethink Retention.

 ## An Assignment for All Seasons

Employee retention is an assignment for all seasons, in good times and bad. The United States has faced two recessions in the 21st century and both times good workers have continued to find jobs because workforce shortcomings involve both quantity *and* quality. And there is good reason to believe that in bad times only the good workers quit. Retaining good workers is an everyday duty, regardless of the economy or your business's current profitability.

My challenge, then, is to present you with real retention solutions, both strategic and tactical, based on credible research. Or, simply, to give you a plan that works. Your assignment in turn is to put these solutions in place, watch key operations metrics improve as turnover falls, and be recognized as a hero by your peers.

How to Get the Most Out of This Book

Because this book is about employee retention solutions, far more pages are devoted to *fixing* turnover than describing its heavy toll. It has been written for practitioners, by a practitioner.

Employee turnover is an easy-to-measure number, and this book focuses exclusively on ways to reduce it. While it is likely that productivity, morale, and other important areas improved as well, the standard for entry into this book is a proven method that caused turnover to fall. Research and best practices are included as evidence that these techniques work, resulting in a hands-on tactical guide rather than a series of academic presentations. Some chapters provide more company examples than others because some practices recommended here are uncommon

To get the most out of this book, study the Rethinking Retention model first in Chapters 1 and 2 so you gain an understanding of the retention principles and strategies. Then read the related tactics described in Chapters 3 through 12 and dig deeply into those that you believe can help you the most and the quickest. The tactics are presented as "Top" lists and provide a handbook for implementing the recommended strategies.These chapters also include a section on "True Stories," which provide real company examples of the tactics in action. The Conclusion provides guidance on how to get started as well as information regarding present and future perspectives on retention.

My goal has been to make this book equally valuable for all types of organizations: large and small, public and private, for-profit or non, with high concentrations of low-skilled and high-skilled workers, and across multiple industries. I've researched extensively to find businesses that fit these criteria to present as examples. To further this cause, Appendix A presents two case studies of extremes: a large company that employs primarily low-skilled workers, and a very small company that must retain higher-educated and higher-compensated professional workers. Appendix B includes a guide through the U.S. Department of Labor's Bureau of Labor Statistics' (BLS) website, and Appendix C contains data on quit patterns in the 2008 recession that is referred to in Chapter 3.

Read this book with a pen in your hand. Circle ideas you like, strike through those you don't, and make notes as to how you can apply these tactics in your company. Then pass it on to colleagues and ask them to do the same. Stir up your company's thinking on employee retention so progress happens—fast.

Part I: The Rethinking Retention Model: Principles and Strategies

The Rethinking
Retention Model

Imagine you are reading this book in the summer of 2007. Surrounded by a blazing economy, you would find data here regarding the high number of jobs versus workers across most industries as well as the challenges U.S. companies face to hire and retain good or even serviceable workers.

But the U.S. economy made a hairpin turn near the end of 2007, moving from very healthy to officially in recession in a matter of months. This stark contrast of economies offers a good look at employees' quitting patterns during down economic times.

For most of 2007, the U.S. economy was riding high and few economists were predicting danger ahead. The recession began in December of that year but wasn't officially announced until a full year later.[1] During that 12-month lapse the United States became a different country.

By the mid-point of 2008 the economy showed the following changes since year-end 2007:

- The Dow Jones Industrials had dropped more than 14%[2]
- Inflation had increased over 4%[3]
- Gas prices had shot up an even dollar[4]
- The Consumer Confidence Index had fallen 44%[5]

- Major layoffs had increased by 22% compared to the same period of the previous year and had put nearly 1 million Americans out of work[6]

These are the times when executives expect workers to hold onto their jobs.

Toward the fall, our government furthered our worry by passing legislation to bail out banks, mortgage companies, automakers, and an insurance company for a total cost of nearly $1.4 trillion.[7] We were told that our financial system would have collapsed without government support. Then in November, President-elect Obama warned that "we could lose millions of jobs next year".[8]

By the end of 2008, the omnipresent media was telling American workers what the year had been like for their peers. Compared to 2007, 43% more had been laid off and unemployment had increased to 7.2%, a jump of 26% over the previous year.[9] Surely, American workers were pleased to have a job . . . any job.

But the data tell a different story. The number of voluntary quits *did* drop during year one of this recession, but only by 11%.[10] This meant that your chance of losing an employee you wanted to keep in 2008 was 89% as strong as it was during the strong economy of 2007.

And while concerns grew deeper as the year went on, the difference in voluntary quits between the fourth quarters of 2008 versus 2007 was just 20%.[11] So there was an 80%-as-strong likelihood of losing a productive worker in the 4th quarter of 2008 versus the same period in the previous year.

More important, there is good reason to believe that those who walk away from their jobs during recessions are usually your best performers. Open jobs declined by 18% from 2007 to 2008,[12] while layoffs and the hike in unemployment put many more applicants on the streets. One study estimates there were nearly three times as many applicants for openings during the recession as there were before it.[13] As a result, companies became more selective and applicants found stiff competition for most openings. Those who left you had probably already secured a new job and beaten out the masses to win it. These are the employees with stronger skills and work ethics, the ones you can least afford to lose. Poor performers, on the other hand, were holding on for their paychecks and knew they must be fired in order to earn unemployment benefits.

Viewed from a higher level, this data tells us we can always lose the employees who keep us in business, in good times and bad.

Senior executives seem to know this. In a study, top execs from the largest 1,000 companies in the United States said their greatest staffing concern was retention, and the survey was conducted in September and October of 2008—a high time for media frenzy about the economy, bailouts, and layoffs.[14]

Forever, organizations have approached employee retention in the same manner as Christopher Columbus, without a map to lead the way. When Columbus left Spain in August of 1492, he set his sails westward toward Asia with hope of securing rich silks and rare jewels there. Capitalist Chris next touched land two months later in the Bahamas. Believing he had crossed the Pacific Ocean, he dispatched his crew to seek out the Great Khan. They came back with sand in their boots.

To his death, Columbus believed he had landed in Asia rather than America. History has since credited him for his courage, as well as for essentially sailing in the right direction.[15]

For many organizations today, solving employee retention is like hitching a ride on the Niña, Pinta, or Santa Maria. With no proven path to follow, they steer themselves by default toward traditional solutions such as pay, benefits, and employee appreciation week. Lacking Columbus's good fortune, they head in the wrong direction.

Let's not be like Chris.

 ## The Price of High Turnover

How much does employee turnover cost? Studies by Pricewaterhouse-Coopers' Saratoga Institute indicate turnover costs organizations more than 12% of pretax income, all the way up to 40% for some.[16] Another study puts turnover's price tag across the United States at $25 billion annually—and that's just to train replacements.[17] A third study indicates that turnover reduces U.S. corporate earnings and stock prices by 38% in just four high-turnover industries.[18]

Turnover touches every aspect of organizations because *people* touch every aspect of these organizations. People answer phones, make sales calls, move products from assembly lines, and make hundreds of decisions every day that impact your customers. No amount of technology will replace the impact of the people you hire, train, and then lose or retain.

So employees *are* your business. And those who manage businesses both large and small face stiffer competition domestically and abroad. In most industries it's now harder to make a buck, making your effectiveness at retaining good workers even more critical. In fact, retaining good workers is *the* tipping point between success and failure for many organizations.

 ## Introducing the Rethinking Retention Model

It's time to rethink retention. We all wish turnover solutions were as simple as tweaking copays for employees' health insurance, but unfortunately retention is more vexing and much more complex. Rather than pulling on one rope, it requires pulling many strings.

Figure 1.1 provides a graphic representation of an organization-wide model for keeping your best workers longer. Follow this map and employee retention will improve and drive all other key metrics in your favor.

The next sections introduce the principles and strategies that comprise the Rethinking Retention model.

 ## The Principles of the Rethinking Retention Model

There are three basic principles at the foundation of retention.

Point #1: Employees quit jobs because they can. Workplace demographics leave employees with too many job choices, even in down economies. Avoid the dead-end road of basing retention solutions on exit surveys and other reasons you believe employees leave. Instead, build a proactive solution you can control.

Point #2: Employees stay for things they get uniquely from you. Who are you as an employer? What does your organization

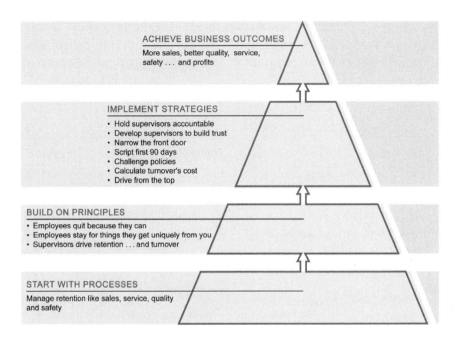

FIGURE 1.1   The Rethinking Retention Model™

offer that others do not? Identify it and build hiring, training, and all other processes on the things that are uniquely you.

Point #3: Supervisors build unique relationships that drive retention... or turnover. Supervisory relationships are unique levers that deeply impact employees' stay/leave decisions. Some employees stay for supervisors, some leave because of them, and some just avoid them.

Chapters 3–5 describe these principles in detail.

 ## The Strategies of the Rethinking Retention Model

Once you've grasped the principles,the following strategies will help you improve retention, productivity, and all other important metrics.

Point #4: Hold supervisors accountable for achieving retention goals. Supervisors won't achieve any other goal you assign them if they lose their best performers, so make them accountable and give them "skin in the game" for retention.

Point #5: Develop supervisors to build trust with their teams.
Communication, recognition, and development all fall behind
trust. Who values information and praise if you don't believe it?

Point #6: Narrow the front door to close the back door. New
hires must align with who you are—your jobs, values, and standards—and give clear indications they intend to stay.

Point #7: Script employees' first 90 days. First impressions
predict how long employees stay, so early activities must be
scripted to present your company in ways that are both positive
and truthful.

Point #8: Challenge policies to ensure they drive retention.
Blow the dust off last decade's thinking and drive your rules
toward retention.

***Point #9: Calculate turnover's cost to galvanize retention as a
business issue.*** Dollars speak louder than numbers and percents.

Point #10: Drive retention from the top, because executives
have the greatest impact on achieving retention goals. Think
about how your company manages sales, service, quality, and
safety and then build those same methods for retention.

Chapters 6–12 elaborate on these strategies.

The core ingredient of the Rethinking Retention Model is the
shared responsibility of operations management and staff support. In
most organizations, operations management drives sales, service,
quality, and safety, with various staff departments providing tracking, training, and other services. When it comes to retention, however, HR tends to manage this on its own.

Making people management work requires organizations to run
on all cylinders, to involve all who can help. Each company has
developed successful, shared-responsibility models for managing
sales and other key initiatives, so why not replicate these ways with
retention?

Driving retention processes from top to bottom is the key. Savvy
organizations manage retention with the appropriate amount of
accountability and other operations-driven tactics to be fully effective.

The following chart represents the types of top-down processes our clients usually had in place before our engagements with them, with "Y" representing yes, that they did have these processes in place, and "N" representing no, that they did not:

	Sales.	Service	Quality	Safety	Retention
Accountability, tops-down in Ops	Y	Y	Y	Y	N
Recognition company-wide	Y	Y	Y	Y	N
Consequences, good and bad	Y	Y	Y	Y	N
Training, skill-specific	Y	Y	Y	Y	N
Coaching for improvement	Y	Y	Y	Y	?

While a few of these organizations provided coaching for supervisors who failed to keep good workers, no retention processes for accountability, recognition, consequences, or skill-specific training were in place. And most of the retention coaching was provided by HR instead of the supervisor's manager.

Organizations that manage retention like the ones represented on the chart turn to HR to solve it. The result is usually programs such as career classes or benefits like vision care. So ask yourself: *Does my company solve retention with processes driven from the top or with programs driven by HR?*

The following chapters discuss research, tactics, roles, and true stories that will help guide you to create your own employee retention action plan.

Two

Principles and Strategies for Steering Your Employee Retention Ship

This chapter discusses the information and logic behind the Rethinking Retention model. Later chapters delve into the details of each of the principles and strategies.

The Principles

The first three points of the Rethinking Retention model are principles that lay the foundation for the seven strategies that follow. I offer these principles as facts, with a strong cast of supporting research for each.

Point #1: Employees quit jobs because they can

Exit surveys and various studies indicate employees quit because of supervisors, pay, career development, and for "better opportunities," or they are fired for attendance or job abandonment. While each of these exit reasons are true at one time or another, the #1 reason employees quit is because our economy and society make it easy for them to do so. Let's consider this thought further by answering this question: Which of the following reasons would cause your turnover to drop the most?

1. You give all employees a 10% pay raise
2. You offer all employees a career development course
3. The U.S. economy tailspins, reducing the number of open jobs

Smart money would probably bet on answer 3. Studies by the U.S. Bureau of Labor Statistics (BLS) indicate that turnover goes up when the economy is strong and goes down when the economy struggles.[1] Said another way, higher turnover can be a price of good economic times.

While turnover has declined during slow economies, good workers still quit.

The 2001 recession reinforced that good workers can still find new opportunities. In the years that immediately followed September 11th, 2001, nearly 50 million employees changed jobs in the United States during any 12-month period.[2] So even though turnover slowed during that time, many workers still chased after new jobs, just not as many as when the economy was strong. So it is fact that historically turnover does slow down when the economy slips, but there are no guarantees that more money or a career course, the other two choices for the question above, consistently reduce turnover.

A lesson learned from both of our 21st-century recessions is that while a struggling economy might deter some workers from quitting, many good employees still find new jobs. Some jobs even appear to be recession-proof. Imagine having to retain skilled salespeople, nurses, or rural MDs in good *or bad* economies.

While the media has done a good job reporting the *quantity* issues regarding our workforce, less has been said about the *quality* issues regarding individual worker's skills. Those who hire entry-level workers feel this quality pinch most.

The BLS data tell us that highest turnover industries are accommodation and food services, leisure and hospitality, and retail trade.[3] During strong economies, these industries provide an endless supply of jobs given that 82% of U.S. jobs are in the service sector and the majority require low-skill workers.[4] Because of high turnover, some managers are pleased to have workers who have minimal skills and can show up. When turnover goes up, these same managers fall into a quicksand of hiring applicants they shouldn't and firing employees only for major violations. The bottom-line decision for many is to keep workers who have good attendance, even if their work is substandard. This is a better alternative than firing that worker and waiting days or weeks for a trained replacement who might not perform the job as well . . . or not show up at all.

Frustrations with workforce quality and quantity are compounded by the astounding increase in young adults who live with their parents. Various studies report that as high as two-thirds of all college grads move back home, with nearly a third of them staying there for more than a year.[5] Managers tell us that employees who don't have bills to pay are more likely to call in sick on Fridays. A call center manager told me that his first boss encouraged him to buy a car and then after that a boat. Asked why, he said "She wanted me to have bills to pay so I needed my job."

Adding to the complexity of keeping good workers is the ongoing increase in entrepreneurs. Eight percent of the U.S. workforce work for themselves, and the BLS projects many baby boomers will leave the workforce early to make it on their own.[6]

So our society offers tall obstacles to retention that include more jobs than workers in good times, too few *qualified* workers, young workers with fewer bills, and a growing number of entrepreneurs. These trends lead us to the #1 reason employees quit jobs: Because they can.

The contrasting opinion is that employees leave for reasons recorded in exit surveys. Many HR professionals question whether their time investment for conducting these surveys is worthwhile. They doubt the reasons employees give for leaving are truthful, and several of the most common reasons close the door to corrective actions. For example, "better opportunity" means different things to different people. Few ask the proper follow-up question, which is, "What did we do that caused you to look?" Similarly, "more money" often results when one looks for another job even though increasing pay is not the real reason they began their search. Too often, exit surveys are inconclusive autopsies that steer organizations toward wrong conclusions. Fast food and other industries that hire entry-level workers often code top leave reasons as "job abandonment" and "failure to meet attendance standards." Neither of these tells much about why an employee left or what the organization can do to improve. Exit surveys can be useful tools if they are constructed and administered properly, but executives should know the limitations of the results.

"Because they can" does not imply that turnover is out of our control and that organizations can wash their hands of responsibility for it. Instead, it just spotlights why turnover is so hard to solve. When employees have more choices in the marketplace, they have less patience for bad schedules, long commutes, dead-end jobs, and jerk bosses. Then they consult online postings and click their way to new companies.

"Because they can" is a no-fault position, and it shapes retention missions to be proactive rather than reactive.

Point #2: Employees stay because of things they get uniquely from you

Let's begin with a brief exercise. Write down the names of five employees in your organization who are crucial to your success. Then write your answers to these questions for each employee:

1. Could this employee leave your organization and get a better job, whatever "better" might mean to him or her?
2. Has this employee ever considered looking?

It's likely that some of your best workers could leave for better jobs but have decided to stay. So the next question to ask is, "Why do they stay?" To complete this exercise, jot down the reasons you believe these top-performing employees stay with your organization. Then consider the following.

Employees stay for things they get uniquely from you. These things might be *tangible*, like being able to walk to work, a four-day/ten-hour schedule, or reduced prices for company products. Or they might be *intangible* things like learning new skills, working with a trusted supervisor, or performing a service that helps others. Some of these stay reasons may come via policies or programs, whereas others occur during the course of doing work.

Retention happens when employees receive things they value that they believe they cannot get anywhere else, and these things create reasons for them to stay. Let's profile some "stay" reasons I've come across as examples.

- A software engineer receives two calls each month from headhunters who promise more money with growing firms, but she continues to say no because her work schedule is flexible and her projects stretch her knowledge.
- A government employee wants no career surprises: His schedule never changes and raises and promotions come as promised.
- A golf course attendant has been promised a promotion to lawn-care equipment mechanic once he completes a company-paid correspondence course to learn the required skills.
- A salesperson stays because his supervisor has centralized all sales tracking and reporting, which lets him focus all of his energy on selling. Competitors try to lure him because he consistently outsells them, but he stays because he knows part of his success is due to his freedom to sell instead of spending time on administrative chores.
- A call center agent works from home on a fixed part-time schedule so he can practice and play with his rock band four nights a week.

These examples feature several of the things employees want most in their jobs: Good supervisors, schedule flexibility, growth opportunities, and work they love. Some of the examples include employees with high ambition who strive for career growth, whereas others are content with the simplicity of a steady job.

Let's call the things that make employees stay the *glues*. Retention, then, is giving employees the *glues* they want that make your organization unique to them.

Our definition of *glues* aligns closely with the landmark research conducted by Terence Mitchell, Thomas Lee, and others regarding job "embeddedness." The three aspects of job embeddedness are *links* between the employee and the organization and its people; *fit*, meaning the compatibility between an organization and the employee's own environment; and *sacrifice*, which indicates the cost of material or psychological benefits that would be lost by leaving the job. Mitchell and Lee demonstrated conclusively that the degree of embeddedness predicts whether employees will leave their jobs.[7] High-retention organizations convert their glues into *value propositions*, which are statements they develop to define their offerings to employees. Then they *brand* these value propositions into marketing materials to communicate their offerings.

How can organizations identify their glues? You must first answer these questions: Who *are* we as an employer? What *do* we offer? And what *must* we offer to attract and retain good workers? While there is much generic data available regarding employee wants, I find that asking your own employees why they stay is more credible. The most effective approach is for supervisors to ask them, one-on-one, with direct questions regarding why they stay. Whereas some will tell you they stay to learn, others might stay because their best friends bowl with them Tuesday nights on the company team.

Who should be asked about their glues? Any employee whose resignation would disappoint you. Much work in the past 15 years has focused on developing and retaining top performers, generally thought to be the top 20% of your teams. But workforce shortages make replacing an okay performer nearly as difficult as replacing a top performer, especially in strong economies. Both can result in significant productivity loss.

It can be useful to divide employees into three groups:

- WOWs, who walk on water
- Wet Socks, who sometimes walk on water but other times slip
- Snorkels, who are underwater—this group must perform its way above water or move aside

Each organization should learn the glues for all WOWs and Wet Socks and do every reasonable thing to meet their needs. Think about how you and other members of your management team would answer these questions:

1. What unique glues do you provide that influence your employees to stay?
2. What glues should you consider providing?
3. When you do provide these glues, how should you communicate them to get the most favorable retention gain?

Point #3: Supervisors build unique relationships that drive retention … or turnover

Supervisor–employee relationships are the Holy Grail of retention efforts because they are your best opportunities to build glue.

Academicians have been demonstrating this link for years, but a series of Gallup studies gave it a megaphone. In the ground-breaking book *First, Break All the Rules*, Gallup researchers Marcus Buckingham and Curt Coffman say on their first page:

> The talented employee may join a company because of its charismatic leaders, its generous benefits, and its world-class training programs, but how long that employee stays and how productive he is while he is there is determined by his relationship with his immediate supervisor.[8]

The authors go on to say that "If you have a turnover problem, look first to your managers." Their book is based on survey results from over one million employees and 80,000 managers, gathered over a period of 25 years.

Other studies report that employees' reasons to leave are often influenced by their relationships with their supervisors, regardless of the reasons they give.

Kenexa studied this relationship by collecting data from employees who left about their fit with supervisors, satisfaction with pay and benefits, and satisfaction with learning, development, and advancement. They found that satisfaction with pay and benefits had an effect on retention, as did satisfaction with learning, development, and advancement. But in both instances, employees' opinions were "mediated," or influenced, by relationships they had with their supervisors. The researchers concluded, "It may be the case that offering employees a higher salary or developmental/advancement opportunities may not be enough to retain employees."[9]

Even though we know intuitively that supervisors have a major impact on retention, organizations often build program-only solutions instead. I asked client representatives (1) "Why have you personally left jobs in your past?" and (2) "What initiatives has your organization implemented to improve retention?" The following are typical responses to these two questions.

Reasons employees left jobs:	Recent retention initiatives:
Supervisor took credit for my work	Pay for performance
Management was insensitive	Employee surveys
Supervisor didn't communicate	Recognition programs
Wasn't learning anything	Improved orientation

Three principles became clear with this exercise:

1. Most retention initiatives are not aligned with the real reasons employees leave jobs.

2. Most of the common retention initiatives do not build glue because they do not make your organization unique.

3. Perhaps most important, relationships between employees and supervisors are personal because employees tend to take all communications from their supervisors *personally*. This multiplies the impact of compliments and criticism and makes staying or leaving decisions *emotional* decisions.

Pay for performance, employee surveys, recognition programs, and improved orientation are all good things, but they are insufficient on their own to improve retention. When was the last time you heard a really good employee say, "My boss treats me like dirt, but I'm holding on for employee appreciation week?" Getting a balloon and a hot dog just isn't enough.

Solving these needs with stand-alone, staff-driven programs is easier, and it's what organizations have traditionally done. But good employees who work for ineffective supervisors will not stay for program solutions that are delivered outside of the supervisor–employee relationship. Poor supervisors will trump good programs, leading to higher turnover.

Earlier I asked you to identify your glues. If your answer included pay, benefits, careers, and company reputation, be aware that these do not qualify as glues if your employees can get the same or better from a competitor.

The research presented by Gallup, Kenexa, and others drives home that supervisors represent the best opportunities to build glue. And for those organizations that offer no unique programs such as the work-from-home convenience for our rock star wannabe, *supervisors might be your only glue opportunity.*

Even supervisors themselves underestimate their retention power. I ask focus groups about this and find the following recurring pattern:

- On a 1–10 scale, with 10 being high, supervisors typically score themselves a 4 or 5 regarding their abilities to influence their employees to stay.
- Using the same scale, employees usually score their supervisors a 7 or 8 regarding their influence on those employees' stay or leave decisions.

The relationships between supervisors and employees are powerful and unique, and offer compelling opportunities for building glue.

The three principles just discussed position us for action. We have now traveled beyond building isolated solutions to recurring symptoms like the need for employee recognition. Let's now begin charting a course toward leveraging our glues, improving supervision, and making other proactive solutions happen.

The Strategies

Recalling the lesson of the three Ps discussed earlier in this book, the most important element is processes. Let's assume that those desired actions that are not part of recurring processes will simply not occur. So now that principles have been established as building blocks for your retention plans, *what actions should you take to cut turnover?*

At their 2007 conference, the Society for Industrial and Organizational Psychology (SIOP) conducted a panel discussion on "Research-Driven Best Practices in Employee Retention."[10] Following the conference, a leading industry publication printed these quotes from the panelists:

- "We've done a lot of research into root cause analysis."
- "It will begin to allow us to do analyses we were not able to do before."
- "We hope in the future to use predictive modeling. Ultimately, we want some retention tools for managers."

But how much money is turnover costing their companies while researchers look for more data? Why the paralysis-by-analysis? Historically, it's been easier to study turnover than to implement solutions to fix it. But in fairness, until now real retention solutions have been in short supply.

HR professionals know solving turnover is a vital concern. In the Society for Human Resource Management's 2008 Workplace Trends survey, the top HR profession trend was a "Growing need to develop retention strategies for the current and future workforce."[11] So let's fast-forward to the new retention tools.

Point #4: Hold supervisors accountable for achieving retention goals

Here's a proposed retention resolution:

Whereas, employee turnover is extremely costly to organizations and
Whereas, employees' decisions to stay or leave are personal and

strongly influenced by their supervisors and *Whereas*, supervisors are typically held to measurable standards for key performance indicators and *Whereas*, the potential for supervisors to achieve these standards is greatly influenced by their retaining their best workers, *Be it resolved* that supervisors on all levels in all organizations should have retention goals, and these standards should have an equal or greater weight than all other productivity and efficiency standards.

Supervisor accountability is the first strategy because you should implement this immediately. Telling supervisors on all levels that they now have retention goals moves your retention efforts from HR into the line management of your organization, which is where nearly all retention activity occurs after hiring. If you do only one thing as a result of reading this book, set retention goals for supervisors.

Most organizations track turnover company-wide or within divisions. Tracking at high levels usually helps companies to observe trends but seldom leads to them taking specific corrective actions that impact employees every day. Tracking must lead to goals and goals must be set from top to bottom, because first-line supervisors are the employee retention point of attack.

How many organizations set retention goals at the first-line leader level? Only 14%, according to a TalentKeepers' recent survey.[12] All readers should seize this competitive advantage.

My experience is that most supervisors have been well-chosen, and they fully direct their energies toward whatever they think is important. They gain these perceptions from management above them based on words they hear, standards they are measured against, and any outcome that impacts their pay.

My first experience with reducing turnover completely changed my career, but only after a bumpy start. When I was HR manager at SunTrust Banks, my CEO called me in to say turnover was high and he expected me to fix it. I pleaded that the HR department had little impact on employees who were located hundreds of miles away, that he just didn't understand. He concluded by saying, "It is you who does not understand," and I was sent off to solve turnover.

Two days later I had lunch with Dan Mahurin, who managed all of the branches and consequently most of our employees. Dan patiently listened and then solved my problem. He suggested that I give him a report that contained turnover by branch. He would then work with all branch managers to set retention goals and add achieving these goals to their incentive plans. Three weeks later we met with all branch managers and presented our reasons why they were critical to our retention success. Dan asked them all to accept a goal to reduce turnover by 10% over the previous year.

Nine months later our turnover had come down 19%, and by our finance division's calculations we had saved nearly $4 million. What is most important is what we did *not* do. We did not change pay outside of our normal processes; we did not implement new programs such as onsite childcare; and we did not provide any new types of management training. All we did was make retention very, very important to the front-line supervisors.

When we asked supervisors what they did to cut turnover, they told us stories of greeting each employee in the morning, asking them about their lives outside of work, and telling them when they did a good job. Some brought in food when work was heavy; others made themselves more visible by walking about and making small talk. From the employees' perspective, the supervisors became "nicer." However, the reason supervisors did these things is because we made retention important by giving them a goal.

Management is like keeping plates spinning on sticks. Facing too many priorities, supervisors decide in five-minute increments which plates to spin and which to let fall. By setting retention goals and holding supervisors accountable, we made retention become fine china and supervisors changed their behaviors as a result.

Not all supervisors will welcome retention goals. You should expect to hear from at least a few that turnover happens because pay is too low, work is excessive, young workers are irresponsible, and so on. At SunTrust Banks we rehearsed our lines for handling objections, and the first "you don't understand" exchange went like this:

Manager from the back of the room: So if I'm understanding this correctly, you expect us to cut turnover. Yet every year when I submit my budget, you send it back and tell me I can't give my employees the raises they deserve. We've also asked for a childcare allowance and you've said no to that, too. How can you hold me accountable for turnover when you won't give us the things we need to keep our good workers?

Dan: I think you do understand this correctly, Robert. I can't promise you that we can give you any new resources for your employees. But the good news is that we are asking you to cut turnover by only 10%. This means you can blame me for the other 90%. In fact, you can blame your dog for the other 90%.

Remember, all I'm asking for is 10%. If I thought you had complete control over all circumstances that lead to turnover, I'd be asking you to cut it by 100%. But I am confident that by using the skills you have, you can cut turnover by at least 10%.

That was the first and last objection.

Point #5: Develop supervisors to build trust with their teams

Organizations by their design represent the intersection of the powerful and the vulnerable. Employees learn in their first jobs that all managers above them can hurt them and peer employees sometimes will compete with them. It should be easy to agree, then, that trustworthiness is an important quality for supervisors to have. But let us present the case that *trustworthiness is the most important retention skill for supervisors to retain their workers*. There is strong data to prove this case; the following are just three examples.

- TalentKeepers surveyed over 100,000 employees representing nearly 100 organizations in all industries and asked what qualities are most important in their relationships with their supervisors. Within each of these organizations, employees chose building trust as the most desirable quality.[13] These surveys also showed that the power of trust in workplace relationships is universal across industries, locations, and cultures.
- Leadership IQ, in a study based on inputs from over 7,000 executives, managers, and employees, found that 32% of employees'

decisions to remain with their organizations were based solely on the amount of trust employees held for their immediate supervisor.[14]

- Sirota surveyed over 64,000 employees to learn their expectations when they join companies. The answers—be treated with respect, be dealt with equitably, and gain a sense of connection on both work and personal levels—applied equally to young and older workers.[15]

So just how important *is* trust as a retention tool? The first survey tells us that trust is the most important supervisory skill. The second tells us that the degree of trust with one's supervisor dominates nearly one-third of stay/leave decisions. The third puts trust at the highest level of employee expectations and dispels the myth that different generations have different expectations.

The dominant role that supervisor trust plays in retention has been a long-kept secret. These studies make known that the narrow concept of trusting one's supervisor is *as important or more* than pay, benefits, and other expensive investments organizations make to keep their workers. Think now about your current and past supervisors, and how hard you worked and how long you stayed based on your degree of trust in them. Then list the retention initiatives your organization has put in place, and ask yourself how important each is compared to building trust among your frontline leaders. Building trust is a magic potion for retention.

The type of trust being discussed here is *personal* trust: Trusting a supervisor to provide feedback and tools for your success, assess your work objectively, tell you when you do something good, be candid when you need to improve, and present your achievements objectively to others. This is an employee knowing that his supervisor "has his back" and really wants him to succeed. This is about the degree of trust a teller has for her supervisor, and that person's trust for the branch manager, and that person's trust for the area manager, and that person's trust for the senior vice president. This is entirely about one-on-one relationships. Positive feelings about trust must travel bottom-up throughout organizations to fully impact retention.

Trust flies way under the radar when most people think about important supervisory skills. When asked to name one skill that is more important than others for retention, supervisors usually respond with "communication," "recognition," or "career counseling." One reason they miss on trust is because employees use code phrases for trust like "nice," "she's cool," or "I like him"; when describing a distrustful supervisor, they say "jerk" or worse, along with an eye-roll. They know when a supervisor connects with them—but don't necessarily know the deep reason why.

The very good news is that trust is usually about behaviors rather than immutable character flaws. Supervisors repeat behaviors they've learned from others and apply them to the many stressful circumstances throughout their days. Acting in trustworthy ways consistently is hard. Let's use the example of telling the truth:

- Do I tell my manager exactly what I think of this new policy?
- Do I tell my subordinates everything I think is wrong with the way they talk to customers or just the main things?
- Should I tell applicants that we are looking to move our facility across town?
- Should I tell my subordinate she'll probably never get that promotion?

Truth-telling requires courage and good judgment. Many supervisors have been raised with the backdrop of 24-hour news stations that report position statements by government and business leaders that are carefully prepared to trumpet some information and shield us from the rest. When you find yourself in the presence of an effective truth-teller, take notes to build your skills.

Point #6: Narrow the front door to close the back door

"Why can't we just give them a test?"

This is the common cry of HR managers searching for the easy solution for hiring workers who stay. While we know of no one-size-fits-all assessment that accurately predicts retention, we can dig into research and best practices to find solutions.

First, let's discuss some basics about hiring and retention. Typical hiring processes include tools such as online applications with screen-out questions, assessments, interviews, simulations, and background checks. Together, these processes should answer three questions about each applicant:

1. Can they do the job?
2. Will they do the job?
3. Will they stay?

Unfortunately, most hiring processes focus heavily on question #1, somewhat on #2, and little on #3. Answering the first two questions is easier because "can" and "will" are exclusively about the applicant. Answering "will they stay" is a far steeper challenge because it requires measuring how the applicant will mesh with the many variables of the total work environment including duties, schedule, peers, supervisor... and more. You will read later in this chapter that research suggests that turnover is more about this meshing than about applicants having "leaver" personalities.

Retention begins with the hiring choices you make. Perfect applicants are those who can and will do the job and also will attach themselves to your glues. So hiring for retention must include two-way learning, where you assess job-related information about each applicant and each applicant learns job-related information about you.

In his book *The 7 Hidden Reasons Why Employees Leave*, author Leigh Branham presents leave reasons from Saratoga Institute's database of nearly 20,000 entries from exit and current employee surveys. Branham found that major turnover drivers included "job or workplace was not as expected" and "the mismatch between job and person." Branham's work drives home the importance of making and securing good matches early on.[16]

Let's take a look at hiring techniques that research has proven will cut your turnover, beginning with employee referrals.

Research by Emilio Castilla, Edwin Cornelius, and others confirm that employee referrals stay longer because they know your business and see themselves as a good match.[17] The referring employee has typically disclosed the good and bad sides of working with you, and the referral then makes a choice to apply. Referrals also tend to be higher performers because the already-on-board employee wants to avoid the embarrassment of referring someone who fails to be hired or fails in the job. Referred employees also start on day one with at least one acquaintance in the company.

Realistic job previews are another tool for fighting turnover. By demonstrating the job's duties, conditions, compensation, and other factors, applicants can choose if there is the right amount of glue for a lasting fit. Studies by Mary Suszko, James Breaugh, P. G. Roth, P. L. Roth, and others confirm that realistic job previews increase the likelihood of lower turnover and in some cases result in higher performance.[18]

Another proven technique for narrowing the front door is to hire older workers. Spherion's Emerging Workforce Study discloses that workers age 51 and older are more loyal than their younger peers and have the lowest intentions of changing jobs among all age groups.[19] And a study by Leadership IQ reports that older workers are the most satisfied with their companies, whereas the youngest workers are the least satisfied.[20]

Even more telling is data from the U.S. Bureau of Labor Statistics. In an ongoing longitudinal study, the BLS is tracking nearly 10,000 workers from age 18 to their current age of 40. They report that "the length of time a worker remains with the same employer increases with the age at which the worker began the job."[21]

So based on the BLS's findings, let's think of "older workers" in a new way. Fifty-somethings are more stable than forty-somethings, and forty-somethings are more stable than thirty-somethings, and on and on. It's not just "hire the gray-hairs." The data clearly suggests that hiring 30-year-olds rather than 19-year-olds will lower your turnover.

This data has major implications for organizations that hire workers into the revolving door of our service economy. Your best solution might be to increase the applicant flow of older workers without discriminating against younger workers who are qualified for your jobs.

Point #7: Script employees' first 90 days

For high-turnover organizations, early turnover often comprises half or more of total turnover. By combining "Will they stay?" hiring techniques with glue-building management processes, you can cut early turnover at least in half. In fact, reducing early turnover tends to reduce turnover at all stages over time because employees build early glue and maintain it. We have found that cutting early turnover also reduces ramp-up time for those who stay.

We chose 90 days as our early-turnover period based on the experience of our clients and other organizations that employ large populations of low-skilled workers. One example is Wal-Mart, the largest private employer in the United States,[22] which has lost as many as two-thirds of its first-year turnover in the first 90 days.[23] You might find that continuing early retention efforts beyond 90 days is right for your organization, especially if your tipping point for early turnover is longer.

The first 90 days is the glue-building period, as employees stay for *things they believe are uniquely available from you.* Having made the decision to join your organization, they are now verifying if their decision was right based on their early daily experiences. New hires are especially vulnerable if they can easily find other jobs in your market, if other organizations where they previously applied call them, or if new peers announce they are leaving and influence them to tag along.

Lest we think early retention is only about low-skilled workers, research shows that professional employees make early stay-or-go decisions too. A University of Florida study of 1,000 professional employees across seven organizations found that employees originally intended to stay for an average of seven years, but many left sooner because of opinions they began forming in *their first month on the job.*[24] Contributing factors included disagreements with supervisors and coworkers as well as reassignment of projects. Professor John Kammeyer-Mueller, who led the study, pinpoints the root of cause and effect: "We had originally thought it was going to be a personality factor, that people would have a kind of 'leaver' personality...but from the personality measures on the survey...we realized personality didn't seem to matter." In other words, it's about us, not them.

This study and others all contribute to an impressive database that reinforces what we intuitively already know. Helping new hires see the good in us immediately is important, just as it is important that we select them correctly. Your solutions, though, must be rooted in targeted *processes*, and these must be carefully designed activities that are locked onto calendars. Without these processes, your new-hire retention plan will consist only of your current new employee orientation program and whatever efforts your supervisors make to bond with new hires. This won't be enough to retain good workers who have other options and find reasons to leave.

Here's one example of an *absence* of process. The Aberdeen Group studied 800 organizations and found 86% of new hires make decisions about staying or leaving in their first six months. Aberdeen also rated these same organizations according to their early support programs and found that among those organizations Aberdeen tagged as "best in class," fewer than half even track their turnover in the first six months. So even the best organizations failed to track turnover during the critical early months.[25]

So our processes must address the fundamental questions employees ask themselves. Sometimes they answer based on detailed information, and other times they go with their gut. These questions include:

- **Regarding supervisors:** Do I trust her? Does she seem to care? Was she ready for me on day one? Has she made it clear what I must do every day to please her? Will she appreciate my work when I do it well?

- **Regarding jobs:** Do I know what to do? Can I do it? Do I have the equipment to do it? Do I fully understand each assignment's desired outcomes and deadlines? Can I adjust my life to this schedule and commute? What new skills am I learning? Whose lives am I improving?

- **Regarding peers:** Do I like seeing these people each day? Do I feel welcomed by them? Would I miss any of them if I left? Why are some of them leaving?

- **Regarding the company:** Do the executives make good decisions? Will the company be in business and in my town for a while? Is there any sign they will deceive me?
- **Regarding administration:** Do I know when I get paid? Do I know ways I can earn extra money? Do I know my benefits?

In a perfect world, *you* want to decide who stays and who goes. Steering new hires to a fully informed, positive-thinking start is essential for you to influence the good ones to stay.

Point #8: Challenge policies to ensure they drive retention

The core belief of these retention strategies is that employees stay for glues, the things they believe are uniquely available from you. We've already discussed *new* processes for building glues, so let's look now at our *current* processes. What things might you be doing that drive workers away?

Pay, healthcare, and work flexibility are three areas that consistently appear as employee concerns across various surveys. The following research for each area leads to pathways for improved retention.

How much does pay really impact turnover? Historically, pay has appeared as a major turnover driver in both internal exit surveys and various industry studies.

Salary.com's Employee Job Satisfaction & Retention Survey gives keen insights into employees' views on pay and their potential to quit. Half of the survey's 11,000 participants chose compensation as the top reason they would quit. The survey put a price on retention, as most participants indicated they would stay with their employers for another year in exchange for a 10%–15% pay increase. Surprisingly, the data also concluded that only 22% of the participants were actually underpaid.[26]

So there is a conflict of reliable employee opinions versus perplexing realities. If half say they would quit because of pay, how many actually *will* quit because of pay? Will they vote with their feet rather than with their keyboards when completing surveys? Next, how likely are executives to make major changes in pay plans when nearly 80% of employees are already paid at market or better?

Let's also explore the employees' position that they would stay another year for more money. A common employee argument is, "It would cost you half of my pay to replace me. Why don't you pay me 15% more to keep me?" We agree with this argument for very high performers. But raising everyone's pay solely to offset the cost of potential turnover requires much more analysis, including what is the likelihood that everyone will leave?

Based on these contradictions, it would be easy to conclude that employees use pay as their default concern in place of other frustrations. But this is not so according to the in-depth research presented by David Sirota, Louis Mischkind, and Michael Meltzer in their book *The Enthusiastic Employee.* The authors surveyed over 4 million employees and report that complaints about pay "are almost invariably about pay," that employees know when they are working for a good-paying employer versus one that seeks to "squeeze the last nickel out of them." They go on to say that employees need both financial and nonfinancial recognition, and employers cannot substitute one for the other.[27]

We believe where there's smoke there's fire, and that organizations can take steps to improve compensation to improve retention. Chapter 10 discusses these ideas.

Healthcare benefits are another lightning rod for employee turnover. On the one hand, TalentKeepers' research indicates that employee benefits in general are more important for *attracting* employees than for retaining them.[28] Even though employees might tell you on opinion surveys that they wish your benefits were richer, we've seen little evidence that employees begin job searches based on benefits alone.

The one exception, though, is the availability of healthcare for employees and their dependents. Organizations that understand the full cost of turnover are wise to offer these benefits and benchmark themselves against other employers to ensure they are competitive or better. Costs are rising for healthcare, such that "healthcare cost containment" was the top compensation and benefits concern among company representatives who participated in a recent Society for

Human Resources Management (SHRM) benefits survey.[29] Yet employees consistently tell us that company-sponsored healthcare is a "must," unlike vision care and similar "nice to have" benefits.

BLS research from 2007 found that 60% of private employers offer medical insurance to their employees and pay an average of 81% of premiums for employee coverage and 71% for family coverage. The average monthly payouts for employees are $81.37 for themselves and $312.78 for their families.[30]

The same study reported that only 24% of part-time employees have access to healthcare coverage at work. Organizations that depend heavily on part-timers and struggle with high part-time turnover might want to ask those employees if healthcare coverage would influence them to stay.

Another way to take a bite out of turnover is to give employees more flexibility with their schedules. Traditional thinkers might object, believing that employees will work less hard and lack required discipline to follow through on work assignments. But those employers who have crossed the flexibility boundary report good news.

Remember, too, that trust is the magic potion for retention. Employees are less likely to trust "traditional thinkers" who don't in turn trust them to manage their work when out of sight or structuring their own work days.

Let's look at some research. CareerBuilder.com and Robert Half surveyed over 1,000 hiring managers and 900 employees to find that the top perks that cause workers to choose one employer over another are (1) flexible schedules and (2) telecommuting.[31] Additionally, Corporate Voices for Working Families studied 29 U.S. firms, including MetLife, Accenture, and AstraZeneca, and concluded that employees with even a small measure of flexibility "have significantly greater job satisfaction, stronger commitment to the job, and higher levels of engagement with the company" and "saved millions of dollars in prevented turnover."[32]

In another study, WorldatWork asked members to rate the impact of various employee benefits on retention. Nearly half the respondents rated telecommuting, a compressed workweek, and flex-time as "high," the top level on their retention scale.[33]

Realistically, it is easier to build flexible options for some jobs than others. The BLS found that "professional and technical services" employees are most likely to have flexible schedules, whereas those in "educational services" are least likely.[34] Certainly there are more schedule restrictions for teachers, retail sales representatives, and others whose jobs require they be available on customers' schedules. Even these employers, though, should heed the calls of our workforce for more flexibility. Small steps, such as enabling workers to easily switch schedules with others and permitting all administrative work to be done from home, can have major impacts.

Employees are telling us they want more *time*. The window will close on flexible schedules as a retention tool as smart-thinking organizations will increasingly leverage technology until flexible work styles become commodities instead of glues. But organizations can gain competitive advantages by offering this flexibility now.

Pay, healthcare, and work flexibility are just three policy areas that merit your scrutiny when seeking retention clues. We'll explore others later.

Point #9: Calculate turnover's cost to galvanize retention as a business issue

Dollars is the most important word in U.S. business, and in many international corporate hubs as well. So in order to move the retention discussion into the boardroom and other important decision-making arenas, the cost of turnover must be translated into bucks.

My first experience with costing turnover was in the late 1980s when we attacked turnover in SunTrust Banks as discussed earlier. Looking back, we did some smart things and made a few mistakes as well. But conducting and publicizing a cost study definitely influenced our 19% turnover decline.

On the smart side, we did the following:

- HR asked the finance department to do the study, understanding that no high-sounding dollar amount would gain traction if finance didn't own and support it. HR participated by suggesting criteria and providing data, but the final outcome was owned and announced by finance.

- Finance expanded the study to include all jobs across the bank. They selected six core jobs, each of which represented larger groups of jobs, and all jobs in that group had similar character- istics that influenced the cost of losing someone, such as the same training time, amount of customer contact, and whether the replacement required relocation. The result was we could put a price on every single departure regardless of the position.
- We reported monthly and annual savings from turnover's decline to all management personnel, which motivated super- visors to share ideas and try even harder.

In retrospect, I would do these things differently:

- Our study focused on the cost of replacing someone but didn't include lost productivity. Measuring the cost of hiring and train- ing is easy, whereas measuring the cost of having the position open and then ramping someone up to do the job completely is more difficult. In fact, for most jobs, the lost productivity por- tion is the greater cost.
- HR reported turnover results to the executive team each month, immediately following the finance department's report on earn- ings. This was the equivalent of saying, "Finance reports the important numbers, and now here's HR to talk about turnover." The executive who reports profits should report retention, with no help from HR.
- While we had well-documented cost amounts, we didn't use them enough. We missed opportunities to report dollars saved or lost because of turnover or compare the cost of losing an employee to losing something more tangible.

To gain executive buy-in on cost, implement this credo: "Top management's buying into the cost is more important than the cost being precisely right." Present the cost to executives and ask if they agree. If they indicate any doubt, ask which number they will agree to. If not $15,000 per exit, how about $14,000? $12,000? Or even $7,500? Any reasonable number will stimulate action once it is mul- tiplied by the total number who leave that job in a year.

Once all executives have agreed to a cost, these figures can be used in many ways to build momentum for retention. Costs can be connected to managers' retention goals: Each manager can be given a "bank" of dollars for turnover costs but penalized if they exceed the bank. In some organizations, retention reports include columns for "dollars saved." And retention savings are always included in tributes for managers who receive monthly, quarterly, or annual awards.

Creative executives find ways to teach their managers the real cost of turnover so they know turnover is important. Here are three real-life examples.

* A call center executive agreed that the cost of losing an agent was $12,000. At the next management meeting, he asked IT to bring some obsolete equipment into the room that originally cost a total of $12,000. The equipment was placed on a table in front of the room. During the meeting, he announced turnover's cost along with each manager's retention goals, and then pushed each piece of equipment off the table and onto the floor. As broken plastic flew across the front of the room, he told the managers that the cost of turnover was as real as the cost of the equipment.

* A delivery company executive accepted that losing a driver cost $60,000, the same approximate value of each driver's truck. The executive then met with senior managers of the drivers and asked what outcome they would expect if a truck was lost due to an accident and the person in charge of renewing the insurance had neglected to do so, resulting in a $60,000 loss. The managers walked away with a fuller appreciation of the cost of turnover and the importance of improving their retention skills.

* Several executives I know have told their managers the cost of turnover and then asked, "Who can tell me a time when you came to me with a new idea that cost the same as losing one of our employees and I said, 'Sure, let's try it'?" Managers snicker at the thought of getting a new expense approved so easily, and then they more fully understand turnover's cost.

Point #10: Drive retention from the top, because executives have the greatest impact on achieving retention goals

Saying that major organizational initiatives must be driven from the top is old news, but this cliché has traditionally not been applied to employee retention because most organizations don't see retention as a major organizational initiative. They instead see it as a major HR initiative, and look to HR to design and implement solutions and accept responsibility for it. As a result, retention initiatives are driven from the side of the organization chart via HR rather than from the top.

Sales, service, quality, and safety are four examples of critical metrics that are usually driven from the top with strong staff support, regardless of industry. To fully understand the power these metrics yield, consider their prevalence in the following:

- Inclusion in your annual report or equivalent year-end financial summary
- Dominance in your annual strategic plans and quarterly progress updates
- Conversion to numerical goals that are established company-wide and then dispersed to managers across divisions and departments
- Percent of all meeting time that is devoted to reporting and improving these metrics on all management levels, company-wide
- Number of support department personnel who provide training, tracking, and other tactical support
- Specific training programs designed to help managers achieve these specific goals
- Rewards and consequences for achieving or missing related goals, ranging from positives such as bonuses and theme-inspired sales celebrations to ultimately losing one's job for consistently missing a goal

Compare these examples to your organization's approach to employee retention. Do you report annual retention success to the owners of your company? Are retention goals set top to bottom among the operation's ranks and real consequences applied? Is specific retention training available to managers and supervisors to help them achieve their goals?

The objection that hovers over our discussion is this: Is retaining the employees you want to keep as important as sales, service, quality, and safety? The intuitive answer is yes, as these are the people who drive all results. None of us would argue that keeping the best salespeople should be managed as less important than achieving sales results, and the same can be said for service, quality, or safety—unless you have morphed into a company that delivers sales and service without people.

Employee retention is a management team game. The CEO or top operations executive must ensure retention goals have been set throughout the management ranks and then consistently drive retention's importance top to bottom throughout the organization. Staff executives from HR, finance, and marketing must play defined roles regarding retention processes, and operations then executes the processes down to the front-line level.

HR's role is premier, as most people-related activities are based on HR policies and processes. Large organizations are now appointing retention specialists to focus a dedicated professional to the role. But the traditional model of putting HR as the frontperson for retention, with full accountability for it, cannot work because operations must implement the processes. A former CEO of mine once said, "HR's role is to never make a decision for a manager and never let a manager make a wrong decision." His message was that HR must change managers with influence rather than authority, but we need authority throughout the operations ranks to improve retention.

Finance is the announcer and protector of all that relates to dollars, so they must put a cost on turnover and then apply that cost to drive better decisions on big-ticket items regarding pay, benefits, and new programs. I find some CFOs are slow to warm to retention initiatives but leap aboard when they realize the potential for improved savings and productivity. Perhaps someday soon all business professors will teach the importance of employee retention to their students so CFOs and other executives can contribute more quickly.

Marketing departments are rightly pointed externally to manage communications with customers. Many high-retention organizations ask marketing to direct some of its talent toward employees, too, by ensuring branding and internal marketing materials are right. Achieving this requires that marketing accept its role as an employee provider rather than consider these internal tasks as extras or one-time projects.

Think sales, service, quality, safety—and retention. Elevating retention to join this group requires strong and constant management from the top, along with clearly defined roles for HR, finance, and marketing.

 ## Next Up: Tactics

With principles and strategies in place, let's move forward to *what specific actions you should take*. The remainder of this book presents tactics and other helpful information for each principle and strategy. Appendix A then presents two in-depth case studies of organizations that have utilized these principles, strategies, and tactics to help cut turnover and enable their businesses to grow.

Part II: Putting Rethinking Retention to Work: Tactics

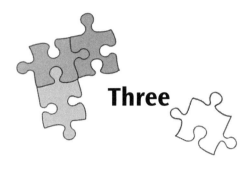

Three

Employees Quit Jobs Because They Can

The first principle of the Rethinking Retention Model says employees leave "because they can" for two reasons:

* The essential driving force for switching jobs is having other opportunities, and strong performers usually have them, even during slow economies.
* Addressing turnover through survey results alone narrows your retention focus to a few reactive strategies that might be off target, whereas building a proactive, organization-wide approach is far more effective.

The data presented in Chapter 1 underscores that more workers voluntarily quit in down times than we might assume. And for most industries, it's likely these quitters are high-performers because they are the ones who can win new jobs. These are the employees you need most, in good times and bad.

You can learn more about quitting patterns for 2007 and 2008 for your industry by consulting Appendix C. This data has been extracted from the BLS site and is for private-industry jobs. The industry groups are those used by the North American Industrial Classification System, and you can learn more about their definitions at *www.census.gov/eos/www/naics/index.html*.

In this chapter, we will look at data and best practices that help us manage our itinerant workforce. The top lists presented are:

Top U.S. Recession-Proof Jobs based on several expert studies, followed by details on the healthcare staffing crisis

Top Reports of Worker Skills Shortages, which show no imminent signs of improvement either now or as our economy improves

Top Ways to Retain High Performers During Layoffs so you keep survivors who are now even more important

Top Tips for Gathering Exit Data, giving you the best opportunity to learn why your employees really leave

The **True Stories** section follows with round-the-world happenings regarding job boards, global aspects of the competition for talent, one public sector solution, the role of traveling nurses, and one executive's approach to learning real reasons employees leave.

In addition, I've included the **Top Sections of the BLS Website** in Appendix B. This is a guide through the most important sections of the volumes of important workforce and retention data that the U.S. government makes available to all.

 ## Top U.S. Recession-Proof Jobs

As an employee, these are the lists where you want to see your job. For employers, though, these are the hardest-to-find-and-keep workers. All of these lists were comprised during the 2008–2009 recession. These list-makers used varying criteria so I offer a few examples of their work. As you will see, not all of the recession-proof jobs require extensive education or training so there are still opportunities in slow times for your lower-skilled workers to switch.

Given the difficulty of filling these jobs during the severe recession of 2008, one would anticipate far worse challenges for filling these jobs and retaining those workers when the economy returns to full steam. But regardless of the *pace* with which the economy improves, the driving force behind impending workforce shortages will be the retirement of the baby boomers, 330 of whom turn 60 *every hour*.[1] During the span of 2006 to 2016, the largest increase of workers will be those aged 65 and older while those who are 24 and younger will decline.[2] And this will happen regardless of the economy.

Here's one bright light to help keep you reading. More babies were born in the U.S. in 2007 than any other year in history.[3] This comes on the heels of 2006 when more babies were born since the post–WW II baby boom period.[4] Some of these babies will join the workforce when they reach age 18, others when they reach 22 or older. So 2024 should be a better year for hiring.

 ## JobFox Top 25

This job board provides a thrice-annual update of the most wanted professions by employers that use their service.[5] Whereas they provide the top 25, we list their top 10:

1. Sales Representative/Business Development
2. Account/Customer Support
3. Accounting Staff
4. Counseling/Social Work
5. Software Design/Development
6. Administrative Assistant
7. Networking/System Administration
8. Nursing
9. Mechanical Engineering
10. Sales Executive

 ## Careerbuilder.com's 10 Recession-Proof Jobs

This report was based on data from the BLS as well as information obtained from various careerbuilder.com surveys.[6] The author lists the following jobs and the following are abbreviated versions of her reasons why:

1. Registered nurse... nurses are always in demand
2. Public relations specialist... advertising and marketing budgets are being cut so public relations departments must do more
3. Post-secondary teacher... more workers are riding out the recession by going to school
4. Police officer... government jobs are more secure and crime goes up in a down economy
5. Insurance sales agent... people are always willing to buy insurance and layoffs lead to being uninsured
6. Pharmacy technician... our aging population plus depression from the economy equals more need for pills
7. Funeral director... death is a fact of life
8. Environmental science technician... the Obama administration plans to create 5 million "green" jobs over the next 10 years
9. Network systems and data communications analysts... companies will always need onsite technical specialists
10. Fast-food worker... it's all that some people can afford these days

 ## A Career Expert Chimes In

Laurence Shatkin is the author of "150 Best Recession-Proof Jobs," which he wrote based on BLS data. In an interview he cited the best industries for workers as:

1. *Healthcare* because it is a great growth industry and a lot of health coverage comes from insurance policies
2. *Government* because jobs there are more secure
3. *Education* because children must go to school and unemployed workers will leverage post-secondary training
4. *Utilities* like water, electricity, gas, garbage pick-up, and sewage treatment because people will need these things in any economy[7]

In another publication, Dr. Shatkin predicts the following jobs will get the greatest boost from the U.S. stimulus bill that was passed in early 2009[8]:

1. Mobile heavy equipment mechanics
2. Mining and geological engineers
3. Geophysical data technicians
4. Construction managers
5. Environmental engineering technicians
6. Electricians
7. Physical therapist assistants
8. Registered nurses
9. Medical assistants
10. Special education teachers

 ## Which Industries Have the Lowest Unemployment?

One sure measure of recession-proof jobs should be how many workers in those jobs or industries were working rather than unemployed. According to the BLS, workers in these industries had unemployment during 2008 that was below 4%, which is considered to be the indicator of full employment:

1. *Hospital jobs* had by far the lowest unemployment at 1.6%; this is part of a larger industry group that also includes *Health services, except hospitals* where unemployment was 3.6%; by this measure, jobs in hospitals are the most in need of workers throughout the United States and all other healthcare jobs are not far behind

2. *Utilities* unemployment was 2.6%, supporting Dr. Shatkin's assertion that utilities will always need workers

3. *Mining* unemployment was 3.1% but mining probably failed to make other lists because there are relatively few mining jobs compared to others that get media attention

4. *Professional and Technical Services* had unemployment of 3.8%

5. *Financial activities* had unemployment of 3.9% and this included sub-groups *Insurance* at 3.1% and *Finance* at 3.9%[9]

The 1.6% unemployment rate for hospitals is just one indication that the employment challenge facing healthcare is the most alarming of any industry. Prior to the 2008 recession, the BLS reported that healthcare and social assistance would have the most rapid job growth from 2006 to 2016,[10] and the data in Appendix C indicates healthcare has been barely touched by the down economy. Healthcare saw a net gain of 419,000 jobs in 2008, with registered nurses growing the most by adding 168,000. Home care aids added 64,000 jobs.[11]

In a survey of healthcare executives, Nursefinders, Inc. found the following:

- The top challenge facing healthcare executives is *severe staffing shortages*
- The most important business initiative for healthcare executives is *staffing issues*
- The greatest positive impact on patient care is *overcoming severe staffing shortages*[12]

The BLS predicts 233,000 additional nurse jobs for each year through 2016, on top of 2.5 million existing positions. But only about 200,000 candidates passed the Registered Nurse licensing exam in 2008, and thousands of nurses leave the profession each year.[13] In fact, the voluntary turnover rate for first-year nurses alone is over 27%.[14]

A study put the chronic nursing shortage in an even dimmer light. Press Ganey Associates surveyed nearly 200,000 employees in 370 hospitals and found registered nurses to be the least satisfied of all hospital employees. The report goes on to say that job dissatisfaction rates are tied directly to nurse vacancy rates.[15] Another study concluded that 6,700 patient deaths and 4 million days of hospital care could be averted annually by increasing the number of nurses.[16]

While nurse shortages are those most widely known, other healthcare providers are coming up short, too. The American Medical Group

Association (AMGA) reports that 19% of physicians now choose to work part-time, adding to the existing physician shortage. Since 1980, the U.S. population has increased by more than a third, while the number of new doctors graduating from medical school has remained the same.[17] And various studies predict a shortage of 157,000 pharmacists in the next decade.[18]

The forces behind our growing need for healthcare are an aging population, new technologies, and demand for national healthcare, which will likely add millions more patients. One encouraging note is that the economic stimulus bill that was passed in February of 2009 includes $500 million to address shortages of healthcare workers.[19]

(NOTE: While the workforce challenge facing healthcare appears insurmountable, solutions provided throughout this book will help; one specific example is referenced at the beginning of Chapter 6.)

 ## Top Reports of Worker Skills Shortages

This section presents the results of several studies about the missing skills of the U.S.'s present and future workers. In good times, these shortcomings have a larger impact on our nation's economic engine when productive workers are harder to find. In bad times, ill-prepared workers face even more disadvantages to find jobs.

One study tells us the skills most needed by our future workforce will be critical thinking/problem solving, information technology application, teamwork/collaboration, and creativity/innovation.[20] Those who employ large groups of low-skilled workers would probably add "show up every day on time."

Ready to work?

The Conference Board joined with other research organizations to ask hundreds of employers "Are They Really Ready to Work?" The report scores workers as either excellent or deficient against sets of essential job skills that vary by educational level. The results include:

* New entrants to the workforce with high school diplomas are rated as deficient on all 10 essential job skills

- Two-year college-educated entrants scored against nine essential job skills received an "excellent" in one—information technology application—and eight deficiencies
- Only the four-year college-educated entrants had the excellence list longer than the deficiency list

The report concluded: "The future U.S. workforce is here—and it is woefully ill-prepared for the demands of today's (and tomorrow's) workplace."[21]

Reading shortcomings

Americans are reading less, with negative implications for our economy. In "To Read or Not to Read," the National Endowment for the Arts (NEA) found American 15-year-olds rank 15th among 31 industrialized nations—behind Poland, Korea, France, and others. Reading scores for high school seniors have fallen significantly, and the percentage of nonreaders among 17-year-olds has doubled over the past 20 years. As likely contributors, Americans ages 15–24 spend almost 2 hours each day watching television and only 7 minutes on leisure reading. Time devoted to video games is not mentioned.

Reading scores for American adults of almost all educational levels have deteriorated, most notably among the best-educated groups. An NEA spokesperson concluded, "This study shows the startling declines, in how much and how well Americans read, that are adversely affecting this country's culture, economy, and civic life as well as our children's educational achievement."[22]

Science shortcomings, too

The Programme for International Student Assessment (PISA) is an internationally standardized assessment that was jointly developed by participating countries and administered to 15-year-olds in schools. In its latest study, American students finished 29th of 57 countries and below the world average. Finland finished first, followed by Hong Kong-China, Canada, Chinese Taipei, and Estonia. Also finishing ahead of the U.S. were Liechtenstein, Ireland, Hungary, Poland, France, and Latvia.[23]

The mixed bag of Americans going to school

If the bad news is Americans aren't learning enough, the good news is more of them are trying. The BLS tells us that over the past 20 years, school participation rates for those ages 16 to 19 and 20 to 24 have increased significantly, and 65% of high school graduates are going to college.[24]

America's Promise Alliance, however, studied high school graduation rates and found that while about 70% of U.S. students graduate on time with a regular diploma, about 1.2 million drop out annually. These dropouts are clustered in cities, as 17 of the largest 50 cities have graduation rates below 50%. Leading the way are Detroit, Indianapolis, and Cleveland.

Former Secretary of State Colin Powell is founder of the Alliance and said this about the report: "When more than one million students a year drop out of high school, it's more than a problem, it's a catastrophe."[25]

Do college majors match forecasted jobs?

The U.S. Department of Education reports the most popular majors among graduates are:

- Bachelor's degrees: (1) business, (2) social sciences and history, (3) education, (4) psychology, and (5) visual and performing arts. Business majors lead by far, as there are nearly twice as many graduates with business degrees as graduates with degrees in social sciences and history.
- Master's degrees: (1) education, (2) business, (3) health professions and related clinical sciences, (4) engineering, and (5) public administration and social services. The gap between business at #2 and health professions at #3 is large; there are more than three times as many business graduates as health professions graduates.
- Doctorate degrees: (1) education, (2) engineering, (3) health professions and related clinical sciences, (4) biological and biomedical sciences, and (5) psychology.

This data is from one academic year, 2004–2005, the most recent data available.[26] It is important to note that far more students earn bachelor's degrees than doctorate degrees, so the number and types of bachelor's degrees are probably a better indicator of the potential to fill open positions. Also, some professions, such as teaching, reward or require advanced degrees more than others, so this might explain why education is the leader for advanced degrees.

Let's compare these majors to the jobs that are in most need of workers, present and future. The BLS study found that the fastest-growing industry sectors between now and 2016 will be in (1) healthcare and social assistance and (2) professional and business services.[27] These sectors will make up more than half the increase in total employment.

While the choice of major is not always a firm predictor of the choice of jobs, it appears the U.S. workforce is far better situated to meet the upcoming business needs than the healthcare needs.

Why the gap?

In their Workplace Visions paper, SHRM analyzes the hard question about why U.S. students don't perform better:

> The low performance of U.S. students compared with students in other countries is not new, but it is, in many ways, counterintuitive. The United States invests much more into education than many countries with higher average PISA scores, and American students enjoy other advantages such as a comparatively well-educated population and higher incomes than many of the countries that outperform the United States. The findings are also counterintuitive given the very high international standing and performance of U.S. universities, not to mention the nation's position as one the the the world's most technologically advanced and economically successful economies.

The report goes on to say that if these problems persist, employers will solve them by shipping more jobs overseas or replacing workers with technology.[28]

Top Ways to Retain High Performers During Layoffs …"Because They Can"

Too often companies strategize about post-layoff perceptions of victims more than they consider the implications for survivors. The price companies pay for overlooking survivors is underscored by a study from the University of Wisconsin where Professor Charlie Trevor and doctoral candidate Anthony Nyberg found a positive relationship between layoffs and subsequent voluntary turnover. In one example in the study, laying off just 1% of the workforce lead to an overall 31% *increase* in voluntary turnover. As important, the participating organizations in the study were those that had applied for Fortune's Top 100 Companies to Work For list, companies that we would assume were managed effectively.[29]

The reality is that those you've chosen to keep should be the better ones and now must do more work. This makes retaining survivors after layoffs even more important than before because any survivor who quits represents losing muscle instead of fat. Or said another way, each survivor is *more important* after layoffs than before.

Losing a good performer hurts companies more in bad times because:

- "Lean" departments have cut to the bone so there is nowhere to assign extra work
- Remaining employees look up to their high-performing peers and might follow them out the door
- Poor performers might slide by and occupy a needed job because managers are reluctant to fire them and potentially lose a position
- Re-assigned managers take on new and larger teams and need full support from their newly acquired best producers

Here are suggestions for retaining survivors during and after layoffs.

Make Other Cuts First

Shedding valuable talent means (1) you won't have it when the economy bounces back and (2) your surviving workforce will think they're next. The important question is "Will we want these employees later?" If you are making permanent eliminations of business units or head-count, cut sooner rather than later. But if you are cutting staff as a temporary survival tactic, look for other savings first because proven talent is hard to replace in any economy. Cutting travel, freezing pay, knocking back executive bonuses and other cuts must be considered first. Doing so not only reduces the chance of cutting staff but it also demonstrates good faith that you've taken all other possible measures first if you do eventually make reductions.

Who Gets Priority?

The priority for all layoff-related decisions should be (1) shareholders, (2) survivors, and (3) those who lose their jobs. Decisions regarding how many to cut should be based solely on the needs of the organization, and decisions regarding communications and future steps should be made for the needs of survivors first and casualties second. This is not to imply that actions taken with those who lose their jobs should be done haphazardly because survivors will be keenly aware of how their peers are treated.

Do It Once if Possible

The first instinctive response of survivors is "Am I next?" Unfortunately, most companies can't promise future job security and know additional layoffs might occur. But those who can give any types of assurances will increase their chances of keeping those they need to keep.

Survivors will dissect every written and verbal phrase to estimate whether they, too, will eventually be cut. From the legal side, written and spoken words might be construed as contracts so messages must be prepared and delivered perfectly. Keeping this in mind, consider which of the following information you can share to glue survivors to your company:

- The business case for layoffs, with numbers of reduced sales or other profit-related criteria

- Industry comparisons if others like you are also cutting staff
- The regretful feelings of the executives who made the decisions as well as whoever is delivering the message
- The fairness of your separation packages, with details if you can share them such as the range of severance, any outplacement support, and types of continuing benefits
- Future steps the company is taking to improve performance and minimize the likelihood of additional cuts
- The most accurate statement you can make regarding future layoffs, always with a caveat such as "We can never make guarantees"

Employees most want to hear messages of hope. Just as those who battle serious health problems or other insurmountable challenges thrive on inspiration, survivors of layoffs must hear words that are truthful but also shine a light on a potentially brighter future.

Which Survivors Matter Most?

Every organization, regardless of size, should always know which employees are most important to retain. This is especially so during layoffs because the most important survivors deserve individual meetings with their supervisors and perhaps higher managers to hear in a personal way the decisions and directions of the company and how this might impact them. Some might merit meetings before general announcements so they recognize their status as important to retain.

"Reduced by Attrition"

Press releases that announce layoffs often say that some or all of the cuts will by "reduced by attrition." This strategy is usually aimed toward low-level jobs and means the company will not replace those who leave over a designated period of time. Taken literally, it also implies that "all employees are equal and whichever ones choose to quit is OK as long as we make our number."

To an employee, this sounds as though my company doesn't care if I stay, and maybe even wants me to leave.

Those that follow this path should select which employees it wants to keep and develop a plan to do so. This might include asking all managers to choose 20% or more of those they cannot afford to lose and then hold them accountable for keeping them throughout this "no replacement" period.

Make Firing Poor Performers Always OK

In struggling economies, smart supervisors aggressively fire poor performers because the market is flooded with qualified replacements. Yet companies oftentimes declare that no one who leaves can be replaced. As a result, supervisors tell each other that any work is better than no work, so why fire someone when their chair will stay empty?

This impacts high performers because they lose faith when poor performers are ignored. Watching a peer fail with no consequences is an invitation to look elsewhere. The solution is to permit supervisors to replace anyone they fire as long as they follow policies to do so. And top management should aggressively fire poor supervisors, too.

Involve Survivors in Planning New Roles

Years ago I read an obscure study that said employees reject change because they think they should have input into all decisions. For example, a policy change regarding customer service might elicit employees to grumble, "What does headquarters know about our customers? They're not with them every day like me."

The solution the authors recommended was to involve employees in post-decision changes that impact them. Employees will leave layoff announcement meetings by asking each other "Now what?" so involve them in planning the answers.

Close your layoff-announcement meeting by scheduling a second meeting where all will have input into planning future work. Organize that meeting to address how to be more efficient, who should change roles, who needs additional training, and other areas where their input makes your decisions better . . . and makes them feel they are part of a survivor team rather than secondary victims of your layoff. Consult with high performers in advance so they know you expect them to prepare and you will act on their input.

Survivors Watch How You Treat Others

Most important, those with the skills to leave are watching how you treat those whom you cut. All will eventually learn about your severance packages, the way you communicated your decisions, and whether you treated employees with dignity. During these times employees measure the hearts of their employers, and disrespectful treatment with peers they liked will be long remembered. These become the stories that replace the ones that used to comprise your company's culture.

 ## Top Tips for Gathering Exit Data

Exit surveys are the first-mentioned retention tool by most organizations. Their logical approach for fixing turnover is to ask employees why they leave and then repair the problems. The traps to avoid are failing to find the true reasons employees leave, and then believing you can solve turnover simply by patching the holes they tell you.

Additionally, it is sometimes hard to match up leave reasons with real causes. For example, an employee leaving for pay might be an indicator that your company needs to pay more. Or it might mean he should have never been hired because your pay doesn't match his needs, or that he might have just married and taken on three children and is suddenly more ambitious.

But we would all agree it is good to learn why employees leave us, if we can find ways to get accurate data.

The primary exit survey methods are the traditional face-to-face interview, paper surveys, online surveys, automated phone surveys, and phone surveys by third parties. Interviews in any form offer the best opportunity to gain more information via follow-up probes if the interviewer is properly skilled. Paper and online surveys are most efficient and offer confidentiality to gain unfiltered information. The following recommendations apply to all of these methods.

Find out why the employee is leaving, period

Some exit surveys have become mini-employee surveys, with questions and scales for how the leaving employee feels about her supervisor, pay, benefits, schedules, and other job factors. The thinking is we should gather as much information as possible, and whichever items get low scores probably contributed to that employee's decision to leave. The reality is that employee dislikes are often not associated with why they leave, and giving them categories for consideration opens the door to their expanding on miscellaneous opinions rather than focusing on the real reason for the survey, which is, "Why did you decide to leave us?"

Providing categories also gives employees a checklist of default reasons to choose from if they want to hide the truth.

For interviews, avoid using categories. Ask questions such as:

- Why did you decide to leave us?
- Of all the things you've told me, what is the top thing that caused you to resign?
- It's great that you've found such a good opportunity, but why did you look?
- What one thing could we have done that would have caused you to stay?

Exit interviews should be structured so all questions are asked consistently and responses recorded in the same format. Interviewers should probe to learn details of leave reasons to fully understand their context. Interviewers should also encourage employees to discuss other job conditions even if they did not contribute to the exit decision, as long as the real leave reason has been determined.

For surveys that are administered without an interview, ask respondents to choose the primary reason they are leaving from a list of possible leave reasons rather than ask them to rate each one. Having them rank factors from most to least reasons for leaving will get you the same data. The goal is to know the most important leave reason rather than learn which three or five things contributed to their decision.

Sort the information you receive into leave reasons that are actionable. Avoid "better opportunities" as a potential leave reason on all survey formats because it gives you no potential direction for change. Include absences and job abandonment with involuntary terminations.

Do not promise confidentiality

Exit information that must remain confidential has little value because what cannot be shared cannot result in change. The best approach is to never mention confidentiality, either when beginning an interview or on any type of survey form.

If employees request confidentiality, tell them you want their opinions to be heard and to make your company better. Worst case, negotiate what data you can share and, if necessary, with whom you can share it.

Exit surveys sometimes surface patterns of abuse. Listen carefully for hints of sexual or other types of harassment. If employees want to share this information but are reluctant, coach them to help your company by telling you, or if necessary make some concessions on confidentiality as long as you can still take appropriate action. Make every effort to hear about abuse, in part because you might be liable for being unwilling to act if you have been unwilling to listen.

Use skilled interviewers

Organizations that conduct face-to-face interviews should choose an employee who is skilled to elicit important and sometimes confidential information from an employee whom they might be meeting for the first time. Skills for this role include warmth, listening, sincerity, trust-building, and objectivity, as well as being able to analyze information and probe to learn more.

This job is often assigned to HR interviewers, and both roles require similar skills. However, interviewers are usually trained to conduct hiring interviews but not to conduct exit interviews. Tell them their most important assignment is to learn why the employee is leaving and then train them to probe to get this data. Meeting with employees who are leaving the company can help interviewers improve their hiring skills, as they will learn about mismatches with your company's culture and specific supervisors.

Special circumstances might require that a senior manager meet with the exiting employee, either in addition to the regular exit process or in place of it. Examples might be when a senior-level or long-term employee is leaving, or someone is leaving for a controversial reason.

Gather data as soon as possible after the employee gives notice

Give leaving employees the opportunity to speak to you before they speak to others. You'll increase the opportunity to keep them if you wish and decrease the likelihood they will say negative things to peers.

Ask what steps they took to resolve their issues

For your benefit, you want to know if the employee took proactive measures to fix their circumstance but met obstructions. For their benefit, they might blame others less for their problem if they realize they failed to take reasonable steps to fix it.

Distribute results to those who can make improvements

Analyze results by reason, supervisor, job, length of service, and other categories that might identify important patterns. Then distribute aggregated results to senior managers and individual results to the leaving employee's supervisor and next-up manager. Too often managers and supervisors report that exit surveys are conducted but they don't see outcomes. First-level supervisors should always receive exit survey results for those who leave their teams so they grow and feel trusted with the results.

Track improvements you make

In one survey, only one-third of HR managers reported positive changes that resulted from gathering exit survey data. With this in mind, keep a list of significant improvements your company makes. Note changed policies, improved supervisors, removed supervisors, uncovered abuses—anything that makes gathering this data worthwhile.

If you find you are gathering data but not improving your company in specific ways, ask your executive team if they see real value in continuing the surveys. If they do, provide a report in 90 days that tells what changes you've seen since they recommitted their interest. If they see no value, streamline the exit survey process to ensure you are at least gathering information on harassment unless you are gathering this data through an employee hotline or some other method.

End on a high

For many employees, the exit meeting is the last meeting they will have with a management representative before leaving. So it is your final opportunity to shape their thinking as they move on and tell others about your company.

Know in advance if the employee is eligible for rehire, and if so make it clear she is welcome to return. Thank her for her contributions that made your company better.

Build solutions beyond exit survey results

If every star aligns and you get true data on why your employees leave, take smart actions to address those causes. And as you do so, move forward to implement the strategies and tactics discussed in the following chapters to strengthen retention across your organization.

 ## True Stories

These stories offer various twists on the competition for talent in good and bad economies.

One easy click away

Strategic planners use terms like "cost of switching" to calculate the degree of hassle or loss a customer must deal with to change providers. One simple example is the amount of administrative work required to change banks versus the ease of driving across the street to switch grocery stores.

A generation ago, applying for a new job required delivering or mailing a typed resume or application and then traveling to the potential employer's office to be interviewed or complete assessments. Today much of this can be done online in minutes while wearing pajamas. Reducing the costs of job-switching benefits employers and applicants alike because all happens quicker and cheaper, but it adds to the conundrum of keeping good workers. Here are just a few examples of the switching capabilities employees have literally at their fingertips:

- The most recent count of Internet job sites is approximately 50,000 in North America and the same number in other parts of the world, far more than the few that advertise nationally.[30]
- The majority of job boards are niche sites that cater to nearly every market: Specific jobs, industries, cities, languages, nationalities, pay levels, gender, and sexual preferences.
- Some boards cross-reference with social networks such as Facebook, MySpace, and LinkedIn to broaden their capacity to connect workers to jobs.
- Other boards offer advanced services like resume screening and development of personal videos.[31]
- A few boards invite anyone to refer a friend and collect a referral award.[32]

Job board guru Peter Weddle surveys users each year and reports the most common profile is a manager, age 40 to 45, who is currently employed. Respondents said job boards were their most used source for finding their last jobs and will likely be the most used source for finding their next jobs. The percent who found their last jobs on a board nearly doubled over the previous year.[33]

Offshoring for quality versus cost

In 2006, AT&T vowed to return 5,000 customer service jobs back to the U.S. from India. Two years later, however, only 1,400 of those jobs had made their way back. The problem? The quality of U.S. workers.

"We're having trouble finding the numbers that we need with the skills required to do these jobs," said CEO Randall Stephenson.

He went on to say he was distressed that high school dropout rates were as high as 50% in some areas. "If I had a business that half the product we turned out was defective or you couldn't put it into the marketplace, I would shut that business down," he said.

While most Americans view cost as the reason businesses offshore jobs, Stephenson made it clear that worker quality matters as much. "We're able to do new product engineering in Bangalore as easily as we're able to do it in Austin, Texas. I know you don't like hearing that, but that's the way it is." He added that the solution was a stronger U.S. focus on education.[34]

Space program at risk

While defense contractors compete with other industries for engineering talent, they face an uphill climb regarding student preferences. "In" jobs are with fast-rising technology companies like Google and Apple, or mission-driven organizations that aim to cure cancer or global warming. Baby-boomer engineers were more interested in building rockets and missiles, and their dwindling numbers is a strong cause for concern. As one industry spokesperson said, "This is not the kind of work that we can just outsource overseas."[35]

Population swings correlate with economic growth

Economists have long debated which comes first: Increases in the population or improvements in the economy. Either way, declining populations usually bring sagging economies along with them.

Russia's population is expected to decline by 22% by 2050 and Ukraine's by 43%. Even China's population will decline by the early 2030s. The United Nations projects that populations will be lower than they are today in 50 countries by 2050.[36] In Japan, deaths have outnumbered births for the first time in a peace period since records have been kept.[37]

Population declines are usually preceded by high numbers of retirements. In Japan, Europe, and North America, the number of retirees will double over the next 25 years.[38]

Any formula for maintaining economic stability as the number of workers falls must include increasing the *quality* of workers, as skilled workers will be in even higher demand.

Canada's labor crunch mirrors the United States

Prior to the recession, the government of Alberta launched a recruitment campaign to pull foreign workers from the United States with a promise of granting them permanent residency status more quickly.[39] Then in early 2009 the government of Saskatchewan invited workers across Canada to relocate, citing their 4.1% unemployment rate.[40]

Prime Minister Stephen Harper has proclaimed Canada will recover from the recession "before any other country" but cautions the country will immediately face a labor shortage when the recession ends.[41] The primary cause, once again, is the aging of the workforce. One study indicates that by 2016 the number of workers will be in steady decline and "the (effective) unemployment rate will go to zero."[42]

International boomerang pulls away needed professionals

The accelerating economies of India and China are providing many new levels of competition, and one is for qualified workers. Estimates are that 60,000 IT professionals have returned to India, mainly from the United States and Great Britain.[43]

The Chinese government has launched the Overseas-Educated Talent Development Foundation. Its mission is to "attract more overseas Chinese scholars to return home and serve the country."[44] In one study, 88% of those scholars expressed interest in returning to China, nearly half of them immediately after graduation. Their targeted cities are Shanghai and Beijing.[45]

Declining dollar brings jobs

Who would have predicted this? While U.S. workers fret about their jobs going overseas, the declining value of the dollar is bringing jobs here. International companies, including Fiat, Volkswagen, Samsung, and ThyssenKrupp, have either talked of moving facilities to the

United States or have begun doing so. Said a PricewaterhouseCoopers spokesperson, "They're worried about the movement of the dollar, so moving to a dollar zone takes a big element of risk out of the equation."[46]

High oil prices bring jobs, too

The sharp fluctuations in the price of oil severely impact the cost of shipping imported goods across the oceans. So as a major importer of world goods, the United States could see more factories and more jobs sprouting up on its soil. Swedish furniture maker Ikea has opened a factory in Virginia and midwestern steel makers are thriving.[47]

States retain talent through double-dipping

Public sector managers have found a way to replace retiring talent—by rehiring it. Legal in most states, governments are following employees' retirement parties with job offers for their same position and then permitting these employees to earn a second pension. While the most prevalent participants are teachers, police officers, and young retirees, double-dippers have also included elected officials, school superintendents, university presidents, and police chiefs. Several states are now passing laws to end or limit double-dipping.[48]

Travel nurses are a booming business

The nursing shortage has been a boon to AMN Healthcare, the largest U.S. travel nurse company. AMN was started in the founder's home with two employees and now boasts 2,000 employees and over $1 billion in revenues.

Travel nurses work for 13-week assignments across the country, filling openings due to staff shortages. Openings are for the usual reasons such as staff growth, turnover, and retirements, but are exacerbated by most nurses being females who are more likely to take time off for children. In a recent survey, about 90% of chief nursing officers agreed with the statement "Our facility could not function without travel nurses."[49]

Double-checking reasons to leave

Sam Panarella manages the consulting practice for Fios, a 175-employee firm in Portland, Oregon, that helps companies nationwide manage their electronic data. Panarella is a very savvy retention leader.

Panarella's method for learning real leave reasons is a three-step process. In step #1, Panarella interviews the leaving employee and asks all the right questions about why he has chosen to leave. In step #2, Panarella asks the leaving employee's manager to send him an e-mail with the reasons why the manager thinks the employee is leaving and what the manager could have done differently to retain the employee. In step #3, Panarella meets with the manager to reconcile any differences and identify lessons learned. As a carrot, Panarella won't sign the replacement requisition until all three steps have been done.

Thinking as a consultant, Panarella's primary objective is to conduct a "root cause analysis" on employee turnover in his area. Deep down, he believes leaving *employees have no reason to be honest because* "there's no upside for them as this is a small business community."

According to Panarella, "The most interesting information always comes from the manager. *Finding the real reasons their employees leave* is a great teaching opportunity for them. And it helps us all learn the types of employees who will thrive at our company and the ones who will not."[50]

Closing Thoughts on "Because They Can"

Here are three major conclusions for rethinking retention based on the data presented in this chapter.

Traditional Beliefs	Rethinking Retention
We take action when turnover goes up.	Demographics make clear that retention must be a major strategic initiative for the foreseeable future.
Workers are glad to have jobs in a down economy, especially after layoffs.	For most jobs, good employees still have choices in any economy and are more inclined to leave after layoffs.
Exit interviews point the way to turnover solutions.	If conducted effectively, exit interviews provide just one piece of a comprehensive retention solution.

The data presented in this chapter can leave us looking for good news, and we have it: *You only have to find and retain productive workers for your company.* If you wake up tonight after dreaming you are The Appointed One who must solve the talent crisis for the world, call it a nightmare and go back to sleep.

Taken in aggregate, the data tell us that employees can leave us for any reason or for no reason at all. The good ones have the upper hand in nearly every field. Avoid at all costs believing the pathway to retention is to plug holes in the dike that surface from exit surveys. Instead, build a company that knows its identity and attracts workers who want to stay with you. Hiring and retaining is much easier that way. Read on.

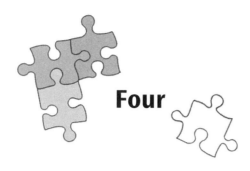

Four

Employees Stay for Things They Get Uniquely from You

S mart companies identify their strengths as employers and market them because they know good talent is essential in any economy. They view attracting and retaining good workers just as they view attracting and retaining customers, with the same levels of strategic thinking and vigor. They recognize the daunting challenge they face and commit the intellectual resources, time, and sometimes additional funding to overcome it.

In a nutshell, they identify their glues and leverage them to the hilt.

I was once invited to consult with the Central Intelligence Agency (CIA). After clearing the security checkpoint, we drove through the Langley, Virginia, campus to the headquarters building and entered the epitome of employment branding. As we walked over the granite inlaid CIA seal on the floor, we looked to our right and saw the Wall of Honor, dedicated to those who "gave their lives in the service of their country." Later we toured various historical reminders, including original spy tools, memorials to CIA leaders, and a statue of Nathan Hale, the first American to be executed for spying.

Certainly the CIA designed its headquarters for reasons beyond attracting and retaining employees. But if I ever had the privilege of working for the CIA, I would know from walking into that building that I worked for a unique organization that has no peers. Flash to their website, *https://www.cia.gov/*, and their employment positioning statement further carves their one-of-a-kind world status: "The work of a nation. The center of intelligence."

While few of us can replicate the uniqueness of the CIA, our job is to attract the right workers so we can then decide if we want to hire and retain them. Here are the tactics included in this chapter to help you do this:

- **Top Q&A for developing an employee value proposition** (EVP) so your top team identifies your employment offerings that separate you from your competitors
- **Top tips for building your employment brand** to help you successfully market your EVP
- **Top ways to conduct "stay interviews"** so you learn what makes your employees stay and your supervisors take the lead on providing it
- **Top strategic employee benefits** to expand your thinking on benefits that match your applicants and employees to you and your mission

The True Stories section explores the actions some organizations have taken to carve their unique niches and concludes with sage advice from an expert on the importance of delivering on your promise.

 ## Top Q&A for Developing an Employee Value Proposition (EVP)

Employee value propositions and employment brands are tools to attract the applicants you want. Both also contribute to retention by reinforcing important company messages to onboard employees.

The Corporate Leadership Council sponsored a global study on employee value propositions and found very encouraging results.

Organizations that developed and managed their EVPs effectively attracted many more passive job-seekers and paid less to new hires. Regarding retention, they found new hires had higher commitment levels after both one month and after twelve months of service.[1]

Developing these tools requires that your top team take a hard look in the mirror to identify your glues. What does your company offer that will attract the workers you want? What advantages do you have to compete for the talent pool?

The quest for your top team is to identify in what ways you are an *extraordinary* employer. Your advantages might be tangible, such as providing extra benefits, or intangible, like improving customers' lives. Regardless of their assets or missions, all companies can offer extraordinary experiences for employees by providing excellent supervision, allowing input into company decisions, upholding appealing values, and providing opportunities to learn. In fact, a Corporate Leadership Council study demonstrated that only 3 of 38 attributes they analyzed drove both attraction and commitment: Development opportunities, future career opportunities, and respect.[2]

The most valuable part of developing these tools might be your top management's taking an objective look at the type of employer you are. The best companies will recognize who they are and set goals to become even better. Conversely, if you find your company offers only an ordinary employment experience, expect ordinary results in return.

Companies that don't script their employee value proposition let applicants and employees script it on their own. Much like a company culture, you always have an EVP. If left unguided, employees will form it by telling each other what's good and bad about working for you. The Corporate Leadership Council study also identified the one source employees find most credible for gaining company information: "Current employees."

Developing your EVP with the processes presented here allows you to formalize your offerings and present them in ways that shape employees' thinking in your favor—as long as what you tell them is true.

The following sections discuss the top ways to develop an employee value proposition and to build an employment brand.

What is an EVP?

An EVP is a written statement that tells applicants and employees what you will provide for them. Designed correctly, EVPs should distinguish your company from others you compete with for talent.

Think of an EVP as a job offer, except it is a *company* offer that articulates the primary benefits employees receive in exchange for their work. "Benefits" in this case goes beyond the traditional ones and might include leadership styles, career opportunities, and what employees will learn. Sometimes EVPs include intangible rewards that heighten emotions such as joining a smart team, helping customers live better lives, or making people healthy with your products.

How do we learn who we are?

Developing an EVP requires knowing what you really offer employees versus what you think you offer. One way to learn this is to conduct a gap analysis between how top management views the company and how employees view it.

Begin by reviewing company documents and lore to learn your stated values. These might include mission statements, strategic plans, marketing plans, target markets, products, media perceptions, and historical business performance. Recall the top five stories that are told repeatedly about your company's founders and current leaders that illustrate the company's roles and beliefs. After considering all this, make a list of *your company's characteristics that make it a good place to work*.

Then test your list against employee perceptions by conducting employee surveys, focus groups, and exit surveys. Large companies might conduct external marketing studies to learn how you are perceived as an employer. Ask college recruiters about graduating students' perceptions of your company.

By comparing inputs from all these perspectives, you'll likely find your strengths as an employer—and some shortcomings as well. For example, you might *not* be a market leader for pay because doing so will cut too deeply into profit margins. But you might also find that 40% of new hires get promoted, so you really do offer career opportunities, or that 90% of your employees are satisfied with you as an employer.

How do we match our EVP to the needs of our workforce?

If you consult the myriad of employee surveys, it seems all employees want the same things: Pay, benefits, careers, flexible schedules, upbeat work environments, and good supervisors usually top the list. But companies that rely on generic information usually develop generic EVPs that read like mush to applicants and employees.

The following are the best ways to tailor your EVP to the needs of your workforce.

- Ask current employees the most important things that make them stay (a process for doing this appears later in this chapter), and consult data from surveys and focus groups used for the gap analysis. Look for niche reasons that might surprise you. For example, there's a warehouse company that refers to its employees as "industrial athletes" because they must be in top condition to load heavy packages. This name is now a source of pride for the team and has become a reason they stay.
- Know the talents you need to attract and the characteristics of those who have them. For instance, young workers want to learn and not be bored, whereas older workers tend to look for stability and positive relationships.

External and internal talent will read your EVP with WIIFM ("What's in it for me?") in mind. Give them a compelling answer that matches their needs.

Should we write about who we are or who we want to be?

Write about who you are, and then rewrite your EVP if you become better. This is a commitment statement, and you must fulfill it 100% of the time or risk breaking trust.

Who should be involved in writing our company's EVP?

Executives, HR, and marketing. Executives will learn from the gap analysis experience, and as a result they'll make hard choices regarding the company they want to lead. HR brings real-world knowledge of employee wants and needs as well as information about the competitor landscape. Marketing is expert at gathering information and presenting it in ways that influence decisions.

Should individual departments have their own EVPs?

Yes, especially in large companies where departments perform different functions and attract different types of applicants. Customizing your EVP makes it more appealing as you differentiate it for IT experts versus sales pros, and for younger or older workers if you are trying to attract them.

What's an example of an effective EVP?

Most employer websites have EVPs but they might fall under another name. One I really like is on the IPsoft website (*www.ipsoft.com/us/careers/employeevalueproposition*) and it includes this line: "We recognize the value of a committed, hyper-driven, rocket-science caliber workforce."

How do we introduce our EVP to our internal teams?

Ask marketing to develop a rollout process similar to a product introduction. Arrange for an executive to meet with all employees, whether in one group meeting or across the oceans via several teleconferences, to describe the reasons for developing the EVP, the process used, sources of employee input, the ways it will be applied, and, most important, the commitments it represents.

 ## Top Tips for Building Your Employment Brand

Design your brand from your EVP

Think of your brand as your EVP's extroverted and highly energized fraternal twin. Brands adapt the content of EVPs and present them with fizz to grab attention. Brands might be presented as positioning statements on posters at job fairs or they might be adapted to video format to show on college campuses. Branding is the marketing of your EVP's content, and it should appear on your website, collateral materials, employee communications, in your employment office, and as part of any other tool you use to shape the beliefs of applicants and employees.

Trigger their emotions

Brands should be eye-catching and trigger one's emotions, because you want applicants and employees to commit their hearts to you as well as their minds. Both want to know:

- How will I grow and change because I choose you?
- How will I impact the lives of others? (It's not what your products *are*, it's what they *do*.)
- What are your values? How do I know I can trust you?
- How does working for you improve my life?
- Will I be proud to tell others I work for you?

New hires must redirect their lives to work for you. On a larger scale, many of them want to improve their lives by improving the lives of others. Tell them how working for your company makes all that happen.

Presume they want to learn and contribute

I worked with a beauty products company that manages several call centers. For years this company hired agents to work in their centers by advertising call center jobs. They have since rebranded to seek candidates who are interested in learning beauty products with the hope of attracting female applicants who will thrive on gaining more knowledge about skin creams and also enjoy the employee discounts. The applicant pool is deeper and better as a result.

Rethink jobs to present them for what employees *learn and contribute* versus what they do. Custodians in schools contribute to education, clerks in computer stores learn technology, bank tellers learn financial services, grocery employees learn food products, food preparers learn kitchen skills, and warehouse attendants learn auto parts or whatever they are shipping. Most learning happens on the job each day rather than in classrooms, so brand your jobs to attract those who have a high interest in your jobs' core learnings and contributions.

Merge your employee brand with your product brand

Your employees already know how you brand your products in the marketplace, and applicants might know too. Leverage this by using the same or similar positioning statements, phrases, examples, fonts, colors, and other ways that will cause employees to adopt and remember your employment brand quicker and easier. One way to reinforce this is to give employees advance screenings of new product marketing materials and then tie these to your employment brand.

Drive brands home with stories

People learn in different ways, but most are captivated by good stories. Think of the stories your company repeats about individual careers, social contributions, civic leadership, product impacts, or the challenges of your founders. If these stories match your brand, script them into prehire discussions, onboarding meetings, training sessions, executive speeches, newsletters, and other ways employees learn about your company.

In Chapter 8, the description of MITRE's hiring process references their online realistic job preview. Included are individual employees telling their career stories with MITRE so applicants clearly grasp that one can advance with MITRE.

Drive your brand through leaders

From executives to first-line supervisors, all who have leadership authority must know and live your brand. This requires integrating your brand into selecting, training, and coaching leaders to ensure they know the values and activities they must uphold.

Likewise, all aspects of your hiring process must uphold your brand as well. If you brand yourself as a company that respects employees, meet candidates on time and get back to them quickly.

Advantage to small companies

Small business owners might shudder at the cost of top-in-class benefits or even consultant help with branding. But according to a study by Salary.com, small businesses have advantages they can market over their larger competitors.

- More bang for the buck: Employees have more responsibility, accountability, and opportunity to gain self-esteem.
- Shorter line of sight: Fewer employees means each one has a greater direct impact on achieving organizational objectives and reaching key numbers.
- Higher levels of collaboration and cooperation: Work groups are more unified and communications are easier, so employees work together better.
- Career development: New products and growth produce more per-person leadership roles, and more meaningful supervisor–employee relationships lead to better career coaching.
- More fun: Small businesses are more likely to celebrate personal achievements and company successes.[3]

Great brand examples

The following are examples of great employee branding available at the following companies' career websites. Although these examples represent large employers, most small companies can design similar branding tools and then carry them over to other forms of advertising. You can view these by searching for "jobs" or "careers" at these companies' sites.

- Texas Instruments' positioning statement is "Think Big. Think Bold. Think Texas Instruments."[4] It implies reaching goals not previously imagined and separating oneself from the pack.
- Herman Miller presents a 44-page corporate values booklet in which applicants view employees at work under titles like "curiosity and exploration," "performance," and "engagement."[5]
- General Mills' positioning statement has a definite retention flavor with "A great place to start. A great place to stay."[6]

- eBay presents a fun work environment using a clever positioning statement and quote. The statement is: "You can find a lot of cool things on eBay. But you won't find anything cooler than our jobs." The quote, from Noel Coward, reads: "Work is much more fun than fun."[7]
- Children's Healthcare of Atlanta maximizes its mission by providing a video on how various jobs impact the health of children.[8]
- Stew Leonard's offers the "Top 10 Reasons to Work for Stew's!" that drives home employer awards, civic contributions, and internal promotions.[9]
- Southwest Airlines presents its benefits as "The Eight Freedoms," capitalizing on their "Freedom" theme.[10]
- Quicken Loans asks applicants, "What does 'THE DIFF' mean?" as a way to differentiate itself from competitors for talent.[11]
- Macy's "Spotlight on our People" has pictures and quotes from employees about their jobs and company.[12]
- Delta appeals to applicants' needs to help others with their positioning statement: "Delta employees don't just travel the world. They work to improve it."[13] Beneath the quote are examples of civic opportunities and ways to improve the environment.
- Publix supermarkets leverages its customer brand, "Where shopping is a pleasure," with "If you think shopping at Publix is a pleasure, try *working* here!"[14]

Let's end this section with dueling positioning statements from competitors. My experience with bookstore employees is they are savvy about their immense product line and genuinely like working with books. The major book retailers know that pulling in candidates with their products is a solid recruitment strategy.

On their site, Barnes & Noble greets applicants with, "If you love books, why not work in a place surrounded by them?"[15] Borders takes a different approach that should also appeal to book readers: "Putting our passion for knowledge and entertainment to work."[16]

Top Ways to Conduct "Stay Interviews"

If companies conducted stay interviews with as much fervor as they conduct exit interviews, turnover would be lower and supervisors would be much more engaged in their retention roles. Unlike exit interviews, stay interviews gather data from employees who are still contributing to your bottom line, and supervisors are in the interview chair instead of HR so they hear stay reasons firsthand.

Stay interviews produce other advantages, too. For starters, they contribute to your research for developing your EVP and employment brand. What's a better way to learn how to attract good applicants than finding out why your current employees stay?

Stay interviews are also important because:

- Supervisors learn why their employees stay, and they can leverage these reasons as retention tools.
- Employees hear directly that staying is important: "Somebody cares that I stay!"
- Employees accept accountability for surfacing their concerns and might accept responsibility for staying, too, if their concerns are addressed.

Supervisors should be trained how to conduct stay interviews so the meetings don't become complaint sessions about company policies that are beyond supervisors' control. We find it helpful to teach supervisors the stay interview process and then have them participate in structured role plays where they coach each other on responses and techniques.

Here are some suggestions for conducting stay interviews. You might find ways to improve this process for your company.

Take good notes

Taking notes enhances listening skills and tells the speaker her words are important. Supervisors will also reference the notes later to summarize the discussion and provide aggregated results to top management.

State your purpose clearly: We want you to stay

"I want to talk with you today about the most important reasons you stay with us, because as long as you continue to do your job well, we want you to work here for a long time."

This statement is direct and flattering, and it protects you from an implied contract if the employee's performance slips. Variations are okay as long as the employee hears she is wanted and the supervisor references "as long as you continue to perform well" in some way.

Focus on what you can control

"My greatest interest for today's meeting is to learn *what I can do* to make this a great place for you to work. As you know, our company, like all companies, has policies that I can make recommendations for but don't have the authority to change—things like pay, benefits, schedules, and the like. Now I do want you to tell me what is important to you regardless of whether I can change it, but I will be listening especially for things I can control."

This statement steers the employee away from noncontrollable issues but leaves the door cracked if saying them is important.

Broaden their awareness

While some employees come to work each day to earn a paycheck, most stay for reasons that are less tangible and may be even less obvious to them. The "less tangibles" also tend to be the areas that supervisors can impact most, such as teaching skills, providing information, or increasing peer social opportunities. So supervisors should ask questions such as these to surface stay reasons that go beyond tangible rewards:

- When you travel to work each day, what things do you look forward to?
- What parts of your job are the most enjoyable—or even the most fun?
- What parts are the most challenging?

- What are you learning here? What more do you want to learn?
- How do you like working with other members of our team?
- And what about me—what can I do to help you stay longer?

Feel free to supplement this list with questions that fit your company.

Summarize stay reasons and seek confirmation

"So based on what I've heard you say so far, let me tell you the main reasons you stay to see if I got it right."

By now the supervisor will have either three lines or three pages of notes, depending on the employee's contributions and the supervisor's ability to probe. With training, the supervisor should be able to cull out the most important items and read them back. Most important, the supervisor should focus on the most important stay reasons in the eyes of the employee rather than the supervisor's wish list of low-hanging fruit. While we might hope all employees tell us they stay for their benefits or relationships with peers, saying they stay mainly for money means they stay mainly for money.

Ask why they might leave, too

"Thanks for helping me understand the main reasons why you stay with us. Let's also look at your staying from another perspective. Are there specific reasons you can think of that could cause you to leave us?"

Supervisors need to know the whole picture in order to coach employees to stay, including specific reasons they might leave. Probing will help them gauge the seriousness of any concerns and the stated or implied timetables for potentially addressing them.

Resummarize and explain next steps

"So let me summarize the reasons you told me you stay as well as things that could cause you to leave. Then we'll make a plan so I can help to make our company a great place for you to work."

This step requires higher skill levels from supervisors, because they must respond to a variety of stay or potential leave reasons. Possible scenarios are:

- *Stay/leave reasons are easy* and can be addressed on the spot: "Let me find a way to get you training on the new printing machine and I'll get back to you by Tuesday."
- *Stay/leave reasons are beyond the supervisor's control,* such as the employee wanting a major pay increase: "Our company policy is..., and the best way you can advance your pay is by ..., but it is very unlikely you will receive that amount of increase at one time or over the next six months."

  During training, supervisors should practice for these exchanges using prepared scripts so all responses are candid and consistent, unless an employee's stellar performance merits a different answer.
- *Stay/leave reasons are more complex,* such as seeking a customized career plan or a flexible work schedule: "Let me investigate ways we might be able to help you, and I promise to get back to you within one week from today."

When high-performing employees ask for nontraditional benefits or rewards, supervisors will push upstream to find ways to say yes. While this might initially stress their managers or HR, it will also challenge historic ways of operating and deepen the supervisor's commitment to retaining her employees.

End on a positive note

"Thanks so much for sharing your candid thoughts with me regarding reasons you stay and could possibly leave. My job is to make our company the best place for you to work, and I promise to do all I can to make that happen."

Making this commitment requires the supervisor to fulfill his initial follow-up commitments and then check in periodically to ensure the employee's stated needs are being met. Savvy retention leaders will also build on the rapport that grows from the stay interview to invite additional "stay" meetings if the employee gives any signs of wanting to leave.

Send aggregated stay and leave reasons up the chain

Your "stay interview" process should include a method for supervisors to send the data they've collected to their managers, who then study the data and continue to send it upstream. Ultimately, managers on each level should know this data for their teams so they can coach supervisors to use it properly and also advocate any smart changes to company policies. On a company-wide level, the data can be used for developing EVPs and branding as well as for reference when considering policy changes.

 ## Top Strategic Employee Benefits

As your top team reflects on your employee value proposition, someone might ask, "If we offered another employee benefit, what should it be?" This section offers examples of unusual benefits companies offer that are all targeted toward achieving their own strategic objectives.

Some would call the following benefits extreme because most companies wouldn't consider them. They don't appear on standard survey lists and applicants don't expect them. But in each case they represent smart, strategic thinking because the benefits are customized to meet unique needs of each company's applicants and employees or the company's own mission.

As you read this list, think past whether your company should implement the benefits mentioned here. Focus instead on the questions that follow each example so you explore new ideas that can link your applicants and employees to your organization.

Las Vegas cabbies get free glitter

The glitter of Las Vegas is its world-class hotels and shows, and taxi drivers and their families experience it all for free. The hotels take the lead, inviting cabbies to see each new show and stay in new hotels, and sometimes they even provide box lunches from new restaurants.

In return, they know the cabbies are more likely to recommend their products to guests.[17]

The cab companies have fallen into offering this great employee benefit because the hotels recognized they needed to make cab drivers their marketers. As a result, cabbies now have a family-friendly benefit they likely could never afford. Cab executives say it's hard to know if these benefits cut turnover, but intuitively it seems sacrificing the experience of seeing each new show with one's family would be a barrier to quitting.

From a strategic perspective, this benefit was born by one industry recognizing it needed another. *Does your company have industries or other companies that need you and might contribute a strategic employee benefit?*

Bring your pet to work

It makes sense that PETCO, "where the pets go," would hire employees who are passionate about pets, and the company's bring-your-pet-to-work policy reinforces its mission. Employees at PETCO's San Diego headquarters are welcome to bring their pets to work—*every day.*

Charlie Piscitello, the senior vice president and chief people officer at PETCO, explains the policy this way: "Bringing pets to work is part of who we are as a company and represents an important aspect of our culture and brand promise. We are pet lovers and our pets remind us of that every day at work."

What's a typical day at PETCO headquarters? Piscitello estimates about 50% of the more than 800 employees who work there either keep or bring pets to their workplaces. Dogs, cats, fish, snakes, rabbits, ferrets, and other types of amphibians and reptiles—it's one big, happy family. Sherpa the hermit crab lives in Piscitello's office, and all employees and pets peacefully coexist.

Calendar highlights each year at PETCO include pet fashion shows, hamster races, and, of course, a Halloween pet costume contest. The "dog fun runs" located on the company's headquarters campus are a common meeting grounds for associates and their pets.

According to Piscitello, "Associates can always leave a company for more money, but they wouldn't want to leave Fluffy at home." Piscitello sees a deep-rooted connection between retention and employees bringing their pets: "The more an organization encourages you to bring your whole self to work, the longer you will stay."[18]

This benefit connects employees to the company mission and helps them have fun at work. For participating employees, quitting PETCO requires the sacrifice of working near your pet and perhaps having to hire someone to take care of it. Is there a similar benefit opportunity for your company that connects employees to your mission?

Concierge services at work

When employees complain about stress, most companies look inward and ask if they can reduce workloads or add better equipment. But some smart companies are now asking, "How can we help you with your life?"

HCA-HealthONE, which operates healthcare facilities throughout Colorado, recognized their employees' need for more time. As a result, the company implemented a concierge program much like hotels have for their guests. Think of this service as a major errand-runner that replaces employees' stress and guilt about driving in traffic before and after work and during lunch—and weekends—to get personal things done. Services include personal shopping, car maintenance, dry cleaning, package shipping, housesitting, gift wrapping, watering plants, planning birthday parties, researching travel . . . and on and on.

Consider the August obligations that envelop your working parents, like registering their children for school, buying school supplies, choosing the traditional new-year backpack, and buying dance or sports equipment. All of these services are covered as well.

Roger Smith, vice president of human resources for HCA-HealthONE, reported that the initial ROI was based on retaining just two nurses, whose exit cost was measured to be almost exactly one year of pay. Turnover has dropped consistently in the first year of implementing it, so Smith feels great about his company's investment. The internal buzz created by the concierge program further supports its impact on retention.

Smith summarizes the value of the program this way: "Eighty percent of our employees are women and many are working moms. We wanted to give them a benefit that would truly help them every day, and also help those who don't have children. The gift of time is often more important to employees than the gift of money."[19]

One study indicates about 5% of U.S. companies have hired concierge-type companies to provide services for their employees, including Google, General Mills, and Ernst & Young.[20]

So how does your company manage stress in the workplace? Would helping employees manage their lives increase productivity as well as retention?

Housing help

Perhaps the best "lock-in" employee benefit is helping employees buy or rent a home. School districts have historically led the way, as some have built teacher-only apartments and supplemented the rent. The New York City Department of Education provides help in another way by offering a housing stipend to experienced teachers who move to that area. The stipend can total up to $15,000 in payments for their first three years.[21]

Homes for Working Families is a nonprofit organization dedicated to helping working families find safe, good-quality homes they can afford. Their website features 14 winners of their recent Pioneer Awards, companies that offer a variety of housing assistance to their employees. This list offers a menu of various ways to help and can be found at *www.bhfs.com/portalresource/lookup/wosid/contentpilot-core-401-5204/pdfCopy.pdf.*

Fannie Mae also offers help for employer-assisted housing. Their most recent report can be found at *www.atlantaregional.com/documents/EAH_brochure.pdf.*

Are you trying to attract and retain workers in a market that lacks affordable housing? Does helping them afford a home make ROI sense for you? Providing shelter addresses a first-level physiological need on Maslow's hierarchy. Are there other physiological needs, like food or clothing, your employees struggle with to provide for themselves and their families?

Repay college loans

Recognizing the highly competitive market for healthcare profession-als, Scottsdale Healthcare in Scottsdale, Arizona, repays college loans for new hires. The company makes monthly payments of up to $5,250 per year and pays the same amount for current employees who are taking health-care courses. The program is simple: Payments are made directly to providers, and employees are not bound to the company in exchange for the loan or tuition support.

These programs have contributed to Scottsdale Healthcare cut-ting its voluntary turnover from 18% to 7.5% over the past six years. Each percent of turnover is estimated to cost $1.3 million, so the loan and tuition programs are a wise investment.[22]

Are you seeking a competitive edge for attracting and retaining professionals? What benefits might mean more to them than to other employees?

Career development as a process

Employees often cite "career development" as a reason to stay or leave organizations. The challenge for their companies is to then build an effective *process* to help employees with their careers rather than depend on individual supervisors to be skilled career coaches. Other challenges exist, too. Can companies help employees build their skills? Are there positions to grow into? Are employees willing to make life sacrifices to move up?

The model company for developing a process for genuine career planning is Deloitte. An early pioneer in addressing the unique career needs of women, Deloitte has now ramped up its career planning to address the needs of all aspects of its diverse workforce across gen-ders and generations. Using the term *career lattice* versus *career lad-der*, they offer their employees various ways to manage their careers rather than rely on the traditional vertical organization chart.

During annual goal-setting meetings, employees choose among four career categories:

- Should my workpace accelerate or decelerate?
- Should my workload be full or reduced?

- Should there be restrictions or no restrictions on my work locations or schedule?
- Should my role be as a leader or individual contributor?

Employees may request changes anytime between goal-setting meetings, too, should they experience any type of lifestyle change.

The outcome so far is that turnover is down, employee referrals are up, and most employees say no to gearing down their careers. In fact, for the 5% or so who want to make changes, most seek more work versus less. But while few employees are leveraging this benefit, it's clear that all appreciate the opportunity to make choices about their careers now and in their futures.

Deloitte has titled its career program "Mass Career Customization," and you can read and listen to information about it on their website at *www.deloitte.com/view/en_us/us/services/additional-services/Mass-career-customization/index.htm*.

Does your organization offer a process for career development that provides employees with legitimate ways to build their careers with you? Or do you offer training programs, job postings, and other processes that fail to integrate into effective career tools?

Crossing language borders

One consequence of our diverse workforces is that many employees cannot speak or understand English. This places risks on productivity and on safety too, as employees and supervisors struggle to communicate during emergencies.

While many companies accept these differences, some are bringing language teachers onsite to provide language training that aligns with specific business scenarios. The ultimate question they must answer is who learns a new language—the supervisors or employees? While "both" is preferred, the new wisdom is to teach supervisors to speak the language of their teams since they are likely to stay with the company longer. Regardless of who gets trained, language training has proven to cut turnover and improve other important business metrics.[23]

Will helping your employees learn fundamental skills such as English, reading, or writing help them contribute more as well as stay longer?

 ## True Stories

Grab an eye-catching credential!

Want to be named as one of Fortune's Top 100 places to work? Or as one of the SHRM 50 best small and medium companies to work for? The gateway for both is *www.greatplacetowork.com.*

The Great Place to Work Institute provides the surveys that lead to selecting winners for both awards, and you can nominate your company via their website. For the SHRM award, companies must have between 50 and 999 full- or part-time regular employees who work in the United States. The *Fortune* award is reserved for companies with 1,000 or more employees. Other criteria must be met, too.

Here's one more motivator. For the 2008 Fortune Top 100 list, only 407 companies applied to participate, meaning nearly one in four made the list.[24] For the SHRM lists, the total applicant number was 321, so about one out of every seven applicants won those distinctions.[25] The list winners really are great companies to work for, so you might find you are not quite ready to join the elite. But by participating you will either make the list and have an eye-catching credential or get valuable feedback for making your company an even better place to work.

"Recruit, Remind, Retain"

Southern Progress Corporation (SPC) publishes books and lifestyle magazines that include *Southern Living* and *Cooking Light.* Voluntary annual turnover at SPC is consistently less than 10% but the executive team thought they could do an even better job retaining top talent. Thus was born the SPC Corporate Culture Marketing Plan, with goals to "Recruit, Remind, Retain."

Headquartered in Birmingham, Alabama, SPC's campus sits on a tree-thick hillside with award-winning landscape and architecture. Using this backdrop, the project has resulted in these new or revitalized employee activities:

- Landscape tours of the company property that include lessons employees can use at home.
- Movie premieres, which are available because SPC is a subsidiary of Time Inc. and Time Warner Inc. SPC employees occasionally screen new releases before they reach the theaters.
- ECHO, the company's Employees Caring and Helping Others program, provides employees with opportunities to get involved in the community and interact with each other.
- Professional development sessions are open to all employees and discuss topics that further engage workers in their jobs. Recent subjects included designing a new magazine, developing a retail book business, and writing a compelling magazine story.

Most important, SPC developed new ways to take advantage of *who they are*. HR Director Carole Cain summed up SPC's "Recruit, Remind, Retain" approach this way: "Highlighting those aspects that make Southern Progress unique has made us appreciate this company even more, which, in turn, strengthens our loyalty."[26]

"Island of Misfit Toys"

That's how Jim Knight refers warmly to the 25,000 employees who work under the brand of Hard Rock International.

Why the moniker? Hard Rock is best known for its rock music, priceless memorabilia, and collectible merchandise. This rock-inspired setting gives clues regarding the types of employees who are attracted to and thrive in this environment: Picture tattoos, body piercings, colored hair, and English as a second language, all focused on providing a great experience for each guest. Turnover for managers and employees is significantly below industry averages.

While Knight's official title is senior director of training and development, he is also known as the founder of the "School of Hard Rocks," through which Knight and his team provide management development and employee training. Themed to its clientele, the school uses manuals that look like comic books and company videos that other companies might call irreverent.

The company brand is blatantly stated in employee recruiting tools. Various print materials shout out to applicants:

* "For Those About to Rock, We Recruit You"
* "Not Working Here Must Really Suck"
* "Kick-Ass Service: Served Fresh Daily"

And for those who think they missed their calling, "Rock Stars Wanted: Come Perform for a Packed House."

The Hard Rock story drives home the importance of knowing and branding your company's true culture. Hard Rock employees have plenty of opportunities to move elsewhere, but they stay because they've worked their way into jobs and a company that fit who they are. The broken toys have found a home.[27]

Stories and symbols

In an earlier life I was asked to give the "company culture" speech during new employee orientation. After much trial and error, I formed a presentation that told the company's values through stories of our employees and executives.

The visible symbol of company pride was wearing the company pin. The pin was our company's shield of honor that all employees displayed to their peers, customers, and communities. It also helped employees recruit applicants as part of the company's employee referral program.

Pin-wearing had been emphasized by newsletter articles, and a question about it was also added to the employee survey to keep awareness high. Wearing pins was so important that employees who left theirs at home would call the HR department each morning for a loaner. So I needed a story that would make clear to new employees that wearing their company pin was expected, every day.

The winning story came from a clever administrative assistant who came to work one day without her pin. Asked how she would respond if confronted by the CEO, she gave the only possible acceptable answer: "I must have left it on my pajamas."

The "pajamas" story became a staple at orientation from that day forward and was subsequently repeated throughout the company as a reminder to wear your company pin.

Bring the hospital in-house

Community builder...free-thinker...most generous...very smart man. These descriptors and more have been applied to Harris Rosen, founder and COO of Rosen Hotels and Resorts. With seven properties located in Orlando's tourist area, Rosen looked for ways to provide great healthcare for his 5,000 employees—and at the same time trim costs. The answer was to build his own healthcare clinic.

The clinic has two doctors and two nurse practitioners, who serve as the equivalent of a primary care physician, as well as a part-time podiatrist and nutritionist. The results are eye-popping:

- Employees pay only a $14.75 per week premium and just $48.25 per week to add two family members.
- Company costs are about half of what Rosen would pay for a traditional insurance program, and costs have stayed about flat for the last five years while competitors' insurance costs have spiraled upward.
- By emphasizing health, company-paid medical care is cheaper for an employee in her fifth year versus her first, so *Rosen is actually helping his employees get healthier.*

And turnover? Just 15% to 20% per year compared to industry averages of 75% to 150%. Disney, Marriott, and Darden have checked out the clinic as a potential way to deliver healthcare to their own employees.

Rosen is pragmatic about his clinic: "When employees are healthy and feel secure in knowing that the medical needs of their families are met, they are happier and more productive. And in an industry that is as reliant on quality customer service as ours, happy employees lead to satisfied customers."[28]

Matchmakers see both sides

Branding one's company to job-seekers evokes thoughts of catchy advertising in order to grab attention. But sometimes branding comes in the form of very important spoken words that can backfire into costly turnover.

As managing director of Magellan International, Jonathan Phillips is the consummate headhunter. With his team, Phillips helps high-priced consultants shift their careers from one major firm to the next. Early on, he says, consultants change jobs for *different jobs* versus careers to broaden their experience base, for more money, or the right fit. Later in life they search for careers where they can match up long-term to their employer's direction.

Phillips cautions that organizations struggle to find themselves just like employees do, especially as companies move in and out of various strategies. "An acquisition here, a redirection there, even the entry of a new competitor can lead to consultants' assignments being changed. The consultant then comes to me, the search executive, saying, 'I'm in the wrong company. I joined to do A, B, and C, but now they have me doing A, B, and Z.'" The price of failure can be losing a star who takes business with her, potentially a seven-figure loss.

Phillips adds one final note: "From time to time, companies call me and ask why we are pulling talent out of their firms. We can tell them the difficulties they have with poor managers, with asking consultants to take on roles that differ than those they promised when they joined... we know."[29]

 # Closing Thoughts on Why Employees Stay

Here are three major conclusions for rethinking retention based on the ideas presented in this chapter.

Traditional Thinking	Rethinking Retention
We advertise our jobs so candidates apply.	We brand our employee value proposition to attract targeted applicants who fit our jobs and company.
Employees seek jobs mainly for pay.	Employees want to know what they will learn and how they will contribute.
Traditional benefits are essential to attract applicants.	Adding strategic benefits connects employees more deeply to our company.

The plans presented in this chapter for attracting applicants and retaining employees are a quantum leap from the approaches most organizations take today. For our current-and-beyond tough labor market, smart companies identify their glues, refine them if necessary, and market them with passion externally and internally to attract and retain the employees they need.

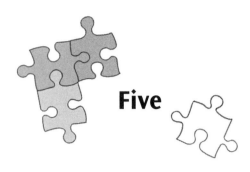

Five

Supervisors Build Unique Relationships that Drive Retention

The first two principles addressed why employees leave, which is because they can, and why they stay, which is for things they get uniquely from you. The final principle moves us from *things* that make your company unique to *relationships* that do the same. By far the most important relationship for retaining your employees is the one they have with their immediate supervisors.

To illustrate this point, imagine that you have accomplished all the suggestions in Chapter 4 regarding employee value propositions, employment branding, and stay interviews, and you've implemented shiny new strategic benefits. However, none of your investment of time, good thinking, and cost will matter to a significant chunk of your workforce if they work for ineffective supervisors. The data supports the cliché that we should all have put on posters: *Employees join for things but stay or leave for people.*

This chapter presents data that underscores the importance of supervisor–employee relationships and the qualities supervisors must have to succeed. Here you will learn about:

- **Top studies on supervisors' retention power**, so you are motivated to select, develop, and reward supervisors who build the right retention relationships
- **Top supervisory skills for retention**, so you have specific ideas for training and coaching them

The True Stories section addresses different approaches for supervising hourly and management employees and other information regarding supervisors' impact on retention.

 ## Top Studies on Supervisors' Retention Power

Being a first-time supervisor is a hard job. Someone above you decides you have supervisory skills, or that you do your current job well, and suddenly people are "reporting" to you. You form a style that combines acting naturally with the good and bad habits passed down from your own past supervisors, mixed in with a native want for your team to like you. As time goes on you find that some members of your team are more difficult to coach than others, you like some of them more than others, and some are just easier to connect with. And some of them quit, too, which derails you from doing your *real* job.

The data presented next make the hard case that these fragile relationships between supervisors and their teams are the biggest drivers of employees' stay/leave decisions. Some of the data tell us that the quality of these relationships influences employees' opinions on *everything* you offer them, including their pay and benefits. Does good supervision influence employees to stay even when they feel cheated on their pay? Yes. Does good supervision enable you to pay less and still retain your good workers? Probably, although I don't recommend it.

It is also likely that some high-impact benefits influence employees to stay even when turned off by their supervisors. Thinking back to the strategic benefits presented in Chapter 4, employees might tolerate more abuse if quitting means they must sacrifice the subsidy you provide for their housing. Or the concierge service might make a working mom hang on for another school year despite feeling snubbed by her boss.

But for those companies that offer only standard pay and benefits, the supervisor–employee relationship is probably your best retention tool. And if that tool breaks, there is no safety-net benefit to catch your dissatisfied workers.

The data presented here bunch all levels of supervisors together—first-line, middle managers, and on up. So whereas new supervisors have a learning curve, it appears some supervisors on all levels struggle to develop retention skills despite having years of experience in people-management roles.

What employees want: a new boss!

This headline is from a report released by Yahoo HotJobs! regarding their 2008 annual job satisfaction survey. More than 70% of those surveyed said they were open to landing a new job in the coming year, and the primary reason was dislike of their boss's performance. Another question asked participants if they agreed with the statement, "People don't leave companies, they leave managers." Over half said yes.

A company spokesperson summarized the results by saying, "It's clear from the survey that employers need to pay attention to the boss–employee dynamic if they want to retain talented workers."[1]

The "stay for people" beat goes on

Florida State University researchers conducted a study to better understand the role supervisors play in employees' decisions to stay or leave. Said Professor Wayne Hochwarter, who led the study, "They say employees don't leave their job or company, they leave their boss. We wanted to see if this is, in fact, true."

The survey respondents said the following about their supervisors:

- 39% failed to keep promises
- 37% failed to give them credit when due
- 31% gave them the "silent treatment" in the past year

- 27% made negative comments about them to other employees or managers
- 24% invaded their privacy
- 23% blamed others to cover up mistakes or to minimize embarrassment

The report goes on to say that "Employees stuck in an abusive relationship experienced more exhaustion, job tension, nervousness, depressed mood and mistrust." They were also less likely to take on additional tasks, and they were more likely to leave if involved in an abusive relationship than if dissatisfied with pay.

Professor Hochwarter puts the findings in perspective by saying some of the results are from "bad manners," noting, "I don't think people roll out of bed thinking, 'How can I abuse my subordinates?'" He also speculates that over the years companies have delayered to the point that supervisors have too many direct reports. The professor added that the expanded impact of poor supervision is that employees "associate that same behavior with the organization as a whole."[2]

"Stay for people" in China

SHRM and Development Dimensions International (DDI) studied retention in China and found three of the top four retention drivers were directly related to leadership: Having a good manager, being recognized for individual contributions, and having great company leadership. They also found that compensation alone is not sufficient for retaining valued talent.[3]

"Stay for people" again

Why do employees stay? For managers first and coworkers second, according to a wide-reaching study by Salary.com. The study goes on to say that employees *leave* for pay, no advancement or development, and lack of recognition, but the clear reason they *stay* is for relationships. Looking deeper, relationships are more important to women than men but are the lead stay reasons for both.[4]

One could argue that the main leave reasons—pay, advancement, development, and recognition—are also greatly influenced by supervisors, as discussed in the Kenexa study in Chapter 2.

Joining versus staying

TalentKeepers' research leads to the same outcome, citing the differences between why employees *join* versus why they *stay*. Employees typically join for issues related to the organization, such as pay, benefits, or reputation, followed by job-related issues such as schedules, opportunities to learn new skills, or challenging work. Last on the "join" list is supervisors, since most new hires know little about them. But within as little as three months, employees' most important stay or leave reasons shift to (1) supervisors, (2) job issues, and (3) organization issues.[5] So whereas supervisors have the least impact on employees' decisions to join, they have the most impact on employees' decisions to stay.

In another study, TalentKeepers found the employees who stay primarily for their supervisors versus pay, benefits, or another "thing" not only stay longer, but they also perform their jobs better and are even more satisfied with their pay.[6]

Poor leadership accounts for more than 60% of all turnover

The Saratoga Institute surveyed more than 19,000 workers across 17 industry groups and found the majority of those who leave their companies do so because they are not recognized for their contributions or sufficiently respected or coached by their managers. The data revealed that poor leadership causes over 60% of all employee turnover.[7]

Is teacher turnover driven by leaders?

Think "teacher turnover" and you might picture rowdy students, low pay, or redundant work. The National Education Association surveyed experienced teachers on what districts and states can do about the "appalling turnover." They found that "When employees stay, it is because of their immediate managers."

An NEA spokesperson went on to say, "Teachers will move to or remain in schools with strong administrative leadership. One board-certified teacher in North Carolina who taught in a high-needs school said, 'I would follow my principal to a shed to teach.'"[8]

Supervisors' retention role is universal

Kenexa studied workers across six countries and found employees are three times more likely to state an intention to leave if they have a manager who is doing a poor job leading their team or organization. The impact is even higher in India and China.

Employees view their manager as ineffective if they do not practice ethical behavior, provide useful feedback, treat people fairly, and effectively manage the workload.

The study concludes: "Given the high cost of employee turnover, it is clear that poor managers within an organization dramatically increase the cost of operations."[9]

 ## Top Supervisory Skills for Retention

The top supervisory skill for retaining workers is to build trust, which is addressed fully in Chapter 7. The other skills listed here aren't in priority order, so consider them all to be close seconds.

Rather than present the usual skill lists that dominate supervisory training programs, let's think instead of the conditions supervisors must create for good workers to stay. What is it that makes employees want to continue to work with us that a supervisor can control or influence?

Abraham Maslow's Hierarchy of Needs provides clues regarding the types of environments where employees will stick. The three items in the middle sets of needs, fitting between physiological at the bottom and self-actualization at the top, provide us with clear direction regarding supervisor dos and don'ts. These three are, from the bottom up:

- Safety: The need to be free from the effect of physical or emotional harm

- Social: The need to interact with others
- Esteem: The need to feel important[10]

My own graduate coursework in counseling and therapy and subsequent jobs drove home a clear message: *Relationships are based primarily on trust and self-esteem.* You stay with people who look out for you and who make you feel good about being you.

Supervision, though, is hard. How can you make someone feel safe when you've laid off half his department? Or feel important when he has blown a major sale and you will fire him if he continues to fail? Or feel accepted by others when in reality he is not?

So based on Maslow's respected thinking, here are the skills supervisors need to retain their teams. No supervisor will do these things right all the time because of their job's level of difficulty, so consider these to be ideal guidelines for retention success.

Give unconditional personal support

Always like them and show concern for them. If for some reason they turn you off, support them from your mind instead of your heart because your job is to help them feel safe and important. Coach them with full confidence they will succeed. Praise them for specific accomplishments in public and private. Coach them on all areas that can cause them to fail and tell them it's because you care. Steer them away from taking your coaching personally by teaching them how wrong behaviors will prevent them from winning.

Ask and remember information about their families, interests, and life concerns so you can support their total lives instead of just their work lives.

They should always think you like them, and only think you don't believe in them if your next step is to fire them.

My supervisor likes me and believes in me.

Connect them to you

Be available, and if not schedule a time when you are. Give them undivided, full eye-contact attention with no multitasking. Smile, be warm, and show no evidence that you have other work to do. Listen intently and tell them back what you heard them say so they know you've understood them.

When you can, ask their opinions as though they are your equal, whether meeting individually or in groups. Invite discussion and hold your opinions until you've heard all others. Call attention to the strengths in others' opinions and how they helped you form your own.

Introduce your family members, share your life interests, and tell them common ground you share so they find easy ways to connect their lives to yours.

My supervisor sets aside time just for me and believes my opinions are important. I feel really connected to her.

Connect them to others

Smart retention leaders take the extra step to ensure employees are connected to their peers and even other managers. Begin by instructing your team on your own expectations for working together regarding listening, respecting opinions, holding each other accountable, and supporting. Compliment positive behaviors and be quick to redirect negative ones. Role model every instruction you give them.

Establish welcoming processes for new employees that ensure each current employee introduces himself and asks questions about background, skills, and what the new employee hopes to learn. Connect each new employee to at least one designated peer for support.

Ask employees individually about peer relationships so you know where to intercede. Use social functions to build peer relationships by observing who connects easily and who seems left out so you can coach later to bring teammates together.

Ask your manager to engage with your team individually and in groups, both to build social bonds and also to increase your manager's likelihood of supporting those who report to you.

The people I work with care about me, so I really enjoy going to work.

Build skills and careers

Work involves many different activities with people, equipment, and assignments, but ultimately there are core things employees must do well. Retention-savvy supervisors are keen to identify what workers do well and enjoy, and make every effort to match them to perfect jobs. All other retention efforts fail if ultimately you misplace a worker's talent.

Matching talents is the foundation step for career coaching. Once employees are aware of their interests and abilities, providing them with additional assignments and training are natural next steps toward establishing and achieving career goals.

My supervisor knows me—what I like and what I'm good at—and keeps coaching me on ways to do better and learn more. I can keep growing here.

Share critical knowledge

Employees need to know how to do their jobs satisfactorily, so they require clear instructions and crisp answers. Supervisors must be job experts who are current on every process, know the limitations of information systems, and therefore know the hot spots where employees need instruction and support. Supervisors who lack job knowledge will lose credibility and fail.

Beyond ensuring employees know how to do their jobs, help them see the line of sight between their duties and the company's goals. Keep them abreast of company success stories and challenges so they feel part of the total team and find ways to contribute more. Point out their specific contributions that fulfill your company's mission so they see their jobs as important.

I know what to do and I know it's important. We do great things here.

Make them win

Supervisors who are driven to achieve retention goals know their employees must feel like winners in order to stay. Winning might mean achieving performance goals, pleasing customers, learning new skills, feeling important, making new friends, advancing to make more money, or knowing you appreciate them.

Retaining them, then, requires your knowing the winning criteria for each employee. Or said another way, what are their motivations for staying?

Supervisors who conduct stay interviews as presented in Chapter 4 will have a clear view of each employee's path to retention. Those who are dedicated to retention will then manage each employee differently to ensure they see their work as a winning experience.

I feel great when I leave work because I know I've done something good. My job makes my life better.

 ## True Stories

Key differences in retaining hourly and management employees

Coca-Cola dug deeply into supermarket retention issues and provides us with good data regarding the different needs of hourly and management workers. For hourly workers, the top three retention drivers were (1) providing directions, (2) equipment and supplies, and (3) immediate supervision. The major retention drivers for management employees were (1) organizational direction, (2) training, and (3) advancement.

Why are the retention drivers so different? The report tells us that hourly workers are most focused on getting things done, whereas management employees approach their work more strategically.[11]

So based on this study, how should we differentiate our supervision methods for hourly versus management employees in order to keep them longer? For hourly employees, the study directs us to ensure they know their duties, provide the right tools, and reinforce them for doing the right things and redirect them when they get off track.

Supervising management employees for retention is more complex because it invites discussion regarding just how much the manager above them can impact organizational direction, training, and advancement. Top managers, then, must accept responsibility for providing information on organizational direction, ensuring their employees receive training and job coaching, and preparing them for advancement. Retaining these employees is their responsibility, and they must find ways to fulfill these employees' needs.

A gift with meaning

A friend who is the top HR executive of a Fortune 500 company was asked to address a ballroom full of top managers on how to reduce turnover.

Searching for a way to reach their hearts, he prepared a carefully wrapped gift box for each manager and had it placed at their tables when they returned from a break. Asking them to refrain from opening their gifts, he then presented data regarding the cost of turnover and the opportunity that was available to all in the room to make great savings for their company.

Having gained their attention, he then told them their gifts contained the single-most important tool available to cut their turnover. All of them opened their gifts to find a mirror inside.

As the story goes, one manager called out, "We could do a better job if your HR people sent us applicants who could fog this thing." But the gimmick worked, as managers left understanding their top-down supervision was the most important tool they had to retain their best workers.

Bullies beware

The fate of jerk bosses is moving into the courts. Aggrieved employees have received six-figure sums for charging their supervisors with assault as a result of verbal attacks, and thirteen states have introduced legislation to stop workplace bullying.[12] Thirty-seven percent of U.S. workers report they've been a bully victim, which is four times more prevalent than illegal forms of harassment, including sexual harassment and age discrimination.[13]

The National Institute of Occupational Safety and Health reports that workplace bullying is associated with "increased symptoms of depression, anxiety, and psychosomatic complaints in those victimized and sometimes in those who were not victims themselves but were witnesses present in the work environment." The study also linked bullying to lack of job security and lack of trust in management.[14]

Supervisors drive safety for outside jobs

Two experiences leap to the top when I think about remote workers, safety, and their supervisors' impact on stay/leave decisions. One was with long-distance truck drivers and the other deep in African gold mines.

Truck drivers hit the road for two weeks at a time, away from supervisors, colleagues, and family, delivering their loads across the country. As one driver told me, "When we're out there, the most important information we need is weather." Dispatchers decide if the driver should take chances. They know that suggesting a round-about route to avoid a potential winter storm might delay shipping for several days and keep that truck from returning and reloading on schedule. This is the bottom-line money decision. On the other hand, directing that driver to take on the storm brings the risk of wrecks, roadside delays, and longer times away from family—the people decision.

Similar to long-distance drivers, African gold miners operate remotely from their supervisors and rely on them for directions that impact their safety. Several years ago I traveled almost two miles deep to interview groups of workers and saw first-hand the dangers they face if the guidance they receive is off course. Entry-level workers are one promotion away from igniting dynamite in hopefully the right location, with tons of earth above them and their colleagues.

Some spoke to me through translators, but their message was clear. Supervisors guide them on which crawl spaces to enter, which tunnels to blast, and how to exit from work spaces that could close behind them—and are a primary reason they stay or leave.

 ## A Closing Call for Introspection

The following are three major conclusions for rethinking retention based on the ideas presented in this chapter regarding the strong connection between supervisors and their employees' stay/leave decisions.

Traditional Thinking	Rethinking Retention
HR-driven programs like pay and recognition are essential for retention.	Ineffective supervisors trump programs and drive turnover.
All aspects of company culture contribute equally to retention.	Supervisor–employee relationships have a disproportionate impact on retention; the supervisor *is* the company.
Centralized communication and career programs impact all employees equally.	Supervisors drive what employees know and learn and help them prepare for careers.

While reading this chapter, you probably reflected on relationships you've had with supervisors, past and present, and considered their impact on how you enjoyed your jobs and how long you stayed. For some, maybe those good relationships led you to promotions and insights into career steps. For others, a poor supervisor might have led you to change jobs, relocate, or even change careers.

But switch your thinking for a moment and consider how your employees view you as a supervisor. Read through the top supervisory skills for retention and score yourself on your own retention skills. Ask yourself how important it is to you to build glue with your team, given all of the other tasks you are asked to achieve. On a scale of 1 to 10, with 10 being high, how important is it to you to be a great retention leader?

Supervisors on all levels must ask and answer this question, whether they work on the front line or have an executive title. The answers will be clear based on how long their teams stay and grow from working with them.

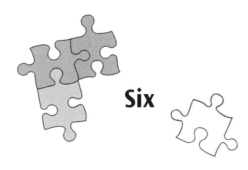

Six

Hold Supervisors Accountable for Achieving Retention Goals

The late Professor Edward Lorenz of MIT once explained how something as minuscule as a butterfly flapping its wings in Brazil could influence the impact of tornadoes in Texas.[1] Dr. Lorenz's work introduced the term *butterfly effect* as a metaphor for seemingly small actions that lead to big changes.

Setting retention goals from the top of your organization down to first-line supervisors will lead to butterfly-effect results. In fact, we believe setting retention goals is the single most impactful thing you can do to reduce turnover, so it is sequenced as our first strategy in the Rethinking Retention model.

In their report on retention strategies, Monster.com's first recommendation is "Make supervisors more accountable for worker retention by tying their compensation to retention performance." They also report that only 11% of HR managers indicate that supervisors are currently held to retention goals in their organizations,[2] similar to the 14% amount reported from another survey in Chapter 2.

While retention accountability is rare, recommendations for it are not. Two studies that call for retention goals address teacher and nurse turnover, jobs for which retention solutions have been in short supply. The National Commission on Teaching and America's Future reports U.S. public school teacher turnover has grown by 50% in the past 15 years, resulting in a staggering cost of $7 billion each year.[3] The report recommends several solutions for addressing teacher turnover including "Amend NCLB [No Child Left Behind] to hold school leaders accountable for turnover and its costs."[4]

As mentioned in Chapter 3, our nation's nursing shortage looks like a problem without a solution. In their report titled "Hardwiring Right Retention," the Health Care Advisory Board of the Advisory Board Company suggests the following: Hold nurse managers accountable to retention goals.[5] Their report describes programs such as performance pay, better communications, onsite child care, and flexible scheduling as "Nice, but not about turnover." They report one hospital that reduced nurse turnover by 41% as a result of setting retention goals for managers, compared to peer hospitals that offered various programs but did not hold managers accountable to retention goals.[6]

The "Hardwiring Right Retention" report, published back in 2001 is an oldie but one that all healthcare executives should review.

This chapter includes:

- **Top methods for setting employee retention goals**, as setting these goals requires careful thinking and decision making
- **Top ways to hold supervisors accountable**, to ensure you treat supervisors fairly and reward the ones who improve

The True Stories section contains examples of retention accountability across different industries.

 ## Top Methods for Setting Employee Retention Goals

Holding supervisors accountable for retention changes the conversation when a good performer leaves. Without accountability, the supervisor's manager approaches him in a consoling, codependent way like:

> I'm really sorry, Bruce, that you have lost Maria. She has been the receptionist at the front door of our hospital for seven years and

was the first person to greet our guests. With that warm smile and soothing voice, she was reassuring to our patients and family members that they had come to the right place. We are really going to miss Maria. It will be weeks before we have someone hired for that job and we'll be lucky to get someone that good, but I'm sure you'll make it work out.

The focus of this discussion is consoling, sharing, and reassuring. The pronoun choice of "we" indicates Bruce and his manager will endure this loss together. An *accountability* discussion, however, sounds like this:

How could you lose Maria, Bruce? We talked about Maria being a key performer who was a difference-maker between us and the other hospitals in town, and you assured me that she was happy and stable in her job. Your team's function is to welcome patients into our hospital and send the clear message to all visitors that if they need healthcare, we are the right place. Maria was by far your best performer, Bruce. I'd like you to find out why she's leaving us and what specific things you could have done to keep her.

The example of a hospital receptionist is a low-skilled, low-paying job, but performing it well leads directly to more company success. Plug in the loss of a sales leader, technology expert, engineer on a time-sensitive project, or a deal-making investment banker and the discussion gets more heated as the consequences rise.

Retention accountability creates a positive stress when a good performer leaves. Rather than just feeling miffed by the hassle of hiring and training a replacement, Bruce now understands that he has failed a major assignment. High-retention organizations take it personally when an employee walks out and use each exit as a springboard to introspection about the organization and the supervisor. Weak excuses like *"We don't pay enough"* or *"You know how young people are"* are replaced by *"What lessons can we learn? What one thing could I have done as Maria's supervisor that would have caused her to stay longer?"* And more important, *"Now that I've lost Maria, I better not lose another good employee. What extra steps should I take to improve retention with the rest of my team, now and ongoing?"*

Here are specific ideas for setting retention goals.

Set an organizational goal and drive it down to supervisors

Goals set at the top of the organization that are not passed down to each management level result in no accountability—except for the person at the top. Subordinate managers listen to turnover reports in meetings and believe all are contributing equally to the good or bad news. Set a goal for the entire organization, a division, or one high-turnover job and make certain every level of management down to first-line supervisors knows the number of employees he can lose to comply with his goal.

Set goals for the most important retention measure

Turnover is typically measured by year or by month, but your turnover patterns might dictate a different metric. Organizations that employ many low-skilled workers often find that half or more of their turnover occurs in the first 90 days, so improving retention during this time might be the most important measure. Those that hire professional trainees often find turnover is highest after the second year, when those trainees are ready to produce but are also vulnerable to calls from competitors. Other organizations are mostly concerned about losing high performers, so they identify them and set a goal to keep them.

For high-turnover jobs, some companies find value in measuring average length of service. Keeping employees for life ended a generation ago, but adding several months to a job's average length of service can represent major gains in productivity. By doubling a job's average length of service, you've cut turnover in half.

Set goals for two metrics at most, and don't let the tail wag the dog by choosing your metric based on what your systems currently measure. Instead, choose the most important criteria for your goals and count your results in new ways if necessary. Some companies have told us they cannot count their most vulnerable types of turnover because they are waiting for a new automated system a year down the road. Instead, decide on the most important data you need and find a way to get it.

Make goals achievable and simple

Build momentum by setting goals your supervisors are more likely to accept and achieve. If turnover has been rising the past several years, a 10% reduction reverses the trend. To keep goals simple, set the same percentage goal for supervisors unless their jobs call for different ones. For example, if organizational turnover last year was 50% and you want a 20% improvement, set the goal for all supervisors at 40% regardless of what their individual department's turnover was the previous year. Adjust a supervisor's target only if she has a particular advantage or disadvantage. For example, weekend shifts might have higher turnover, so that supervisor might merit a goal that is higher than the others but still shows improvement. Or another supervisor might manage only part-timers, who historically turn over more.

Ideally, set goals for turnover that is voluntary, controllable, and undesirable

Looking back at the story about the hospital receptionist, the supervisor might have later found that Maria resigned to move out of town to take care of her sick mother. Bruce would have then raced to his manager to plead that this exit was out of his control.

We all agree that some turnover is good, especially when a poor performer leaves. Even then, though, one can argue that someone was accountable for hiring this employee, and maybe someone doomed this employee by not providing enough training and coaching. And all turnover costs money because it represents the loss of an investment.

Setting goals that limit which turnover is included require (1) knowing the real reasons employees leave and (2) managing performance closely. Let's look at some examples:

- Are "staying home with my baby," "going back to school," or "early retirement" real lifestyle changes or excuses to get away from a bad supervisor?

- Do we accept that the employee who voluntarily quit was a slack performer even though he was rated satisfactory on his last three performance reviews?
- Is job abandonment voluntary or involuntary? Do you fire them because they don't show up or are they quitting on you for reasons you can't identify?

These examples argue that all exits should be counted against a supervisor's retention goal. Coming from the other side, some object that including all exits will result in supervisors not firing poor performers because they'll be afraid to miss their goals.

Companies must work their way through these scenarios to decide which turnovers to count. However, most companies:

- Don't know the real reasons employees leave, so counting only controllable turnover is inaccurate
- Exclude employees who are fired or quit while on probation, which is okay although they still represent cost and a hiring or coaching failure
- Have supervisors who might hold back on firing a poor performer in order to make their retention goals, but their managers should be accountable for making sure they don't

If you cannot discern true reasons for exits, here's a way to implement retention goals that addresses most of these concerns: Tell supervisors you will begin tracking their team turnover immediately and assign them retention goals in three months. From this day forward they should make hiring decisions with retention in mind, and also begin addressing poor performers so they improve or move out. Then set goals that include all types of turnover so your tracking is simple, and your coaching discussions are about improving skills rather than disagreeing over why someone left.

Supervisors who don't make hiring decisions will put more pressure on HR to provide quality hires and this will make your organization better. These same supervisors might then blame HR for their turnover but this argument becomes stale if their peer supervisors have better retention and are getting new hires from the same HR-provided pool.

The ideal message to supervisors is, "You own your team. You hired it, you coach it, you are responsible for its outcomes. And you must retain a high percentage of them to make your retention and production goals."

Set continuous improvement goals

Your objective when setting retention goals is to improve retention performance against your past. If you set an annual goal, compare progress against the same month of the previous year to account for seasonal trends. If you are looking to improve 90-day retention first, increase your goal each quarter until you've reached an adequate level of performance, especially if you plan to add new retention tools along the way.

Adjust your goals, of course, if some event makes the current period very different from the comparison period, like a major reorganization or severe change in the economy.

Many organizations search for external data to benchmark their performance, but retention is one area where benchmarking comes up short. Differences in what gets measured along with local market factors make comparing your turnover to others' turnover fruitless. You know your turnover and you know it must improve, so shift your "comparison" energy toward fixing it.

In *Good to Great: Why Some Companies Make the Leap... and Others Don't*, Jim Collins writes about the dangers of comparing ourselves to average companies. I've seen executives who respond to competitors' turnover data by reaching the wrong conclusion. Believing that their own turnover is the same or even a little better, they decide that turnover is solved and they move on to other priorities. Meanwhile on the shop floor, employees are quitting and production is behind schedule. The greatest risk when comparing your turnover to others' is that their turnover can become your standard of excellence. It's easy to slip into "If ours is the same or better than theirs, we must be doing okay" thinking. You will be "doing okay" when you stop losing your good workers.

Think "goals and tools" when introducing goals to supervisors

Tell supervisors they are accountable for retention and that you will be giving them new tools to help. Describe improvements you are making regarding hiring, onboarding, policies, and practices, as well as the skill building they will receive to build trust with their teams. Tell them, too, that accountability goes all the way up, including the CEO.

Be sure to acknowledge that some turnover is beyond their control. That's why their goal is a fraction of 100%.

 ## Top Ways to Hold Supervisors Accountable

Supervisors are accustomed to being accountable for sales, service, quality, and safety. Retention goals are new, though, and raise red flags. Some will argue that employees leave because of reasons they cannot control or not having the right support from above regarding pay and other reasons.

Let's compare retention to sales. Goals are set for both and supervisors are accountable. Both are also driven by complex variables. For sales, supervisors must ensure that customers are attracted to the product and that they choose to buy it and are not swayed to buy competitors' products. Breakdowns might occur via product quality, marketing, competitor products or pricing, or other things beyond the control of the person who manages the sales personnel.

Your best evidence that a sales manager is underperforming is when she struggles against peer managers who are selling the same product to the same or similar markets. This controls for the "uncontrollables" and puts the emphasis on whether her team can close deals.

Historically, supervisors have readily accepted responsibility for achieving sales goals but they are less likely to welcome retention goals because they've had personal experiences of losing workers for reasons they believe were beyond their control. And they might be right. So retention goals must be introduced and managed with extra efforts to ensure fairness. And like sales, you will know if your supervisors are effectively retaining their talent by comparing their results to those of peer supervisors who are operating with the same "uncontrollables."

Some turnover really is uncontrollable

Good workers sometimes leave because they tire of the commute, want to do something different, or really *do* want to stay home with their babies or go to school. So supervisors must be held accountable for *high patterns of turnover compared to their peers* rather than for an occasional exit. Supervisors who repeatedly miss retention goals deserve close scrutiny by way of exit surveys, focus groups, and other means to learn what behaviors they must change to keep workers longer.

Remove supervisors who drive good workers away

Move them permanently from jobs that require managing people, and only retain them in another position if there's a good fit. Make this your strict policy for managers up the chain as well, as too often long-term managers retain their jobs in spite of managing teams that don't grow and eventually leave.

Coach retention accountability top-down every day

Managers should discuss retention's importance in staff meetings and in one-on-one coaching sessions with subordinate supervisors. Ask for lists of top performers and action plans to retain them. Have supervisors rank-order employees by vulnerability to leave and coach them on steps to take. Ask them what makes each employee stay and how they will leverage it. Teach them retention's importance by the amount of time and energy you devote to helping them make their goals.

Work with them to conduct a postmortem when an employee leaves. Dig deep for reasons they think along with other reasons that might have contributed. Leave the discussion by asking them what they might have done differently to keep this person longer, and what lessons that teaches for how they manage the rest of their team.

Tell them, too, that your retention goal includes you retaining *them*. Be a perfect role model by asking why they stay, leveraging those reasons as best you can, and building a trusting relationship.

Reward supervisors who achieve retention goals

Choose the type of reward that fits best for your organization: Award a retention cup for the supervisor with lowest turnover; provide a widely distributed monthly or quarterly report that indicates supervisors' retention performance, top to bottom; publish or discuss specific retention initiatives supervisors are taking; or spotlight a supervisor in an executive management meeting who continually meets her goals—and perhaps have her address your board on her retention techniques.

We once knew a manager who awarded a trophy with a spatula on top to his best-retention supervisor. The spatula represented turnover as one is used to "turn over" food that is cooking in a pan. His idea was hokey, but it worked.

Above all else, make employee retention a requirement for promotion

Broadcast widely that no supervisor will move to a higher role without an outstanding track record of hiring, developing, and keeping her best workers. When announcing such promotions, be sure to include specific retention information. If you can't find it, you might be making a wrong choice.

 True Stories

Wegmans' mantra: "Continuous improvement"

The late Bob Wegman was known to be caring and competitive by his colleagues at the supermarket chain that bears his name. So when his leadership team raced to his office to report their company had climbed from #67 to #10 on Fortune's 100 Best Companies to Work For list, his snap response was, "Who's number 9?"

That was in 2003. Wegmans did reach #9 the following year and has finished in the top five for each of the past four years. The *Fortune* articles tell many good things about Wegmans, such as great benefits, flexible scheduling, and a warm environment. The result is a phenomenal 9% annual full-time turnover, and part-time turnover is less than half of the industry average.

But Wegmans has another trick in its bag that contributes to its stability: Frontline management accountability for retention. Team leaders are the first line of management and all are held accountable for retention.

Ask a team leader her employee turnover compared to last year and she'll likely tell you both numbers. Her manager will know them too. The goal is to increase retention each year, in the spirit of continuous improvement.

Retention accountability for frontline leaders at Wegmans doesn't make the headlines because various employee programs dominate the criteria for most "best workplace" surveys. But Karen Shadders, vice president of people, knows its importance: "We must retain our good workers to meet the needs of our customers. Our team leaders know they are our main point of contact and are accountable for retention."[7]

Insurance company leverages technology for accountability

Chuck Moore is a technology guru by training who continuously finds his way into human resources roles. As a result, he is savvy regarding data tracking and the opportunities to track turnover.

As an HR officer for a 20,000-employee insurance company, Moore's first major project was to buy a new HRMS payroll system. At the same time, his CEO challenged all of HR to reduce turnover. "The solution was clear," Moore told me. "We now had a system to track who quit, when they quit, and who they worked for. My first move was to present data to the executive team so they could see that turnover happens disproportionately across the company and is concentrated among a few supervisors."

From that report came retention goals that then lead to consequences. Supervisors who retained employees were rewarded with increased bonuses, while others were held accountable for driving away talent.

Over the next 18 months, annual turnover dropped from 38% to 14%. Moore makes clear that other retention initiatives were put into place too, but he believes retention goals drove improved retention behaviors at the front line.

"My experience is that nine out of ten employees who leave do so because of their supervisors," says Moore. "What is a better first step for improving retention than holding supervisors accountable for retaining their good employees?"[8]

 ## Closing Thoughts on Holding Supervisors Accountable for Retention

Here are three major conclusions for rethinking retention based on the information presented in this chapter.

Traditional Thinking	Rethinking Retention
Supervisors cannot control all reasons employees leave.	Like managing sales, supervisors can manage in ways that lead to more good outcomes.
Pay and other policies are controlled centrally, leaving supervisors with few options.	Comparing peer supervisors' turnover rates controls for the impact of pay.
Supervisors won't fire poor performers if they are accountable for turnover goals.	Manage supervisors top-down to ensure they make the right decisions for their teams.

This chapter spotlights the importance of retention accountability across several industries. Wegmans uses retention goals at the first-line supervisory level to help retain low-skilled workers, many of whom work part-time. On the professional side, recommendations are included to apply accountability to retain teachers and nurses, perhaps the standard-bearers for hard-to-retain jobs.

Like trust, retention accountability flies under the radar of best practices because surveys don't ask about it. Instead, they focus on programs such as pay, benefits, work–life balance initiatives, and flexible schedules. All are important, but right-directed retention requires working for a supervisor who takes actions that make you want to stay. As a general rule, effective supervision plus good employee programs equal high retention, but poor supervision will trump good programs most of the time.

Accountability is a cousin to natural selection, as both require us to adapt to survive. Both require real change.

Driving accountability top-down to all levels of management will improve your retention chances exponentially. Recalling that only 11% of organizations hold supervisors accountable for retention, seize this competitive advantage before others apply the secret.

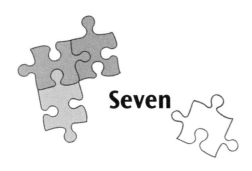

Seven

Develop Supervisors to Build Trust with Their Teams

Building trust is the make-it or break-it retention skill for supervisors. Chapter 2 presented data from TalentKeepers, Leadership IQ, and Sirota to establish this point, and Chapter 5 included information regarding the strong impact of first-line supervisors on employees' stay/leave decisions. Let's look back on the studies discussed in those chapters and highlight the comments that involved trust.

Those that describe what employees want in a supervisor were:

- "recognized for individual contributions"
- "sufficiently respected"
- "practice ethical behavior"
- "treat people fairly"

Those that describe ineffective supervisors included:

- "failed to keep promises"
- "failed to give them credit when due"
- "gave them the 'silent treatment' in the past year"
- "made negative comments about them to other employees or managers"

- "invaded their privacy"
- "blamed others to cover up mistakes or to minimize embarrassment"

This last group of comments is from the study conducted by Dr. Wayne Hochwarter and his team from Florida State University. In an interview describing his study, Dr. Hochwarter concluded, "There's a bigger dynamic going on not only in organizations...this bigger issue of who's looking out for me." He went on to say, "The more training that managers, especially new managers, can get to tap into issues related to fairness and trust and balance, the more productive everyone's going to be."[1]

Other studies arrive at the same conclusion. In their most recent "Loyalty Report," Walker Information found that employee loyalty reached an all-time low for the years Walker conducted the study. Additionally, the number of employees categorized as "high risk," the least favorable category, exceeded the number who are "truly loyal," the most favorable category. When asked what work experiences most influence their degree of loyalty, employees ranked them in this order: (1) fairness at work, (2) care and concern, and (3) trust in employees.[2]

The case for the primary importance of trust in retention is clear. This chapter provides tools and information so you can elevate trust's importance in your company and build supervisory skills to improve it. The "top" lists are:

- **Top behaviors that cause mistrust**, which gives you a framework for the behaviors that break trust and the frequency with which they occur
- **Top components of a trust training program**, which you can adapt to your own supervisory training curriculum to develop trust skills with your managers and supervisors
- **Top ways to spot a nontrusted supervisor**, to help you identify supervisors who need help

The True Stories section includes a personal trust-building story that has guided me throughout my career.

Top Behaviors that Cause Mistrust

In their study titled "Trust Factors at Work," Randy Pennington and his team dug deeply into the real behaviors that organizations and supervisors do that break trust. After surveying a global group of employees who represented various jobs and demographics, they obtained a valid sample and then evaluated these responses against an existing database of over 800,000 employee responses.[3] The results tell us which trust-breaking behaviors happen most in organizations.

The resulting behaviors were then grouped into five categories: Communication, competence, consistency, character, and courage. The following sections discuss these traits; the percent of respondents, definitions that follow, and sample behaviors are directly from the study. I've added the priority behaviors.

Trust behavior: communication

Thirty-three percent of all responses focused on behaviors that reflect the individual's and/or organization's commitment to share and receive information.

Sample behaviors. These included the amount or availability of information, listening and valuing others' opinions, openness, and style.

Priority behaviors. From the employees' perspective, supervisors break trust because they choose to withhold information. The action steps, then, are to:

- Avoid withholding information about your jobs, department, and organization unless the information is confidential.
- Sort information by saying what is essential to know versus optional, so employees feel accountable for knowing the most important information and not overwhelmed by having to know all of it.
- If employees want to know something you can't share, tell them you can't share it.
- Practice listening and then saying back, "Let me tell you what I heard you say to see if I got it right." Your employee will know you listened and you'll build your listening skills.

Trust behavior: competence

Twenty-one percent of all responses described behaviors that reflect the individual's and/or organization's ability to perform responsibilities.

Sample behaviors. These included awareness and knowledge of the job, decision-making, having direction or vision, and not micromanaging.

Priority behaviors. To build trust through competence:

- Become a complete expert on jobs that report to you; give employees clear direction and uncluttered answers; move past valuing employees below you only because they know processes you don't.
- Make decisions on the spot or explain your process and timeline for doing so, then meet the timeline and announce your decision.
- Avoid the halitosis effect of micromanaging and let employees complete their work; if you have to manage them too closely over time, fire them. The good ones won't trust you if you don't trust them to do their jobs without you.

Trust behavior: consistency

Twenty percent of all responses described behaviors that reflect the individual's and/or the organization's ability or willingness to maintain agreement between word and deed, and the ability or willingness to respond in like manner to similar situations.

Sample behaviors: These included following through on promises and commitments, fairness and playing favorites, and providing consistent direction.

Priority behaviors: To build consistency, take the following steps:

- Make commitments carefully and keep them. Think through the steps you must take, timeframes, and potential outcomes, and then commit with specifics: What, when, and how you will fulfill your commitment, and then keep your word or give advance notice if you cannot.

- Treat people differently only if based on performance, but otherwise ask your manager or a peer to be your sounding board so your personal preferences don't interfere with your business decisions.
- Tell your team you trust them to let you know if you contradict yourself by giving conflicting directions, then thank them when they tell you.

Trust behavior: character

Nineteen percent of all responses discussed behaviors that reflect the individual's and/or organization's moral strength.

Sample behaviors: These included keeps confidences, does not take credit for others' work, honesty, does not act in a self-serving manner.

Priority behaviors: To develop and show character:

- Guard against disclosing confidential information in order to gain favor with someone; they will only know that you broke a confidence and therefore think less of you.
- Give more credit to your team than they deserve to ensure you minimize credit to yourself; err on their side to overcome a tendency to promote yourself to others.
- If you find you are giving yourself too much credit, ask yourself who you are trying to impress and monitor your behaviors when that person is nearby.

Trust behavior: courage

Seven percent of all responses listed behaviors that reflect the individual's and/or organization's willingness to stand up for principles, take unpopular positions, or provide support in the face of resistance.

Sample behaviors: These include supporting and being an advocate for staff, standing up for one's beliefs and principles, and being assertive in the face of conflict.

Priority behaviors: Ways to develop and show courage include:

- Involve top management with your team so management supports your promotion and pay recommendations.

- Gather staff input on issues and if you agree, present a business case for change one level up.
- Support new policy decisions with your team by sharing your belief that management's decision-making track record is good.
- Broaden your team's opportunity for input by inviting their ideas for implementing new policies, whether they affect customers or employees.

Top Components of a Trust Training Program

Because trust flies under the radar as a supervisory skill, most companies have structured training programs for other subjects but not for the most important one.

The following are some ideas to consider as you design a trust training program. The thoughts presented here are generic and need to be adapted to the ways your company conducts supervisory training. The facilitator should be chosen and trained to ensure she conducts the program effectively, especially the fishbowl sessions that are the most important skill-building parts of the program.

This training is best delivered from the top down, starting with senior managers and progressing down to first-line supervisors. Then supervisors will have full support and good coaching from their managers when they confront a tough trust-related issue.

Think of this approach as Trust Training 101. Consider additional courses that address more complex issues or provide refresher training for the participants after they've applied their newly learned skills with their teams.

Identify your company's core trust skills

Prior to the session, consult the Pennington study cited earlier in this chapter to broaden your thinking about trust-building and trust-breaking opportunities in your company. Then prepare a list of specific trust skills that participants should develop along with a real-life scenario in your company for each where a supervisor might struggle to act in trustworthy ways.

Begin with your employee value proposition

Comb through your EVP for phrases that reflect the trustworthiness you promise to applicants and employees. Include branding examples such as positioning statements, videos, and other ways you communicate who you are. Also consider incorporating your company's mission statement or other declarations that say you can be trusted.

Whichever tools you use, make clear to participants that being trustworthy is important in your company and you expect them to role model trust skills with their everyday behaviors.

Distinguish trust from other supervisory skills

Tell participants that building trust is the most important skill for retention rather than have them believe trust is one of many equal skills. Support this by using data presented in this book or from other studies. Contrast trust to communicating, providing feedback, and career coaching, and clarify that employees don't care about those things if they come from a supervisor they don't trust.

Make it personal

Develop an exercise that requires participants to reflect on past supervisors and reasons why they left past jobs. One way is to ask them to describe three events where they believed they were treated unfairly, the emotions they felt, and the resulting actions they took. Ask them to specify their emotions at the time so they relive those moments. Track events, emotions, and consequences on a flip chart so all participants see the connections.

Ask them then to give one example of a supervisor who treated them in a trustworthy way. Post those events, emotions, and consequences on another flip chart so they all see the positive outcomes of building trust.

Then ask the group to describe the differences they have all seen between supervisors who build and break trust, and the consequences for their teams and organizations.

Provide a reflective experience

Now that you've heightened their emotions about the power of trust, invite them to share times when they've broken trust—and built it. One way is to ask them to form small groups and share an example of when each took an extra step to build trust and one where each broke trust, and the lessons they learned from both. Encourage them to give their strongest examples and not to be modest or embarrassed. When the groups have finished, invite anyone to share their stories with the larger group if they choose.

If you find participants are reluctant to share their stories, ask the facilitator to be prepared to share her own examples. The group will likely match the degree to which she discloses her best and worst trust performances.

This is also the time to share recent employee survey data that contains individual information on trust for those in your group if you have it.

Solicit in-company trust opportunities

Ask each participant to write down five opportunities she has to build or break trust with her team, targeting ones if possible that are specific to your organization. These might include withholding truths about an upcoming merger, taking full credit for team achievements, sugarcoating feedback during performance appraisals, and similar trust-breaking examples. Record these on the flip chart.

Fishbowl the core trust skills

Distribute a list of the core trust skills that you identified prior to the session. Some of the skills will be basic, such as "tell the truth" unless the information is confidential, and then say you cannot disclose it. Others will be more complex, like how to respond to questions about actions taken above you or how to apologize for embarrassing an employee.

Compare the core skills you've distributed to the trust opportunities the group just shared. Feel free to add a skill to your list if the participants identified a skill area you missed.

Discuss the first skill with the group, and then invite two participants to sit in the center of the room to role-play the scenario you developed for that particular skill. One should play the role of the supervisor and the other play the role of the person who is likely to be included in the discussion, usually a subordinate, but this might also be a manager or peer. Explain each role and circumstance to the full group, and give the role players brief individual coaching and a script outline to follow to ensure the real-world complexities of the circumstance are addressed. For example, the first role play might involve an employee who asks the supervisor to never correct her performance in public again.

After the role players have delivered their scripts to the group, invite the group to critique the positions taken and the statements made by the "supervisor." When you hear a suggestion you want the group to use, ask the participant who contributed it to take the "supervisor" role-play seat and replay that section of the discussion with the other role player.

Ask participants to write down any helpful hints on their core trust skills handouts as they observe and make suggestions for the role play. Conclude the fishbowl for the first skill by summarizing key points of the discussion and then move on to the second skill. Continue this exercise until all skills have been addressed.

Seek commitments

After concluding the fishbowl sessions, give the participants a "lessons learned" form and ask them to record the following:

- Key trust-related statements from your employee value proposition, mission statement, or other document you referred to at the beginning of the program
- The emotions they felt from being treated unfairly in the previous-experience examples they used
- The times they broke and built trust with colleagues at work
- The five best lessons they learned from the fishbowl experience

After they've completed the "lessons learned" form, ask them to study it to identify the most important changes they should make to their own behaviors to improve their trust skills with their teams. Then provide them with a form on which they can write out these changes in detail. Once they've completed the form, ask them to meet for no more than ten total minutes with another participant to share their plans.

Conclusion and next steps

Conclude the meeting by recommending each participant share their commitment lists with their teams and also with their managers. Remind them of the dates of your next employee survey so they can set improvement goals on the trust scores and aim to achieve them.

 ## Top Ways to Spot a Nontrusted Supervisor

Like scientific experiments that involve stimulus and response, employees indicate their lack of trust by changing their behaviors. Top managers and HR must be on the lookout for these behaviors, especially for departments that are led by supervisors who tend to manage better "up" than "down." Some who successfully manage up show their best interpersonal and business skills to their managers but are far less effective when managing their teams.

The following sections describe some of the best ways to identify teams that are stifled by a supervisor they don't trust.

Rumors abound

Sometimes grapevine action is understandable, like when stories on the Internet identify your company as a takeover prospect. But when rumors abound in one area of your company more than another, employees might be telling you they don't trust their supervisor. These rumors might be about company issues or local specifics about peer employees' pay, who-said-what, why someone didn't get promoted, or even details about their supervisor. Employees start and spread rumors as subconscious ways to get even, to establish power in an organization when they resent not having enough influence or not enough of a voice.

Employees clam up

Management visitors notice employees are polite but not engaging. All comments are politically correct but disclose no specifics of how things really are. Employees tend to visit for socially required short periods of time and then say they need to get back to work. Nonverbal cues have no genuine warmth, just the right smiles and handshakes to get through the visit.

Complaints bubble up

When employees initially stay silent regarding their work environment, the objections they hold in eventually find ways to escape. Whether using formal grievance processes or by complaining upstream, they begin to expose circumstances regarding too much work, unjust treatment, playing favorites, or various forms of harassment. These might be real, exaggerated, or imagined, but the increase in complaints compared to peer departments is a clear indicator that something is wrong at the top.

Pay is a problem

Often these complaints focus on pay, both from the team and the supervisor. For the team, the mantra is, "If you expect me to put up with this…" The supervisor, on the other hand, sees pay as a way to quiet the employees who are now expressing concerns. And solving the problem with pay shifts the root cause away from his nontrustworthy style.

Fewer individual meetings occur

In our experience, supervisors who break trust with their teams feel the backlash and then respond by creating distance. Group meetings are okay because they have tight agendas and employees are more likely to stay in line. Individual meetings, though, offer more opportunity for confrontation, and supervisors tend to postpone or eliminate them as a way to "save time."

Survey scores dive

Even in small companies, employee surveys only have value if the data is reported for each individual supervisor. Surveys should include items that clearly address whether the team trusts its supervisor and a few other questions that ask about trust specifics, such as telling the truth, keeping commitments, or giving versus stealing credit.

Confidential surveys are one way employees know they can get even. Compare trust survey results across peer supervisors to identify which ones have integrity issues with their teams.

Production is down

When numbers fall, top managers ask supervisors for explanations and should listen carefully to their answers. When supervisors blame down, they open the door to investigation that might reveal deep problems between the supervisor and her team. The top manager or HR can conduct individual interviews, focus groups, or surveys to learn real causes and might uncover the supervisor's trust behaviors that are disengaging the team.

Turnover is up

Increased turnover is always cause for alarm, but especially when it comes in groups and is higher for one supervisor than his peers. Losing good workers is forever, so investigate swiftly and make a hard choice whether the supervisor can be saved or risk losing more members of his team.

 True Stories

Channeling the Great Place to Work Institute

Chapter 4 mentioned the Great Place to Work Institute as the one-stop online location for applying for the *Fortune* and SHRM best-places-to-work awards. Employees from companies that apply for these awards are asked to complete the Trust Index. The Index consists of 57 statements that cover credibility, respect, fairness, pride, and camaraderie.[4]

The Trust Index is just one way the Institute declares its opinion of the importance of trust in the workplace. They go on to say:

> Any company can be a great place to work. Our approach is based on the major findings of 20 years of research—that trust between managers and employees is the primary defining characteristic of the very best workplaces.[5]

The Institute and their associates *Fortune* and SHRM are making clear that the pathway to achieving the most enviable workplace awards is the amount of trust employees place in their supervisors and organizations. So organizations that apply for these awards not only have a chance to earn a prestigious credential, but they will also learn the degree to which their teams trust them, which is another reason to apply.

Truth-telling cuts turnover and increases profits

Kent Thiry is CEO of DaVita, a leading dialysis-treatment company headquartered in El Segundo, California. When Thiry took over DaVita, loans were in default and turnover was 45%. Employees who left included those with the most knowledge for fixing the company's problems.

Six years later, turnover has been cut by 50%, revenues exceed $5 billion, and DaVita has achieved the industry's best clinical outcomes. Thiry attributes much of this success to encouraging candid feedback and building a truth-telling culture. Through town hall meetings and other communication methods, Thiry opened doors to frontline employees to give inputs on decisions large and small. In a program called "Reality 101," Thiry asks every manager to spend a week working in a dialysis center to see firsthand the challenges faced by patients as well as employees.

Thiry tells employees to think of DaVita as a "village where there's shared responsibility and a shared vision of reality."[6] His good work connects the dots between building trust, improving retention, and making more money.

My favorite true story

Most of us can readily identify our best boss ever, and Bob Bowen was mine. Bob was smart, caring, and always kept his emotions under control. His charisma came from listening.

After we had worked together for six months, Bob called me into his office and said the following:

> Finney, I want us to work together for a long time, so I'm going to make you an offer. If you accept it, we'll shake hands and our bond is our word.
>
> You're going to have some tough days here because I might be difficult, our team will have conflicts, or management will run us in circles. When those days happen, you might decide to look for another job.
>
> So here is my offer. If you ever decide to start looking, I want you to promise that you will come tell me on that day. And my promise to you is I will make every effort to make our company a place where you want to stay. But if you ever place an envelope on my desk that tells me you're leaving and we haven't talked about it before, you've broken the deal.

I shook Bob's hand, of course. We never had to use our plan, as I stayed another 17 years, and it is no coincidence that I resigned six months after Bob left, even though by then we worked in different cities.

Any of us can repeat Bob's words and hope the person in the chair will stay, but the real test is whether that supervisor can build relationships that are based on trust.

 ## Closing Thoughts on Building Trust

The following are three major conclusions for rethinking retention based on the ideas presented in this chapter regarding the very strong link between supervisors, trust, and retention.

Traditional Thinking	Rethinking Retention
The most important supervisory skills for retention are communication, feedback, and career coaching.	Supervisors who cannot build trust have little credibility regardless of their other skills.
Trustworthiness is a character trait and cannot be changed.	Building or breaking trust is usually about behaviors that can be improved with training and coaching.
To reach their positions, supervisors and managers have already learned trust skills.	Our own experience tells us some supervisors are trustworthy and some are not.

All of us have encountered people who've lost our trust because they told us a lie or deliberately sold us a defective product. This chapter is not about them.

Being promoted to supervisor on any level brings with it the assumption that people in the know think you are basically good. You want to be trusted, liked, and respected but might not know the right ways to achieve this. Then stress from too much work or other conflicts gets in the way and you perform like your worst past boss instead of your best one. The consequence is that your team has no tolerance for any of your shortcomings, whereas trusted supervisors are given plenty of leeway to make mistakes.

So let's assume that trust in the workplace is not about being right or wrong, acting morally or immorally, or having indelible qualities that cannot be changed. It's our behaviors that determine whether others trust us, and these are within our control. The very good news is that with training, coaching, and direct feedback, most of us can improve our trust skills and retain our teams longer as a result.

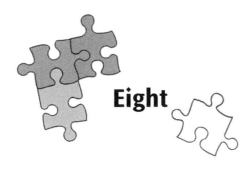

Eight

Narrow the Front Door to Close the Back Door

Hiring wrong employees puts us on the straight path to turnover. Seek applicants who *can* do your job, *will* do your job, and *will* stay. Assessing the "will stay" part can be elusive, though, as there is no selection method or product that can give us guarantees.

We do know, though, that *employees stay for things they believe are uniquely available from us.* Chapter 4 discussed how to develop an employee value proposition and employment brand, with both processes targeted to attract the candidates you want. This chapter addresses the best ways to screen these applicants in or out, based on that slippery "will stay" criteria, and presents the following top lists:

- **Top tips for hiring workers who stay** focuses on both daily activities and new research
- **Top extreme employee referral ideas**, because employee referrals tend to stay longer and perform better
- **Top methods for building realistic job previews**, because we must be expert at making applicants know our jobs, both to attract them and encourage them to opt out if the job isn't a right fit

- **Top tips for hiring and retaining older workers** is included because older workers are a steady supply of applicants who are usually loyal when matched correctly
- **Top questions to ask selection vendors**, because so many of us base our hiring decisions on assessments that have been designed elsewhere, and we need to become smart buyers

The True Stories section includes data-driven examples of organizations that have used these techniques to reduce turnover and improve productivity.

Top Tips for Hiring Workers Who Stay

Hiring workers who stay requires doing many things right. Some of these ideas are old, but so are blocking and tackling, and teams work hard each year to perfect them. Read these tips and score your company on how thoroughly you do these items. Do them better and your turnover will fall.

Increase your applicant-to-hire ratio

None of us will be choosy if filling openings requires hiring half of our applicants. High-retention companies turn down nine out of ten who apply. Set an applicant-to-hire ratio goal and use online services, community contacts, professional networks, social networks, and other methods to achieve it.

Between 2008 and 2012, companies are projected to spend $11 billion on online employment advertising. Over half of all job seekers search Internet websites, and 75% of Fortune 500 companies recruit applicants using their own websites as their primary tools.[1] These numbers are increasing as you read.

One way to spruce up your site to attract more applicants is to see how the best sites do it. Each year Peter Weddle surveys users to identify the best 30 job boards, and you can see the most recent results at *www.weddles.com/awards/index.htm*. Check out these sites and you might find improvements you can make to your own.

Conduct in-depth reference checks

Using reference checks sounds old-school because legislation now limits how much companies will tell you about past workers, but there are no laws that say you can't ask. Put the burden on applicants to tell you names and contact information for past supervisors and call them. HR departments will be tight-lipped, but not all supervisors read the e-mails that tell them to stay silent. Ask questions that require answers on a scale of 1 to 10, and if a supervisor says "7," probe for more information. Seek the real reasons the applicant left. Just knowing the applicant is eligible for rehire isn't enough.

Track 90-day/1-year retention rates

If nonexempt workers stay fewer than 90 days or professional workers stay less than 1 year, something is broken at the hiring gate. Check your processes and the people who make hiring decisions. If HR makes hiring decisions or recommends candidates for hire, they are responsible for early exits. If hiring managers have a poor track record for hiring workers who stay beyond early periods, retrain them or remove them from hiring responsibilities.

Probe incessantly for reasons applicants left past jobs

"I just really needed a change." "I found a better opportunity." "It was time to leave." Many interviewers accept these answers, especially if they've already decided they like the candidate. But these answers only tell us that the candidate is choosing not to tell us the real reasons she left.

Follow up with, "Tell me the one or two things about that job that caused you to look elsewhere." "Was there one event or recurring thing that pushed you over the edge and made you know it was time to leave?" "What was the real reason you left?"

Once you know the real leave reasons, probe to learn if applicants might apply that same thinking to leave your job. Know the top three reasons your employees leave and match the candidate's past leave reasons against them. If the candidate can't give you firm reasons for leaving, maybe she just doesn't know what she wants.

Hire interns to learn if they qualify for permanent employment

For professional jobs, internships are the ultimate realistic job preview. Give interns a complex project they can complete from start to finish under the tutelage of a good supervisor. Then the natural match between you and them will unfold—or it won't. Know that interns will use blogs and other electronic means to spread the word about your company.

Hire rehires, refugees, and people with disabilities

Be selective, of course, but best-practice companies report higher retention with all three groups.

Google professional candidates

Much background information is available on the web on free and pay sites. Thirty-five percent of executive recruiters report they have eliminated candidates based on information found there.[2]

Look especially for high-level accomplishments like awards, conference presentations, or leadership positions in professional associations to confirm what the candidate told you and expand what you know. Look also for cities of residence, degrees obtained, convictions, and other information that might disclose the candidate is not shooting straight.

 ## Top Extreme Employee Referral Ideas

Imagine that six months from now your company has undergone the following transformation:

- Good workers are eager to invite their friends to apply
- Recruiting is now a job for all versus a few
- Your applicant-to-hire ratio increases with quality applicants
- New hires begin with a friend at work
- And, most important, new hires stay longer

Most organizations implement employee referral programs by establishing a reward, announcing it in their newsletter, placing posters in the break room, and telling new employees during orientation. The ideas presented here take employee referrals to a higher level of success. These ideas will light a fire under your referral program.

Set a goal that up to 50% of new hires will come from referrals and hold one person accountable for achieving it

Goals, accountability, and measured results drive action. Set interim goals so progress happens quickly, such as 25% for the first quarter, and then raise the goal another 5% each subsequent quarter. Appoint one person to be in charge, likely from HR, and help her build a plan for success. The referral role might be full-time or part-time depending on the size of your company. The employee you appoint will build planning, organization, communication, and creativity skills, and your company will have lower turnover as a result.

Marketing more than money

When HR peers discuss employee referral programs, the first question asked is, "How much money do you pay?" The better question would be, "How do you market your program?"

Employees *are* motivated by money, but our experience indicates they are more motivated by clever and varied marketing and by being asked. Solicit your marketing department to help and to address your employees as they would a prospect. They will then ask about target markets, value of repeat sales, and most effective reach techniques— all the things marketers research when building a marketing program. Emphasize that this is not a short-term campaign, but rather a forever initiative that must occasionally take on a new look.

Obviously, marketing is better at marketing than HR. Less clear, though, is the importance marketing places on helping with HR-related initiatives. When executives lead the retention effort, marketing is more likely to see helping as part of their ongoing role. This is less likely to happen when HR leads the retention effort on its own.

Assign referral goals to managers on all levels

Missing from most referral programs is a direct, verbal request from supervisor to employee. You can make this happen by including in the marketing plan a goal for each supervisor and suggested ways for achieving it. The goal should be reasonable and based on a number of referrals gathered from a department that are hired anywhere in the company, such as three per quarter. Here's one example of a supervisor's pitch during a team meeting:

> As you know, we are down about twenty people across our plant and two on our own team. We need people who can do the job you have and really want to work. With the weekend coming up, this is the time you visit with friends and family, see people you know at church, and go to shopping centers and restaurants where you notice employees who do a good job. Please ask all the good ones who can do what you do if they'd like to come work for us.
>
> On Monday morning, I'll ask you all to meet like this for just a few minutes to tell us how you did. We can share ideas that worked and talk about ways we can get better. Thanks so much for helping our company perform even better.

Clone your best performers and long-service workers via an employee committee

Invite the employees you want to replicate to take a lead role with recruiting. Choose employees who perform well, demonstrate stability, have leadership skills so they influence others, and might contribute a good idea. Ask these committee members to provide company-wide ideas, encourage peers to recruit, and recruit on their own. Ask the committee to meet monthly and begin with a company-wide progress report versus goal, followed by individual reports on actions they've taken since the last meeting to rally others and find referrals on their own. Rotate the committee every six months or so to keep the energy and ideas fresh.

When forming your committee, recall the BLS conclusion referenced in Chapter 2: "The length of time a worker remains with the same employer increases with the age at which the worker began the job." Presuming peers will refer peers, thirty-somethings and those older are more likely to refer stable workers than those who are just entering the workforce.

Ask exempt workers to accept outreach assignments

While HR is responsible for recruiting from various community organizations, it is usually challenged to do so effectively. To fix this, list every community agency, church, school, and other organization that might help, and then solicit an exempt employee to take on the recruiting task. The employee must have influencing skills and present your company in a positive way. Equip her with some company information and an elevator speech about your jobs, and set her initial goal as getting a top agency official to experience your realistic job preview. Her reward will be receiving the employee referral bonus for each successful new hire she brings in.

Increase awards for top referrers

Expect a version of the 80/20 rule: A few will refer the most. Stoke these employees by stair-stepping the rewards so they increase significantly after three successful referrals in a twelve-month period. During the mid-1990s technology boom, one Silicon Valley company gave employees a Jeep Cherokee once they reached eight successful referrals in a year. Scale your rewards appropriately.

Expect professional employees to participate too

Professional employees network via associations, conferences, and viral networks, usually on your nickel. Expect them to seek out qualified potential colleagues at conferences and schools and bring back business cards with recommendations.

One major bank consistently expanded its core of corporate lenders by way of employee referrals. The top executive knew his team worked every day with peers in other banks with whom they shared responsibility for multimillion-dollar loans. As a result, these bankers knew each other and knew who they wanted as colleagues.

Build smart rules into the program

Open the program to all employees, customers, and vendors, even if you have to adjust the rewards. Move past the old notions that HR and managers should already be referring people, because they'll refer more if you reward them.

- Include taxes in the gross award amount, so you don't promise $100 and then give $73.23.
- Give employees generic business cards on which they can write their own names, and require referred applicants to present these cards when applying. Expect cards to be lost and other snafus, and give employees all the benefit of the doubt to keep the program positive.
- Match rewards to your employees' needs. Time off or free parking might be more important than cash.
- Add a referral program link to your employee portal so a reminder is never far away.
- Present awards publicly with a check, even if it's a fake check. Ask the winner what she plans to do with the reward so all of her colleagues can hear.
- Raffle off a trip each quarter, allowing one entry per successful referral. Include a camera so you can post pictures throughout the work area to encourage participation.
- Pay the full award when the new employee starts, unless the referring employee can impact retention during the first few months. The referring employee's job is to get the applicant in the door, whereas HR and the hiring manager must take responsibility for whether the employee stays.

 ## Top Methods for Building Realistic Job Previews

Realistic job previews (RJPs) provide applicants with a clear, candid experience of your job so they can opt in with enthusiasm or opt out to save you turnover later. This is a top-tier retention tool that is underutilized by most organizations because they don't dedicate enough people, time, or resources to build it correctly. Instead they settle for a walking tour of the facility or a handout that duplicates a job description.

RJPs should communicate the varied aspects of your job such as duties, working conditions, schedule, pay, benefits, opportunities, and other people the applicant will be working with. This can be done through observation, job simulations, talking with incumbents, and/or videos—any form of communication that works for your job.

RJPs must deepen applicants' convictions about your job either positively or negatively, so your choice regarding the form of communication is critical.

The following section outlines recommendations for building a top-notch RJP.

Onsite RJPs must be led by a trained facilitator to ensure that applicants take in all key points

In the spirit of "I'm going to tell you what I'm going to tell you, then I'm going to tell you, then I'm going to tell you what I told you," RJPs must be facilitated by great communicators with effective scripts. If leading a tour of a factory floor, the facilitator would begin with one or a small group of applicants in a conference room, telling the group what they are about to experience and five key points they should learn. During the tour the facilitator stops to point out each of these five key points, then returns the group to the conference room to ask each applicant their opinions of the key points. The facilitator concludes by asking each applicant what concerns she might have about the job and whether she wants to continue with her application.

RJPs must reach the applicants' senses

Sights, sounds, smells, feels, and maybe even tastes can all be critical components of a job. So, ideally, the RJP will provide a sample of these experiences. Examples might include standing all day, lifting 50-pound bags, climbing on and off a truck, working in a room with no natural light, working in a refrigerated room, working on a wet floor for eight hours, dealing with angry customers, hearing loud machinery or working in a library-quiet environment, working among many or totally alone, or having to wash your clothes out every night to remove the stains and smells. I once worked a summer job in a food factory making Worcestershire Sauce, and that smell has never left my memory.

Facilitators must point out sounds, lighting, sitting or standing, and other job conditions. Job slices might include asking the group to focus for one full minute on the sounds or smells of the workplace. Where possible, ask the applicant to participate in a job slice by handling the product, listening to a real or simulated caller, riding in a truck, or wearing the uniform. Or ask them to return to observe the work for an hour or more so they really understand the pace.

Use subject matter experts to learn the job's true content

Interview those who manage the job to learn its full details, including the parts most incumbents don't like to do, so you can build an RJP that includes the job's attractive and less attractive parts.

Tell applicants the high-turnover issues

Tell them the main reasons employees leave: Work pressure, sore backs, schedule changes, or whatever the real reasons are. Tell them why you fire workers, too. Make certain they understand these job aspects and then ask each of them if they are willing to accept them.

Be brutally honest

Don't sugarcoat customer emotions, extreme temperatures, forced overtime, holiday requirements, or the amount of their first raise. For professional workers, speak clearly about performance standards, travel, and hours of work. All applicants will respect you for your honesty, and some will leave you now versus in their first few weeks.

Do the RJP early in the hiring process

It is better to screen nonqualified applicants out early, and they are more likely to screen themselves out before they've invested more time in your process.

Schedule applicants to meet individually with a high-performing employee

This technique can yield information from the applicant that you won't get elsewhere. Employees can demonstrate aspects of the job and ask casually about the applicant's real reasons for applying and how long they intend to stay. Applicants tend to be more comfortable and therefore more open with a peer, and you might learn new information.

Include unique information about your area for relocating employees

Tell them commuting times, the cost of housing, or even the cost of milk. A client in Hawaii lost several employees who found that moving from the mainland to paradise was just too expensive.

Track the percent of hires screened out by the RJP

PetSmart shows job applicants a 10-minute RJP video that screens out about 15% of their applicants. They believe those applicants would have left in the first 90 days.[3]

RJPs that don't screen anyone out are too weak, whereas those that screen out too many might be exaggerating concerns about the job. Aim for 20% screen-out and continuously review your results and your RJP's content.

Build remote RJPs using video and other technology tools

Video provides the opportunity to show job areas that cannot be shown in person. Another advantage is that online applicants can view video RJPs before applying, so those who don't fit can screen themselves out early.

Residents of the Mid-Atlantic states know that Sheetz convenience stores are a step above their peers, as each store employs about 35 workers and serves fresh food. RJPs for Sheetz stores can be viewed at *www.sheetz.com/main/*, then click "Job Opportunities," then "Job Preview." You will have to enter a first name to proceed.

This is a slide show that first presents the "Sheetz DNA," which is a list of company values, followed by details of the job and then a compatibility questionnaire. The sales associate presentation describes the 24/7 scheduling, working with customers, and doing diverse jobs such as stocking shelves and cleaning bathrooms. Store level pay ranges are also disclosed. The compatibility questionnaire makes clear that Sheetz employees must have no beards, no excessive jewelry, no visible tattoos with a short-sleeved shirt, or "extreme hair style or colors." Applicants are presented with a summary score to the questionnaire in the form of a fuel gauge, and then offered an online application if their compatibility score permits them to proceed.

Annual turnover at Sheetz is roughly 55% for hourly workers and 5% for managers, significantly below industry averages. Manager of Employee Programs Earl Springer attributes much of his company's good retention to the RJP. The top prehire screen-out reason is appearance, and consequently the number of terminations for appearance after hire have been greatly reduced. Each hourly exit is calculated to cost $3,200, so the RJP has paid great dividends.[4]

 ## Top Tips for Hiring and Retaining Older Workers

As noted earlier, trusted research tells us older workers stay longer and have better attitudes about their work. In this section, we will explore ways to hire and retain workers 50 and older.

Many older workers want to work after normal retirement age, and there are plenty of them. They are part of the 76-million-strong baby boom generation, and their age group represents the largest of all generations in our workforce. By 2012, nearly 20% of the total U.S. workforce will be age 55 or older,[5] and various studies report between 60% and 75% of them plan to keep on working past normal retirement age.[6]

Down economic times place extra pressure on older workers because their retirements slip further into the future. In one study, 60% of workers above the age of 60 say they will put off retiring because of the 2008–2009 recession, and nearly three-quarters of this group plan to work up to six years longer to re-coup their savings.[7]

So embrace the good news: There is a large pool of workers who want to work and are prone to stay. Imagine replacing the young and misdirected members of your team with mature workers who show up and work hard.

All the reasons older workers are more loyal might be contained in a quote from a 50-something employee who was being recognized for her consistent high performance: "When I graduated high school, there was no plan B; you got a job, kept your job, and if you lost your job you got another job."

The following are suggestions for employing older workers.

Convince older workers who work for your company to stay and not retire

Healthcare administrators have especially strong reason to fret, as nearly half of all nurses will reach retirement age within fifteen years. Twenty-eight percent of nuclear power facility employees will be eligible for retirement in five years, just as that industry is expected to expand.[8] For any industry, good-performing older workers who retire just create more turnover. So ask them what they need to stay. Satisfying their answers might require changes in scheduling, retirement and health benefits, training, or giving them new assignments. But the cost of changing might be less than the cost of replacing. You might want to conduct retirement planning sessions, too, so some understand that they need to continue earning an income.

Beat back misconceptions about older workers' productivity with your management team

In a recent study conducted by the National Council on Aging, 97% of respondents said older workers are thorough and reliable when completing work.[9] A *BusinessWeek* analysis found that by increasing productivity and labor-force participation of older Americans, the U.S. could add 9% to its gross domestic product by 2045, which would add more than $3 trillion a year to overall economic output.[10]

An AARP/Towers Perrin report indicates that employing older workers costs marginally more when considering healthcare costs as well as pay and other types of rewards that tend to increase with longer service. This is more than offset, though, by the additional productivity older workers bring and the cost of hiring and training their replacements.[11]

Build your organization to attract older workers

Various studies tell us that older workers want flexible schedules, healthcare benefits, competitive pension plans, time off for elder care, innovative growth opportunities, and financial literacy skills so they can plan to retire. However, it would be better to develop your own list of what your current older employees want by asking them. Not only will you increase your odds of providing the right things, but they will thank you for caring enough to ask and also refer their peers.

Market your company effectively to older workers

Recruiting older workers used to mean sending letters to senior centers, whereas most of today's older workers are working somewhere else. Target marketing might mean reaching out via radio, magazines, member organizations, or anywhere that people 50 and over connect with the media.

One opportunity for large employers is to participate in AARP's National Employer Team. This is a group of employers that have lived up to AARP's standards as a choice employer for older workers. These employers are noted on AARP's website with a link to pitch their jobs. Click on *www.aarp.org/money/work/articles/national_employer _team.html* to learn more about this program.

 Top Questions to Ask Selection Vendors

Many organizations buy tools from vendors to improve employee selection. These vendors might sell hiring tools only or they might combine them with temporary help services, so their product is workers who have been selected with their tools.

These tools include, among others, online and paper-and-pencil assessments, simulations, and structured interviews. Vendors also offer tools to recruit applicants online or via interactive voice responses, and then screen out applicants based on a predetermined set of questions. Some offer tools to select supervisors as well. Organizations buy these tools primarily to improve sourcing and hiring, but vendors should be asked about the impact of their tools on retention.

Selection tools measure job skills and personal characteristics. Depending on the job, skills might include data entry, equipment operation, or customer service. Personal characteristics might include managing change, honesty, or working with others. The logical assumption is that the closer the candidate fits the job characteristics, the candidate will do the job better and the candidate will stay longer.

Vendors sometimes *claim* that their selection tools impact retention, but you need to look past those claims and seek hard data to support them. The following questions represent a demanding test. Even highly reputable vendors might not have tracked enough data to answer each of these questions, but collecting whatever answers they give will lead you to know their tools' impact on retention. If answers are general and without supporting data, assume the tools do not impact retention.

I studied the websites of five leading vendors and found that three of the five made no mention of retention or any related term. All used phrases one would expect such as *talent management, assessment,* and *development,* but the absence of any retention-related statements leads me to believe these organizations might not have confidence that their products can lower turnover. One stated their products will help users know which applicants "can and will do the job," omitting the obvious question of "Will they stay?"

The following are questions you should ask selection vendors before you hire them, or as soon as possible if you work with them now.

How does your product impact employee retention?

The response to this open-ended question will tell you how acquainted the representative is with retention and data. Ask this question and then resist the urge to expand. Listen instead to the degree of specificity you hear. General responses such as "I can assure you our products cut turnover" have no value. Better are responses that contain data or say that data is available, even if the representative must call you back or involve someone else on the call.

What data do you have regarding how your product impacts retention in my industry? And for the specific position for which we need help?

These questions require data-driven answers. Listen carefully for how much turnover dropped once clients began using the tools. All that matters is what was turnover when the engagement started, what is turnover now, and when did it begin to drop. Comparisons to industry averages matter less.

Listen also for whether the data presented is for all clients or a selected few. Push to learn the vendor's average outcome for your industry and your job, as well as the best and worst case. Feel free to arrange a follow-up call so the representative can gather this data and report it to you if it is not readily available.

If your product is so effective, will you take responsibility for early turnover?

If vendors get paid by the hire, they make money on your turnover. So linking this knowledge with their claims for their products, it is fair to ask them to accept and achieve retention goals for some period after hire. Ask them to refund your money for any new hire who fails to last through training or for some period afterward. If they refuse, negotiate a standard for 30-, 60-, and 90-day retention and hold them accountable to it.

How would you separate the impact of your product on our retention from other retention initiatives we have underway?

Readers of this book will likely implement several retention initiatives at once, and measuring their individual effectiveness will be difficult. This is okay, though, because lowering your turnover solves a greater problem than wondering which solution mattered more. You will know intuitively and with reasonable accuracy over time which initiatives changed behaviors and generated high energy for retention.

But you want to challenge any vendor *to accept responsibility for measuring their own success.* Otherwise they will climb aboard the declining-turnover train and tell you they are the conductor. So ask them to provide you with a concrete answer as to how they will separate out their product's impact on retention.

Their responses should focus exclusively on the retention and job performance of the new hires they help you select rather than look to overall changes in retention. One way is to compare 30-, 60-, and 90-day turnover for the employees hired using their tools to turnover during those periods of those hired immediately before using the vendor's tools.

Think creatively beyond these examples if necessary. Some organizations don't hire enough new employees to get a significant sample size in 30 days, and for others turnover happens later rather than sooner. Most important, put responsibility on the vendors for measuring their tools' impact rather than permitting them to lump the success of their efforts with yours.

Do your supervisor-assessment tools measure the supervisor's likelihood to manage in a way that leads to high employee retention?

Vendors that offer supervisor-selection tools should disclose to you whatever answers they have to this question. They might tell you the skills their tools measure and draw a logical connection that having these skills will lead to retention, but we want to know data. Value highly any convincing data they present, as we know that much turnover is driven at the first-line leader level.

If they have no data, make sure you ask for several references from clients in your industry who use their supervisor-selection tools and ask their opinions.

 ## True Stories

Refugees are a new-age hiring pool

Hiring refugees has paid off handsomely for several companies:

- Dee Zee Manufacturing in Des Moines, Iowa, attributes its turnover reduction from 60% to 20% to hiring refugees. Their absentee rate has dropped from 6% to 0.1%.

- A Wells Fargo manager hired ten refugees into his department, which he believes has contributed to a 34% turnover decrease. Refugees tend to stay four or five years versus others who stay a year or less, and their productivity is higher.[12]

Structured interviews create big payoff

A midwestern manufacturing company had a 30% involuntary turnover rate of administrative assistants in their first year. Examining why, they found these employees were unable to perform complex spreadsheet calculations. They corrected this by implementing a structured interview with appropriate skill testing and there were no further early terminations. Net savings were $54,000.[13]

Employee referrals lower turnover and hiring costs

Houston employers were surveyed regarding outcomes of their employee referral programs. While the programs were designed independently, all found employee referrals to be more reliable and less likely to leave. Additionally, costs per hire were reduced by 75% to 90%. Participating companies included 3M, Texas Instruments, Fidelity Investments, and McDonnell Douglas.[14]

Since implementing their "You've Got Friends, We Want to Meet Them" campaign, AmeriCredit has filled 45% of all openings with employee referrals, and they credit the program with helping cut turnover by more than half.[15]

Branding your referral program

A Florida bank took employee referrals to a new level and significantly cut turnover as a result. Developing a pink flamingo logo named "Hire-Em," they awarded winners with hats, t-shirts, and mugs with Hire-Em's likeness. Those who won stayed costumed for a day to remind employees and customers that they were always looking for good referrals.

RJPs and structured interviews make for better coffee

Coffee Bean & Tea Leaf, a Los Angeles-based coffee house, has cut turnover by more than half with solutions that include a four-hour realistic job preview for managers and structured interviews for all candidates.[16]

Small businesses benefit from referrals

As mentioned earlier, SHRM publishes its list of the best 50 small and medium businesses to work for, selecting 25 from each category. On their most recent list, more than half hired at least 25% of their employees from employee referrals. Leading the way was Badger Mining Corporation of Berlin, Wisconsin. With 177 employees onboard, all of Badger's new hires in the past year came by way of referrals.[17]

Older workers like to work

The YMCA of Greater Rochester was recognized by the MetLife Foundation as one of ten nonprofits that excelled at hiring older workers. Their turnover rate for those 50 and older is 2%.[18]

Borders has partnered with AARP to hire and retain workers over 50. According to a Borders' representative, "Their turnover rate was 10 times less than those under 30." Older workers' satisfaction rates were also much higher than younger workers'. Important benefits were a high 401(k) match, good healthcare for part-time workers, and flexibility. Borders also worked with Merrill Lynch to offer a "Pension Builder" program that allows retirees to buy into a gradual annuity stream. All store leaders take a "Generations" course, and some older workers have scored "snowbird" transfers to change locations during the seasons. Borders sales are probably higher because of extra efforts to hire older workers, since half of all their books are purchased by people over 45.[19]

Innovative thinking on employee referrals

Destination Hotels & Resorts employs 7,500 workers across its 33 properties. To keep positions filled, the company implemented an innovative employee referral program that leverages technology. Some of the features are:

- The system places an electronic tag on all employee referrals, so the candidate is interviewed ahead of others and receives frequent status updates from the system.

- Employees who pass on a posting can refer a friend by sending that friend an e-mail or inputting their data directly as an application.
- The referral portal page is designed for all generations and includes open jobs grouped under headings like "tech guru," "innovator," and "entrepreneur."

Robert Mellwig, Destination's top HR executive, reports the following results:

- Half of all jobs are filled via employee referrals
- Jobs are filled 60% faster with referrals versus other methods
- Average length of service for referrals is at least 20% to 30% longer than other employees

Building on these results, Destination Hotel's referral program goes one step further. Anyone, including nonemployees, can make referrals and get paid for those who get hired. Know someone who can fill an opening? Go to *www.destinationhotels.com/refer-a-friend. php* and enter their information. You might earn $500, and external rewards have been as high as $1,500 for tough-to-fill positions.

Mellwig explains the employee referral ROI this way: "It's simple ... we have data. We know that referrals help us to fill jobs faster, they stay longer, and they do better work. We wouldn't even compare this cost to the cost of putting a job online or in a newspaper because those candidates just aren't as good."[20]

Smart thinking: matching referral awards to your culture

I've never met a truck driver who didn't want a Harley.

—Karla O'Malley, HR Director,
OIX Trucking Company, Kansas City, Missouri

When David Orscheln founded OIX Trucking 13 years ago, he learned early that how you treat employees will determine your success. In 2006, OIX was locked into the usual high turnover and driver shortages that all trucking companies seemed to face. One year later, an employee referral program resulted in 22 new drivers and turnover had fallen from 70% to 42%, a significant improvement compared to a national average of greater than 100%.

The most important ingredient to OIX's referral program was a Harley Davidson, a hunk of steel that was universally coveted by all drivers. The rules were simple: Refer a driver who stays six months and you get one tally, and whoever gets the most tallies in the year wins the Harley. Second prize was $3,000, and monthly leaders earned a $50 Harley Davidson gift certificate.

Not only did new drivers stay, but they performed above standards, leading to 2008's prize: A Hawaiian vacation. Taking a cue from his owner, executive vice president Jeff Lamble knows topside leadership is more important than ever as drivers deal with the consequences of rising gas prices. "Our drivers have always been proud of our company," said Lamble. "We know the more they believe in their leaders, the harder they will work to find good drivers."[21]

MITRE narrows the door

MITRE puts the front-door retention practices to work better than any organization we know, and it has been on *Fortune*'s Top 100 list for eight consecutive years.

Based in Bedford, Massachusetts, and McLean, Virginia, MITRE is a not-for-profit company that provides technology research and development for several large federal government organizations. Total employees number 6,700 with annual turnover of 5.5%.

For starters, MITRE hires 48% of new employees via employee referrals. Referrals are hired at an applicant-to-hire ratio of 18:1 versus 60:1 for other applicants, so referrals are more than 3 times more likely to be hired.

MITRE also deliberately markets to mid- and late-career workers. The average employee age is 45, and many employees are in their 50s, 60s, and beyond. MITRE sponsors eight specific initiatives for developing, motivating, and retaining older workers.

MITRE's realistic job preview is testimony to its technology talents. Presented in video-game format, it challenges technology applicants to navigate the campus, meet potential teammates to learn about their jobs, and then assign those team members to participate in the design of a project. You can use their RJP's interactive game at *www.mitre.org/employment/*.

"Even though MITRE currently enjoys a high profile in the employment marketplace, we frequently reassess our employment value proposition to ensure our recruitment and retention practices successfully address the ever-evolving needs and expectations of our employees, applicants, and sponsors," says Gary Cluff, manager of MITRE's corporate recruiting.[22]

 ## Closing Thoughts on Narrowing the Front Door to Close the Back Door

The following are three major conclusions for rethinking retention based on the ideas presented in this chapter regarding narrowing the front door to hire employees who stay.

Traditional Thinking	Rethinking Retention
We source all employees who meet our qualifications.	We take extra efforts to source older applicants because they stay longer.
We pay good money for employee referrals.	We market our employee referral program and meet our referral goals.
We give applicants a tour of our workplace.	We conduct facilitated realistic job previews and track the percent of applicants who drop out.

So, based on the data presented here, and assuming the candidate demonstrates that she *can and will do the job*, here is a profile of one who is more likely to stay than others:

- Is chosen from many applicants versus only a few
- Reference checks and structured interview indicate she left past jobs for acceptable reasons and thinks long-term
- Was referred by a long-service, high-performing current employee
- Became more interested in your job after experiencing your realistic job preview

- Older is better
- If selected with the help of a vendor, that vendor is held to strong standards for early retention

Hiring workers who stay requires a lot of skill—and a little luck. The solutions offered in this chapter will help to stabilize your workforces, but only if you challenge some beliefs, implement new processes, and hold people accountable for smarter hiring. Increasing employee referrals, designing top-notch RJPs, focusing on older workers, and taking tougher stands with hiring vendors require commitment and hard work.

Here's a final thought regarding older workers, from the AARP/ Towers Perrin report mentioned earlier:

> Some companies may be able to escape the talent crunch entirely if today's 50+ workers do, in fact, stay in the workforce longer than previous generations.[23]

Rethink sourcing, hiring, training, and rewarding older workers. Abundant research and our experience say 55 is almost always better than 19, especially for those jobs where you struggle to retain workers due to motivation and attendance.

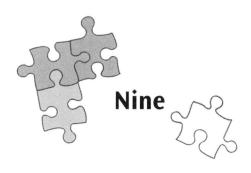

Nine

Script Employees' First 90 Days

mployees' first few months on the job give us a chance to prove ourselves, both to them and to us. So far in our model, we've now interviewed employees to find why they stay, converted their inputs into employee value propositions, branded those ideas to attract applicants, and then hired employees who match who we are. Locking them in early is the first real test regarding whether we can keep them.

Research tells us the stakes for early retention are high. The aforementioned Walker study says that only 26% of first-year employees are "truly loyal" and 45% are "high risk."[1] Another study by Sirota discloses that while 69% of new hires feel satisfied and enthusiastic during their first 90 days, that number continues to plummet throughout employees' first year.[2]

Until recently, new employees started by signing forms, completing orientation, receiving formal or informal training, and then going to work. The term *onboarding* was then introduced to lump these activities together and suggest additional ones to strengthen early ties.

Organizations can easily address the administrative aspects of onboarding and also introduce new hires to their company's mission—two of the standard pieces of traditional orientation programs. More challenging is weaving in specific tactics for getting relationships right with their supervisors and their peers. No onboarding program is complete if processes are not included to solve this important objective.

Before moving forward, let's contrast "old school" versus "new school" thinking regarding an employee's first week on the job. A generation ago, new-hire Harry would be thrilled to accept any job offer, eager to sit for an hour to complete paperwork, gladly yawn through boring lectures in orientation, and then trudge off to impress his boss. This was an accepted part of work.

Today's new hires expect much more. Having accepted your job, they want early evidence that you are living up to your promises. If orientation is dull, they'll text their friends—or their grandkids. They want to know if they joined the right company and can achieve their own goals—unless you hired the wrong applicants. So the first 90 days is test-time for them and glue-time for you.

Some studies tell us employees make decisions to stay or leave in the first month, others up to six months. We offer 90 days as our scripting duration, but you should adjust yours to match the turnover patterns and other symptoms you see in your workforce.

This chapter discusses:

- **Top retention tactics for new professionals**, so you can take extra steps to retain high-priced talent
- **Top retention tactics for new hourly employees**, so you can fully utilize your management talent to focus on retention
- **Top inclusions for your onboarding program**, so new hires learn your company in ways that are both positive and truthful
- **Top questions supervisors should ask new hires** to build strong early connections
- **Top guidelines for successful mentoring programs** to help connect new hires to the guidance-givers you choose

The True Stories section presents some additional perspectives on early retention as well as best practices from Whole Foods Market and Wyndham Vacation Ownership.

Top Retention Tactics for New Professionals

In his very helpful book *The First 90 Days: Critical Success Strategies for New Leaders at All Levels*, Harvard professor Michael Watkins details the ways newly appointed leaders should approach their roles and develop their skills. He points out that nearly half of all senior outside hires fail to achieve their desired results. Estimates of the direct and indirect costs of a failed executive-level hire are as high as $2.7 million.[3]

While Watkins' book addresses ways senior leaders can help themselves, the following sections discuss ways those leaders can retain the newly placed professionals who report to them in their first 90 days. The list is tactical and presents specific retention activities.

Set up early wins

Assign a task you know she can complete successfully by the end of the first month. To avoid micromanaging, tell her the result parameters such as objectives, scope, timeline, and budget if appropriate, and ask her to come back in a day or two with a plan. Once you approve the plan, assure her of your availability but stay out of her way. Let her contribute the work and the thinking behind it rather than just follow your instructions.

Give specific feedback, focusing on the positives but provide improvement areas, too. Teach her how you react to good work and also to work that is insufficient if necessary.

Involve the new employee in a team project too

Give her a way to know and work with others by assigning her to a group project. If possible, connect her with at least one peer who is skilled, positive, and likely to lead. Again, give her and the team distance to complete the project and give feedback to all. Ask her about her experience working with the team.

Connect to multiple managers

Recalling the primary importance of trust, ask three or four of your peers to meet individually with your new hire. By broadening her familiarity with the management team, she will gain more insight into your company's culture and hopefully make some strong ongoing connections. These connections will be especially important if for some reason she feels she cannot connect with you.

Tell your peers this is an important job and ask them to:

* Briefly share their history with the company, including what they've learned and who they've helped
* Bring four or five open-ended questions so the discussion moves on to the new hire
* Send a follow-up e-mail mentioning one or two highlights of the meeting and volunteering to always help

As a result, your employee will feel known, will feel listened to, and will acquire informal mentors.

Connect also to top executives

Aggressively seek out local executives for at least a five-minute meet and greet, even if you have to wait at their door when you know they will arrive. Help your new hire make an early impression, match names and faces, and have some basis to form her own opinions.

Discuss scheduling options

During the hiring process you likely covered the implications of travel and other out-of-office times, but what are your expectations for regular days in the office? New professional hires usually have to guess at office protocols for start and stop times, being out for doctor appointments and family emergencies, working from home, sleeping in after a late-night flight, and the like. You can clarify scheduling issues and relieve her pressure by proactively addressing these scenarios.

Socialize with partners and families

Nearly half of all executives say their top advisor on potential job changes is their spouse.[4] Knowing this, give the spouse or partner his own opportunity to form an independent opinion of you rather than have it framed by dinner table conversations. Include your spouse or partner, too, so both see you in a role other than a boss.

One of the best ways to disclose yourself to others is to invite them to your home. There they meet your family, see the setting of stories you tell, your commute to work, furnishings you like, and photos of those you love. Consider the value of this experience when pulling closer is important.

Check in frequently with relocating employees

Life-change surveys tell us that changing jobs and locations leads to high stress, for employees as well as for each member of their families. New home, new job, new schools, trailing spouse, transporting cars and boats, new doctors, new bills—all offer many opportunities for things to go wrong.

Ask your employee about all aspects—spouse's job, schools, commutes—and be the bridge between her and any centralized relocation administrator if issues arise. Verify also that her former home is sold or progressing toward closure in the unlikely event a family member becomes homesick. Employees worthy of company-sponsored relocation are costly to replace.

 ## Top Retention Tactics for New Hourly Employees

Those who manage people in high-turnover industries know the importance of taking extra retention steps during employees' first 90 days. In call centers, retail, fast food, and restaurants, companies seek every edge for early retention.

The following ideas expand on the first strategy of the Rethinking Retention model: Accountability for retention. Designing this accountability for new hires is complex, because many staff and operations employees are usually involved in influencing employees' stay/leave decisions early on. There are a lot of moving parts.

As you read these ideas, note that they are about changing management processes rather than developing new employee programs. Often the best retention tools are those that influence key personnel to fully utilize their retention skills.

Measure early turnover and set retention goals

Organizations with high early turnover must choose the right measurement criteria and then set goals to improve. For many, measuring early turnover is more important than annual or monthly turnover. The sequential steps are:

1. Identify your tipping point: The length of time during which most early quits leave. This might be one month, three months, six months, or even a year.
2. Measure the percent of new hires who have historically quit during that period.
3. Set a reasonable goal to improve retention over time as you implement retention tools. For example, if you find that you retain 60% of your new hires during the first 90 days, set a goal to retain 75% of them for that same period.
4. Track your success monthly or even weekly, knowing that your ultimate goal is to retain 75% of your new hires three months out.

Share goal-setting among all who work with new hires

Identify all who impact early retention and find ways to hold them accountable. For example:

- If HR makes hiring decisions or hiring recommendations, track each recruiter on how many of his new hires achieve 90 days.
- If training representatives are responsible for training new hires, track their success at graduating employees who reach 90 days. Their mandate should be to graduate only those who are likely to succeed and stay, and hold others back for additional training or fire them.
- Track supervisors who take on new hires on their success at retaining them for 90 days.
- Track those supervisors' managers as well so they are more likely to coach their supervisors on retention skills.
- Hold department managers accountable, too, so they are invested in the successful completion of these goals.

Assign all new hires to one or a few supervisors

Acknowledging the power of supervisors and their varying abilities to build trust, choose your best one and assign all new hires to her immediately after they complete training. Tell her that her primary job is retention, to coach with all of the skills she brings to get her team to the 90-day mark. Then eventually assign those employees to other supervisors to make room for your new-hire supervisor to take on more new employees.

If you cannot assign all new hires to just one supervisor due to issues related to shifts, locations, or the volume of new hires, narrow the new-hire supervisor pool to include your best, and hold them all accountable for early retention.

Install weekly tracking

During the 13 weeks that comprise employees' first 90 days, those responsible for new hires should record their weekly opinions on the likelihood each new hire will reach the 90-day retention goal. The criterion for success is whether the supervisor or trainer thinks the new hire will be with you through the 90th day. Reasons for failing include the employee might quit or he might fail and you fire him. The coding should be reviewed each week with the supervisor's or trainer's manager, and that team should decide who to coach to succeed, who to encourage to stay, and who to terminate now rather than later.

Hold 91-day retention meetings

Now that you've identified your 90-day retention team, the top executive should gather them for periodic meetings to review their retention performance. If you bring on new hires in classes or teams, schedule the meeting 91 days from the class's first day so you will know the percent you retained and whether you achieved your collective goal. If you hire individuals who are not in teams, schedule a 91-day meeting as often as necessary to review all individual employees who were hired in the past few months, so you are tracking their individual success at achieving 90 days.

Think of these meetings as the type doctors hold to review patient files. Each person around the table will have a unique and qualified viewpoint on what the management team did to retain each employee for 90 days, or what the team failed to do for those who left. The executive should probe to understand better why HR hired someone who quit three days later, or why training graduated an employee who failed to grasp a basic skill to succeed. The weekly tracking provides helpful information, too, as reasons should be explored for employees who left but those around the table thought would stay.

These types of discussions will improve everyone's retention skills and also imbed accountability for achieving the 90-day retention goal.

Fire early

Send a message to your workforce that those who cannot do your jobs early on or who show signs of negative influence will not be tolerated. Give extra credit to those who try hard, but otherwise draw boundaries regarding the types of employees who deserve all you give in your value proposition and those who do not.

Train new hires on their working shift

Hiring employees to work a night or weekend shift that they've never worked before is risky, and training them on a shift other than the one they will be working multiplies the risk. Ask trainers to work the same shifts their trainees do and train on their schedule. You'll use your training rooms more efficiently, too.

Top Inclusions for Your Onboarding Program

Let's think of *onboarding* as all the processes you implement for new hires to acquaint them with your company. These likely include new employee orientation, administrative steps involving payroll and benefits, initial training, and more. Whereas the previous sections in this chapter involve tactics management can use to improve early retention, these onboarding ideas can help you design specific programs for your new hires.

One size cannot fit all for onboarding programs. Multinational corporations will design onboarding programs that seem to have little in common with small nonprofits. However, these ideas can apply to any organization.

Make your EVP your guide

Traditional orientation programs present company mission, culture, and goals, but employees ultimately want to know the WIIFM: What's in it for me? Your EVP has been the common thread for all activities that brought these employees to you, so drive it home throughout your onboarding process. Think of the message as, "We said we would do these things for you and now we are already doing them."

Focus on mission and culture, too, with an emphasis on how each job provides a good service to others. If you manufacture sporting goods, you help customers have fun and improve their health. Bus drivers enable people to get to their jobs and see their families. Accountants help companies make more money so they can add jobs and give more to their communities. Physical therapists help injured people put their bodies back together.

Start immediately after "yes"

Your first onboarding move should be within 24 hours after a new hire accepts your offer. Some might overnight a welcoming kit to her home with a package of company products, whereas others might send a welcoming e-mail from the recruiter, supervisor, or CEO. The message should be "thank you, you made the right choice" and again reinforce all or parts of your EVP.

Certify all presenters

Presenters must know their content and deliver it with high, positive energy. Regardless of the role they play, anyone who speaks to new hires in person or on video must be trained against skill-driven criteria and certified to perform that role. This means the primary presenters are always the "A" team, and no other scheduled speakers can arbitrarily send a substitute.

Dispense with administrative tasks

Once the centerpiece of new employee orientation programs, completing payroll and benefits forms can now be done online at work or from home. Likewise, new hires can accomplish other chores, like ordering uniforms or parking passes, or reading and checking off on written policies, at another time. Highlighting the quality of pay and benefits during your in-person sessions is a good thing, and you might have to distinguish between health insurance options and other details. But interrupting a high-energy presentation to ask the group to complete forms is like directing them to read a policy manual. Don't permit form-filling to take the air out of your program.

Avoid "death by PowerPoint"

Curriculum design pros can interview you, spew back carefully constructed program objectives, and then design experiences that both teach and entertain. If no curriculum pros work for your company, stretch your skills to develop group exercises, games, contests, and other methods to involve employees in learning. Then teach your facilitators how to make the best use of these processes in your certification training.

Large companies should ask their marketing department to participate in or own the design of onboarding programs, since they are the inhouse influence and communication pros.

Spotlight retention as an important part of your culture

Dedicate one section of a group presentation to retention. Consider disclosing your turnover percentage, the number of employees with long service, and the cost of losing a good employee. Invite in one or more long-service employees to explain why they have stayed and what they've learned. Tell the group you are proud of your retention and the careers employees have built, and you expect the same for them. Add that they have a responsibility to alert their supervisor if for any reason they are considering leaving so you can coach them to stay.

Design all tours to connect the dots

Whether facility tours are live or virtual, the most important objective is to give new employees a clear sense of how what they do impacts other employees and customers. As a result, facilitators must be aware of the jobs represented in the group and speak to each of them. Tours offer many distractions, as new hires might focus on equipment, other employees, or learning their way around. Facilitators, therefore, must be trained during the certification process to connect the dots from the most common jobs to the duties of other employees and the end result for your customers.

Leverage stories to build legends and memories

The "company pin" story in Chapter 4 is an example of communicating your company's culture. Imagine now that you could have your company's founder at each onboarding session. (She would have to be certified, of course!) Every organization was started by one or a handful of people who had an idea and developed it into the foundation of the company where you work today.

So select key historical and culture points you want to communicate and then seek out stories and presenters who can deliver them. Most won't care about history unless you can bring it to life. For small organizations, ask the founder to speak to all new hires to personalize your company and drive home the importance of its success.

Give new employees distinctive ID badges

This seems like a lightweight idea unless you influence all of your ongoing employees to spot the new-hire badge and introduce themselves. Imagine a culture where new employees are approached during their first week by strangers-who-become-colleagues in your halls, cafeteria, break room, and parking lot. We know feeling welcome and developing relationships at work are important retention tools. This "hello" culture will gain traction in your town as each new employee tells others—and they will.

Schedule ongoing onboarding events throughout your tipping point

Onboarding events will only continue if they are scheduled as non-negotiable parts of an ongoing process. Consider department welcoming socials, new-hire focus groups with executives, and supervisory introductory meetings (described next). Many companies provide supervisors with checklists of activities they should perform with new hires with recommended dates. Savvy supervisors watch carefully to ensure new hires are connecting socially with the team, and call on peer leaders to welcome them in if needed.

 ## Top Questions Supervisors Should Ask New Hires

Every onboarding program should include a structured meeting between each new employee and her supervisor to ensure that relationship starts right. This meeting should be structured and rehearsed as part of supervisory training so supervisors know what to ask, how to listen, when to probe, and how to identify any resulting action steps for retention. Topics included are job duties, important relationships, desired learning, and supervisory style. This meeting will be most effective after the new hire has begun her job, no earlier than after two weeks of performing actual job duties. As always, taking notes is required to build listening skills and show you care.

Once the supervisor has greeted the new hire, use these questions as well as your own favorites to build an early connection.

Why do you think I hired you?

This question requires the employee to compliment herself and gives you the opportunity to agree and expand. Expect modesty and even embarrassment at first, but hold back further prompts so the new hire knows you expect her to answer this important question.

She will leave your office having dug reflectively for an answer and will know you concur, or that you also see talents she didn't see herself.

How is working here compared to what you thought it would be?

This is like dragging a net across the ocean searching for fish. The new employee might tell you all is well, the duties are stifling, or her colleagues don't like her. Most important, probe to learn the importance of each item she describes so you know what to leverage and what to improve.

What do you want to learn here?

This moves the discussion to development and tells the employee the supervisor cares. If the employee struggles to answer, ask probes like "What would you like to be really good at?" or "What can you do here that will make you feel good when you leave work every day?"

Which task has been the hardest to learn so far?

Compare this question to "What has been your greatest challenge so far?" The "task" question directs the discussion to job-related activities versus a more general question that would probably yield a nonspecific answer.

How are your relationships with others on our team?

Careful listening is required here. If the employee becomes enthusiastic and says all relationships are great, smile and move to the next question. But if she changes her expression or hesitates in any way to say positive things, probe to learn more. Feel comfortable probing for specifics, asking "who," "what happened," and "who said what." Her answers will give you the full picture and let you take steps to give her feedback and improve her comfort with the team.

Do you have the training and equipment you need to be successful?

Draw out her opinions regarding her job skills, success with training programs, and comfort with tools she must use. Remove any obstructions to her having every opportunity to succeed.

How do you see your work each day contributing to our company and our customers?

The value of this question is that it forces her to form an answer and hear herself say it. Add to her response if necessary to ensure she appreciates the role she plays for her colleagues, you, your company, and those you serve.

How can I be a better supervisor to you?

Most will dodge this one or just not have an answer. Take this opportunity to surface any instances when you wondered if you were both on the same page regarding work assignments or style. She will appreciate your bringing those moments into the conversation so they can be addressed and cleared.

What else would you like to talk about today?

This question invites her to address any other topics and communicates your interest.

May I summarize our discussion today?

Reviewing your notes, summarize three or so key points you learned from your meeting. Then ask her what she learned as well. End the meeting by thanking her for sharing her opinions and addressing any items that require follow-up by either of you.

 ## Top Guidelines for Successful Mentoring Programs

Research tells us that mentoring programs can help improve early retention. Experience tells us that mentoring programs must be planned carefully in order to succeed.

The mentoring concept is sound. Wise veterans take newcomers under their protective wings and steer them to success through the maze of unwritten rules. Employees, in turn, lock onto these carefully selected role models and trust them with their inner thoughts and respond to their directions. Both can avoid those messy conversations about performance that must happen when one is accountable to the other on the organization chart.

But mentoring can fail when mentors and their employees can't connect or their relationships have loose boundaries. The following guidelines will help make your mentoring program work.

Choose mentors instead of accepting volunteers

Mentors must have supreme judgment and focused listening skills, honor confidentiality, know the political ropes of your company, show strong loyalty up the chain, and above all else really enjoy helping people and coaching them to win. They are your point-people for steering talent with influence rather than authority. Imagine each potential mentor advising a new hire on handling a disagreement with a colleague, responding to unfair negative feedback, or ways to step up to a challenging assignment. Issues might cross over to personal ones, too, like coping with health problems or relationship issues with spouses, parents, or kids. The best mentors eventually hear it all.

So identify the qualities you want and invite those who qualify to apply. Make being selected to mentor an honor in your company rather than a casual assignment based on interest alone.

Certify mentors to ensure they know their roles

Tell mentors their job descriptions and help them build required skills. For some, participating in one group meeting that clarifies roles and other conditions presented here will be sufficient. Others might need some initial and early coaching to succeed. Avoid overdoing training, reporting in, form-completing, and other administrative tasks. If too much structure is required, you've selected the wrong group.

Match employees to the best available mentor

Matches are usually made by the mentoring program administrator, or in some companies employees choose their own mentors. If administrators choose, they might make alignment decisions based on skills or styles such as asking a mentor who listens well to draw out a shy employee. When employees choose, they might select a mentor who has a particular job or reputation. Either way can work well.

Regardless how you make matches, be sure your mentor pool is diverse with reference to gender, race, and ethnicity, and honor employees' specific requests if you can.

Coach mentors to set goals with their employees

During their initial meetings, mentors should agree to goals with their employees. To seed the discussion, they might recommend these three topics or others more specific to your organization:

- Provide guidance on company protocol, such as the unspoken dress code, start/stop times and other schedule expectations, ways to greet executives, and other sticky subjects that employees normally solve by trial and error
- Coach on relationship dos and don'ts, such as managing conflicts with your supervisor, building more productive bonds with your team, and making connections with other managers who can influence your career
- Be a sounding board on all issues related to working here, with no boundaries except those chosen by the employee

Once these subjects have been presented and discussed, the mentor then asks what other objectives the employee wants to include. Whether she recommends others at that time or not, she now knows the mentor is open to helping on all company issues.

Set confidentiality boundaries

Mentoring times should represent safety zones, so both must agree that all they say here stays here unless both concur to specific exceptions. But regardless of this agreement, mentors must be certain to (a) never betray a confidence lest they break trust, and (b) say nothing they wouldn't want to be shared. Mentors must ask employees for confidentiality but not expect it. Imagine being new to a company and hearing a juicy story about an executive. How many employees would keep it totally to themselves?

Agree to rules of engagement

Set a predetermined end date of one year or less for new-hire mentoring programs. This tells both parties that there is limited time to surface and resolve key issues and also frees the mentor to move on to other new hires. Many times the relationship will continue informally if it has been successful. Both sides should be able to opt out early, too, if the mentor and employee can't find ways to meet their objectives.

The mentor and employee should agree to contact protocols in the first meeting that address how often to meet, in what settings, the appropriateness of phone or e-mail as ways to meet or schedule, and any other details. Some global companies manage mentoring relationships entirely by e-mail and have proven it can work successfully.

 ## True Stories

Effective onboarding cuts turnover

The following are three examples of companies that aggressively improved their onboarding processes and cut turnover as a result:

- Corning Glass Works found that those who attended a structured orientation program were 69% more likely to remain with their company after three years versus those who did not.
- Hunter Douglas upgraded their onboarding process and reduced their six-month turnover from 70% down to 16%.
- Designer Blinds believed upgrading their onboarding process played a major role in reducing annual turnover from 200% down to 8%; they also reduced their recruiting budget from $30,000 to $2,000.[5]

These improvements are staggering and likely represent millions of dollars in improved productivity for these companies. A closer look would probably reveal that "orientation" and "onboarding" for these companies included ongoing processes that linked new hires to their supervisors and teams rather than consisted of only one-time group events conducted immediately after hire.

Mentoring from a distance

For companies that span broad geographies, technology has brought mentoring programs close to home. Employees can now choose mentors online and communicate with them, many using the various social networking tools that are now available.

Intel has pioneered online mentoring, resulting in employees having mentors who work oceans away. Kevin Gazzara was program manager for Intel's "Leading Through People" program and the concept developer behind their copyrighted program. Employees log on, input what they want to achieve, read mentor profiles, and then click the "Match" button to express interest. An e-mail races to the potential mentor, who reads the information supplied by the employee and then suggests a next step or asks them to choose another mentor.

Mentors are usually one to three pay grades higher than the employee, are in another department or separate chain of command, and should have more expertise than the applying employee in an area where the employee wants to grow. Mentors do not participate in formal training, and employees must only want to improve their skills.

Gazzara summed up the program's impact by saying, "It's been very successful, so well received. We get all levels of employee participation, up through senior managers."[6]

Voting on the island

Long before television popularized "voting off the island," Whole Foods Market asked its employees to decide who stayed and who left after 90 days. Work teams have power, and as a result they help decide if new hires make the grade for performance.

Teams conduct hiring interviews together, so once they say "hire" someone, they also take on responsibility for the new employee's success. Performance criteria includes following all policies and procedures, going above and beyond for customers, demonstrating team awareness versus self-interest, and completing required orientation training. Most are voted to stay on the team after about 90 days, although some are asked to leave. Others might have their orientation extended with a development plan. Those who win the vote are then called *team members* rather than *new members* and are welcomed by their teams.

Since team voting has been in place, six-month retention has improved by 23 %. Other process improvements have contributed too, including customized interview questions and other selection tools that identify better applicants. It likely helps as well that the average age of Whole Foods employees is 34, which should go up even higher if turnover continues to fall.[7]

Wyndham solves retention, productivity via *iGoWVO*

Wyndham Vacation Ownership (WVO) is the timeshare division of Wyndham Hotels. Recognizing the high price of turnover, WVO recently upscaled its onboarding program. The results are in for the corporate group, and first 90-day turnover has been cut in half. The program also earned WVO a prestigious award at the recent American Resort Development Association conference.

The comprehensive onboarding program spans 180 days and includes administrative sign-on, an "enculturization program" called *iGoWVO*, customer service training, and specific activities managers and supervisors undertake as employees learn and perform their jobs.

The centerpiece of the program is iGoWVO, a three-and-one-half-hour experience designed to make an emotional connection. The program follows a travel journal where employees learn about the company by visiting:

- Who: Wyndham Worldwide and WVO overview
- What: The timeshare industry
- When: The WVO story, past, present, and future
- Where: The properties
- Why: The owners and you
- How: The brand and business

Interspersed throughout the trip are video clips from executives and employees who speak about WVO's strategic direction, the magic of their brand, company values, ways to grow with WVO, and "how we make memories here." The program is conducted both in person for headquarters' workers and online for those who work remotely.

Says Barry Ogle, vice president of leadership enrichment, "Our goal with iGoWVO is simple: To make every new hire say, 'Wow, did I ever make the right decision to come here!' The program is working really well."[8]

 ## Closing Thoughts on Scripting Employees' First 90 Days

The following are three major conclusions for rethinking retention based on the ideas presented in this chapter regarding scripting employees' first 90 days.

Traditional Thinking	Rethinking Retention
Employees stop looking for other jobs once they say "yes."	Employees are least loyal early on and are vulnerable to offers from other companies.
Onboarding should disclose our company's culture and mission.	Onboarding's first role is to reinforce our value proposition.
Supervisors introduce new hires to their teams.	Onboarding must include well-designed processes to ensure new hires build relationships with those they work with.

Whether working in a global company or a mom-and-pop store, we can all stack hands on the importance of getting new hires off to a positive start. The difference between success and failure, once again, is *processes*. What locked-in steps must you take to ensure new hires see your company both *as it is* and *the way you want them to see it?*

So your assignment now is to list each step of your onboarding process, evaluate the effectiveness of each activity, and then consider adding the ideas presented here and others you know from experience or research. Once you've developed a plan you like, ask top executives to give it their unwavering support so participation is mandatory for employees, supervisors, and on up. High-retention companies bypass the temptation to hold employees back from onboarding sessions because the work must get done, and don't tolerate high-ranking mentors who procrastinate meeting with their employees.

New employees test you to see if your EVP and all other implied commitments are for real, so you must build early glues in order for them to stay.

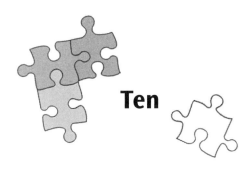

Ten

Challenge Policies to Ensure They Drive Retention

So what are the policies and practices employers do every day that drive workers away? Chapter 2 detailed research behind the three areas that deserve your scrutiny: Pay, healthcare benefits, and worker flexibility. This chapter offers specific recommendations for turning these and other policy areas into retention tools—versus exit reasons—for your employees.

The following are the top ways to help you achieve this goal:

- **Top compensation and benefits ideas to improve retention**, because rewards have tangible and intangible consequences for staying or leaving
- **Top ideas for increasing schedule flexibility**, including a starter checklist of ways to give employees more time
- **Top ideas for retaining part-time employees**, because their turnover tends to be higher and it costs almost as much as losing a full-timer
- **Top ideas for managing telecommuters**, because remote workers require different types of support
- **Top additional people-management practices to build glue** based on best practices I've seen that work

The True Stories section includes examples of organizations that have successfully implemented several of these tactics. These include paying for performance, affordable healthcare, schedule flexibility, managing call center agents who work from their homes, stock ownership, and cafeteria benefits. Both large- and small-company stories are included. The common thread among all stories is that these organizations took targeted actions that departed from traditional policies to improve retention—and their actions worked.

Before reading further, ask yourself which policies and practices in your company cause employees to leave. Think beyond your company's policy manual and explore all of the traditions, habits, and behaviors that sum up to how you treat your people. Thinking from a clean slate, you might identify areas not included here. Address these areas in your retention plans.

Top Compensation and Benefits Ideas to Improve Retention

Since all compensation and benefits entries are debits on organization's financial statements, they must be balanced carefully against the cost of turnover. Managing rewards correctly will lead to improved productivity as well as retention, whereas managing rewards poorly leads to employees doing the wrong things, doing them less well, and potentially leaving you.

As stated earlier, employees rarely leave jobs that satisfy them for benefits alone. Benefits do, however, become retention factors when already frustrated employees add rising healthcare costs to their daily woes, or when they investigate other employers and see better benefits that then become secondary reasons to leave.

The following sections discuss ways of managing compensation and benefits to help you keep those employees you want to keep.

Really *pay for performance*

Organizations must move past the "pay for performance" cliché and make hard choices in order to reward top performers. These employees know they outperform others and expect you to pay them fairly, which means to them that you leapfrog their pay past their peers. Historic excuses about peer employees' time in position or time with the company mean little to high performers who can easily leave you for other jobs that pay more. And for some, achieving higher pay is a reward for their egos as well as their wallets.

Rewarding top performers requires separating your WOWs from your Wet Socks, as you can likely provide extra merit increases only for your WOWs.

WorldatWork surveys point out the tiny amounts of average merit increases that are actually based on merit. For the past few years, merit increases have averaged between 3.75% and 3.8%, but slightly more than 2.5% of this amount has been based on upward movements in salary ranges to match inflation. This leaves just 1.2% that is devoted to merit.[1] This, then, is the same amount that boosts your average employees' spending power each year. For example, here's one way to calculate the actual increased weekly spending power for an employee who makes $30,000 per year:

1.2% of $30,000, minus taxes, divided by 52 weeks per year, equals
…about $5 a week

So, average merit increases don't lead to better lifestyles.

In today's compensation environment, top performers can get significant raises only if some lesser-performers get none. Giving bonuses and stock contributes to paying for performance, but ultimately base pay must align with productivity when compared to peers. For those who need big chunks to catch up, distribute raises over a year or so and tell them your plan in advance in exchange for their commitment to stay. They'll appreciate your candor and be motivated by your recognition.

Align pay plans with strategic objectives

A recent Towers Perrin study confirmed that organizations rarely develop customized pay programs for nonsales personnel, and there is increased use of company-wide performance as a payout criteria. The results are that most employees are being paid based on non-specific, highly subjective criteria, and any bonus-type payments are based on team performance versus their own. In other words, top performers are on the common assembly line that results in near-average compensation even if they greatly out-perform their peers.

Performance-based incentives must be *tied to the right accomplishments* and be *within the employees' control.*[2] For example, salespeople should be rewarded for achieving and exceeding their sales goals, regardless of their team's or company's performance. For less quantifiable positions, rewards should be tied to the most important job objectives, even if these are difficult to measure, rather than to objectives that are more easily measurable but less important. Top performers need assurance that they are contributing in ways that drive their companies forward, and that they will be rewarded for their achievements regardless of others' work.

Drive stock down into the organization

Company ownership is a win-win proposition for employers and employees. For companies, various studies confirm that employee ownership leads to increased productivity, profitability, and longevity.[3] Also, a review of several "best companies to work for" lists shows that employee stock ownership is usually associated with low turnover. Given stock, employees become eligible for ongoing financial benefits, and the emotional thump of "owner" provides strong glue for retention. Most employees will never own stock of any kind unless their employers provide it for them. Employee stock ownership plans (ESOPs) offer tax advantages for companies in addition to all of the benefits of improved employee retention and productivity.

Obviously, stock ownership works best in times of bull markets or when your company's stock soars. Research supports that companies can increase their chances of raising their stock's value when sharing it with employees.

Give performance appraisals and pay raises on time

In its internal studies, a leading grocery store chain found that those supervisors who habitually conduct performance appraisals late also had the highest turnover. Perhaps the late appraisals are actually just one example of several supervisory duties they perform poorly, or maybe employees lost patience.

How can supervisors build trust when they delay conducting annual reviews, especially if these reviews must precede employees receiving a merit increase? Supervisors who are late conducting reviews are telling employees they are less important than every other activity supervisors do in the interim time. Organizations should implement no-tolerance policies for this practice and remove supervisors who are consistently late.

Nonprofits should pay for performance too

Mission plays a major role in attracting and retaining employees in nonprofits, but research indicates that dissatisfaction with pay and career advancement can trump the warm feelings that come from helping others.[4] My own experience as a board member of several nonprofits is that executives and volunteers expect employees to work for less, and that dollars spent on staff versus service are seen as a reflection of poor management. Most nonprofit employees must stretch dollars to live comfortably, and they know their worth on the for-profit side. Consider for-profit organizations that have jobs like yours as your competition for talent, and feel good about paying your best performers competitively.

Provide better benefits for some

You pay nurses more than you pay nurse's aids, so why not give them better benefits as well? Too often organizations pass on implementing the types of strategic benefits listed in Chapter 4 because they cost too much to implement for all employees. Why not implement them just for the hardest ones to keep?

A few of the "left out" employees might grumble, so tell them in advance why the favored job is more important to your company and give them a career path to achieve it.

Factor turnover's cost into health insurance decisions

All decisions regarding the addition or subtraction of healthcare benefits for employees and their dependents should be made in light of their impact on retention. Executives have a sharp eye for healthcare's costs and future company cuts are likely. These decisions will impact recruiting and retention. Organizations that rely heavily on part-time employees should implement healthcare for them in some form, even if they require a minimal period of service for eligibility.

Use cafeteria benefits plans to minimize employees' health care costs

In a recent survey, 76% of employees said they would rather receive $7,500 in employment-based health benefits than an additional $7,500 in taxable income.[5] Given this loud mandate to reduce healthcare costs, employers can provide tax advantages for healthcare and other benefits for their employees by implementing a cafeteria plan under section 125 of the Internal Revenue Code. Once implemented, HR should communicate the plan's advantages clearly so employees fully leverage its benefits.

 ## Top Ideas for Increasing Schedule Flexibility

Employees want more time, and you can provide some with flexible schedules. The ideas presented here are "low-hanging fruit" that can be applied by most organizations, large and small, and across most industries. These ideas have high glue potential based on the data presented in Chapter 2, as employees are far less likely to leave jobs that offer flexibility they cannot easily replace.

For benchmarking, participants in SHRM's most recent benefits survey reported 58% provided flextime, 38% provided compressed workweeks, 33% provided telecommuting on a part-time basis, and 21% provided telecommuting on a full-time basis.[6] Consider how your company stacks up against your competitors for talent and which of the following ideas you can implement.

Promote ways for employees to easily swap work times

Establish online or bulletin board trade sheets and minimize advance notice. Expand the pool of employees who can replace others with cross-training to increase the likelihood that one can trade. Point out in staff meetings the number of employees who have successfully traded so others know they can and that trading is encouraged.

Accommodate flexible in-office work schedules

Some organizations can achieve this by permitting employees to start and end their days on fixed schedules that vary from each other's. This can accommodate difficult commutes, childcare schedules, or second jobs. Other organizations might take a more liberal approach and permit employees to work any in-office hours as long as work is completed. Some restrictions might be included to ensure core hours are covered for high customer traffic or other reasons.

Question traditional assumptions that all employees must be in the office for the same hours, or that all must be treated identically for consistency's sake. Use length of service where one employee must be given preference over another, as that measure is indisputable and reinforces retention.

Invite employees to work from home when assignments permit

Trust employees to work responsibly from home, in part because they want you to continue this privilege. Be clear on what must be accomplished by when so all know the expectations. Individual assignments such as completing administrative work, planning projects, and writing copy can be done just as well in one's home.

Offer 4×10 schedules to nonexempt employees

For many industries, creative employers can find ways to distribute work across four days instead of five. Retail sales, office workers, nurses, call center reps, and warehouse attendants are just a sampling of jobs that can likely be accomplished in forty-hour workweeks that can be scheduled over four days. The ideal is for employees to work four consecutive weekdays, giving them perpetual three-day weekends, but employees will stay with you longer regardless of which four days they work. Imagine if you worked a four-day schedule and another company tried to pull you away into a five-day schedule. Wouldn't it be hard to give up about fifty extra days off each year?

Those who schedule work might object, and even say that positions must be added to accommodate four-day weeks. Invite them to meet with finance to develop a new staffing model that involves the cost of turnover and potential savings for reducing it.

Loosen schedules for employees after heavy travel

Missing evenings and weekends with families is regular fare for employees who travel for their jobs. Acknowledge these contributions by encouraging travelers to sleep in, stay home, and work on their own after trips as long as work gets done. These employees have earned privileged treatment over those who never leave town for their jobs.

Force schedule changes only as a last resort

Requiring employees to change schedules from day to evening, night to day, or weekdays to weekends completely disrupts childcare, school, and other parts of their lives. Even though realistic job previews might announce the possibility of schedule changes, steps must be taken to minimize them. Many call centers hold "shift bids" as frequently as once per quarter, which puts employees at risk for completely new schedules. These centers should consider turnover's cost before deciding to force schedule changes and then accommodate good performers who cannot work new shifts. Finding employees who can work our jobs and also completely revise their lives is an uphill climb, especially if other employers are offering them fixed-schedule jobs.

Involve employees with nontraditional schedules in team activities

Part-time employees and those with flexible schedules can be easily overlooked when planning training programs, employee activities, and team celebrations. Leaving them out not only makes them feel less important but also reduces opportunities for them to develop glue-building relationships with colleagues.

One sure way to increase participation of employees with nontraditional schedules is to ask representatives of this group to join the event's planning committee. This ensures that events are held at times that accommodate most schedules and sends a message that all employees' needs have been equally considered.

Provide flexible scheduling equally for all

Many of us associate "work–life balance" with working mothers, maybe at the expense of other employees who value work flexibility as much or more. A study sponsored by Simmons School of Management found no differences in how much men and women value their time away from work.[7] Additionally, some organizations report that unmarried employees have expressed concerns regarding perceived favorable treatment for employees with families.[8] So all policies related to flexibility should be equally available and consistently applied.

 ## Top Ideas for Retaining Part-Time Employees

Employing part-time workers is attractive because they cost less in pay and benefits than full-time employees and can fill in during peak times and others' absences. Yet turnover is historically higher for part-timers than full-timers, and employers struggle to fix it. The following ideas will help.

Hire applicants who want part-time vs. full-time work

Review applicants' recent work histories for consistent patterns of part-time work. Question changes from part-time to full-time and any gaps in employment. Ask why they are applying for part-time work and listen carefully for lifestyle reasons that require hard stops such as "My doctor told me to work no more than four hours each day," "Our sitter can only work from noon to 3:00," or "I have a class that begins at 1:30." As a final test, tell them the same or a similar job might be available full-time and ask if they are interested. A "yes" answer means they really want full-time work.

Hire older workers

Older workers are more fixed in their lifestyles and their expenses, giving them a clearer understanding of their wants and needs.

Ask applicants which hours they can work before you disclose the job's schedule

Hiring part-time workers into variable schedules is challenging because applicants might exaggerate their flexibility to get your job. Ask them to speak first regarding their flexibility before you disclose the job's schedule and potential for change. If they respond by asking the hours of the job, tell them there are many schedules and you want to hear their preferences and limitations first so you can match them to the best one.

Train new hires on schedules that match their work schedules

Training new hires on full-time schedules invites two risks for turnover: They might quit because they can't make the training schedule, or they might permanently adjust their lifestyles to accommodate full-time work. Ask your trainers to change their schedules instead. Trainers who work in call centers, retail stores, and other extended-hour industries should learn in their own realistic job previews that their own schedules will change based on the hours when employees need to be trained.

Provide as many benefits as possible

I mentioned previously that organizations that rely heavily on part-timers should offer them some form of health insurance. All organizations, though, should review each full-time benefit and decide which they will provide for part-timers as well.

For benchmarking, the BLS reports the following percentages of all U.S. part-timers are offered these benefits: Holidays, 39%, with an average of 7 holidays per year; vacation, 38%; work-related educational assistance, 24%; healthcare, 24%; prescription drugs, 23%; sick days, 23%; dental, 16%; and life insurance, 16%. Part-timers with health insurance pay an average of 21% of individual premiums and 31% of family premiums. All other noted benefits are company-paid.[9]

Pay market rate or better

While this seems like an obvious tactic, a study by the BLS found that part-time employees are typically paid less per hour than their full-time peers in the same jobs.[10] Combining this with the usual shortage of comparable benefits, organizations are asking part-timers to perform as well as full-timers but compensating them less. Perhaps organizations compensate part-timers less to save money, or because they expect to get less productivity per hour than full-timers. Paying more and expecting high performance back should lead to better work and higher retention.

Provide complete performance appraisals and daily feedback

Part-time employees sometimes get part-time support, including perfunctory reviews and feedback. Like other employees, they want to know they are contributing and are eager to learn additional ways they can help. Effective supervisors will provide them with full-time-equivalent feedback and support, rather than assume part-time employees are less interested or less likely to improve.

Include part-timers in incentive and bonus plans

If incentives and bonuses are designed to improve contributions, why wouldn't you want part-timers to improve their contributions as well? When part-timers are denied rewards that full-timers receive, organizations are telling them their performance is not as important. Well-designed incentives are usually self-funding, based on the added productivity of the incumbents. Payouts should be proportionate to hours worked. Be sure to schedule any payout ceremonies at times when part-timers can participate.

Make a part-timer the employee of the month

Recognize part-timers as you do full-timers with public recognition, awards, and gifts. Honoring them in public will motivate peer part-timers once they know similar recognition is available to them.

Assign part-timers additional training and responsibility

Seek out ways to reward high-performing part-timers with additional knowledge, skills, and work. Assume they can provide more productivity in their limited work hours and give them tools to do so. Small steps such as observing an employee in a related job, crosstraining to learn new skills, or reading a work-related article will increase their contribution and tell them you see past the limits of their schedules.

Top Ideas for Managing Telecommuters

Few glues have more retention power than enabling employees to work from home or another remote location. The advantages of working remotely include no commutes, no travel expenses, no work clothes, no micromanaging boss, and on and on. The prime disadvantage, though, is remote workers lack ongoing human contact unless organizations take special steps to provide it. These ideas address connecting telecommuters with others as well as giving them structure, tools, and inspiration to do their jobs well.

Set specific performance expectations weekly

Supervisors must paint a clear picture of the job's objectives, responsibilities, and tasks, and then break those tasks into the smallest components. Weekly assignments should include activities along with measurable and immeasurable outcomes and timelines, followed by feedback based on performance.

Telecommuter supervision requires proactive goal-setting and coaching. Supervisors should be selected for and trained to initiate continual discussions regarding expectations, performance, and improvement coaching until telecommuters demonstrate independent competence.

Establish communications guidelines

Geography permitting, supervisors should meet individually and in person with telecommuters at least once per month to develop comfortable relationships, review progress, and coach. Phone meetings should be scheduled at least once per week, and ongoing communications usually occur via e-mail. Telecommuters might also be directed to contact support personnel directly, such as IT or operations, to resolve typical issues that surface in their jobs.

Set remote workplace protocols

Organizations might set specific "office hours" for jobs such as administrative support, while salespeople are more likely to work their own schedules. Establishing guidelines for returning calls, checking e-mail, and related administrative tasks ensures timely flow of information.

Provide initial training in the office if possible

New hires for all jobs need to work initially with supervisors and key support personnel in person to build the basis for trust and support. Experiencing the office environment builds the foundation for teamwork, as telecommuters seek becoming part of a team despite working independently and being physically alone.

Organize peer networks for support

To reinforce team membership, supervisors should organize peer networks for support. This could include establishing a designated online chat room or assigning a fellow telecommuter as a mentor. Just as in-office employees seek out peers with questions and ideas, telecommuters benefit from having available peers.

Conduct team meetings to resolve issues and share best practices

Supervisors should schedule a weekly meeting to address common concerns, swap helpful techniques, and reinforce teamwork. These might be conducted remotely. Peers will grow from sharing, learning, and building relationships for continuing peer support.

Establish and implement developmental plans for each telecommuter

Telecommuters' inevitable feelings of isolation can transfer to feeling pigeonholed in one stagnant role forever. Supervisors should develop learning plans with each telecommuter to help build additional skills and vary their duties in whatever ways they can.

Provide the best technology to enable top performance

As technology is the lifeline for telecommuters regardless of their roles, supervisors should know and advocate the most modern technology for their teams. Leading-edge hardware, software, PDAs, GPSs, and other tools enable workers to do their best and feel supported.

Ensure supervisors build trust

Supervisors must build trust in two ways. During monthly individual meetings, supervisors should begin by complimenting the telecommuter with specific feedback examples and then ask for input on the agenda for the remainder of the meeting. By asking questions, listening, and taking notes, the supervisor will build trust by building esteem.

During daily interactions, the supervisor should share job-related information and feedback in positive ways and respond to questions or needs as soon as possible. Supervisors are the strongest human link for remote workers, and building trust is essential for retention.

Monitor attitudes of others

A downside to telecommuting is those left in the office might be less satisfied. A study conducted by Rensselaer Polytechnic Institute reports that those who work in the office might actually have *higher* turnover because they have less in-person time to accomplish work with telecommuting colleagues who are not physically there. The study recommends ensuring more face time when all employees are in the office and giving office workers more autonomy.[11] Smart managers might also take extra steps to avoid office worker envy by clearly communicating to them the telecommuters' efforts and accomplishments.

 ## Top Additional People-Management Practices to Build Glue

Most of these practices touch high numbers of employees and help improve retention and productivity. Whereas policy changes can be implemented at the top or within HR, several of these are practice changes that require supervisors to grow skills and change habits. Ultimately, some will perform them better than others and will have improved retention as a result.

Celebrate employees' service anniversaries better than you celebrate their birthdays

Which means more to you: An employee ages another year or that same employee provides you with another year of good work? Employee anniversaries present us with a retention opportunity. It's a common practice that supervisors announce in monthly staff meetings the names of employees who are celebrating either a birthday or service anniversary that month. Birthdays, though, are also celebrated on the employee's actual birth anniversary with a card or luncheon, whereas service anniversaries are relegated to only the monthly roll call. Supervisors should thank employees on their anniversary dates for another year of good service, in part so employees know their supervisors care enough to track their anniversary dates. Included should be a specific, prepared message that distinguishes that employee's contribution from others' such as, "In this past year, Juan, I've seen you work especially hard with new employees so they learn to do things right from the start. Thank you for being such a good role model for others." Whether written or spoken, these types of messages are the ones employees remember and share with others at work and at home.

Birthday celebrations are usually done defensively so employees don't feel forgotten, whereas service anniversaries can be strong retention tactics.

Provide learning opportunities in place of career opportunities

Employees often cite "career opportunities" and "career development" as reasons to leave. Their employers translate this to mean "I didn't get promoted," presuming that *development* implies more responsibility and pay. In reality, many employees who seek promotions are not qualified, and others who are qualified get stuck sometimes because there are no openings above them. But for many employees, development means they just want to learn new things, either to contribute more, to become more marketable, or to overcome the boredom of their jobs.

The good work of Michael Lombardo and Robert Eichinger shows that employee development results 70% from challenging job experiences, 20% from observing good work and getting feedback, and 10% from coursework, books, or mentors.[12] These findings offer many ways for supervisors to develop individual learning plans with their employees, far beyond the usual method of sending employees to internal or external training courses. Whereas responsibility for "development" has often been assigned to HR or training, it is supervisors who have the nearest and best opportunities to help employees grow.

Supervisors need to discover all the ways they can help their subordinates learn, so consider this training activity. On a prepared form, ask supervisors to list the names of their past supervisors, then next to each name list what they learned and how they learned it while working for each one. Then score each supervisor on their effectiveness as a developer on a 1-to-10 scale, with 10 being high. On a second prepared form, ask them to list names of each member of their teams, what each would benefit from learning, and the activities and timelines they commit to for helping each of them learn it. This exercise moves supervisors to accept their roles as developers and to commit to develop each member of their teams. If increasing development leads each employee to stay an average of just three months longer, the productivity payoff is high.

Fire poor performers

Organizations tend to develop firm positions regarding firing as parts of their cultures. Some fire poor performers quickly and move on, whereas others fire only for tangible offenses such as absences or theft and otherwise tolerate slipping performance. The employees whom you most want to keep will appreciate your taking fair, firm, and, if necessary, final action with poor performers.

Proactively communicate upcoming changes that might impact employment

Layoffs, mergers, acquisitions, and reorganizations are breeding grounds for employee rumors, distractions, and mistrust. From the executives' side, some information just cannot be shared because of legal agreements or common-sense restrictions. Employees, though, feel like potential victims of bad outcomes they can't control. This is also a time when headhunters ramp up calls to transitioning companies to leverage employees' fears and frustrations.

Executives should place integrity first and protect their bonds of trust by doing the following: (1) tell employees all that you can from the start, as openly as possible, (2) communicate all information from the executive level directly to employees so all hear the same precise message, and supervisors are protected from spinning it, expanding on it, or answering questions about it, and (3) give clear timeframes for future communications and meet them.

Manage all exits for any reason with dignity

Employees identify with peers who leave and look carefully at how supervisors and organizations treat them. Whether terminating for performance, accepting a voluntary resignation, or laying off due to position reduction, supervisors should announce exits with positive comments about leaving employees whenever possible. Employees who choose to leave are exiting for a good reason *for them* so congratulate them openly on a bigger job, new career, or cutting back on work. Security-related activities such as walking a terminated employee to the door or observing them clean out their work areas should be handled discreetly and after hours if possible.

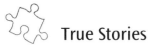 **True Stories**

Paying for outstanding performance

Pacific Service Credit Union, located in Walnut Creek, California, pays salaries that are in the top 2% of comparable credit unions. Recently retired President and CEO Tom Smigielski said the organization was able to afford this because "We have a third as many employees as other credit unions our size—one for three—but we manage because our employees are really good." Pacific Service also pays full healthcare premiums for employees and their dependents. Turnover is less than half of the 30% industry average.[13]

Making healthcare affordable

Seeing that healthcare is "one of the top three benefits employees insist on," McDonald's has shifted more of the premium increases to higher-paid employees to limit recent employee increases to no more than 7%.

Costco caps employees' healthcare costs at 10% of the total, which is below average for retail, to attract and retain better employees.[14]

Communicating benefits cuts turnover

At Yahoo.com, voluntary turnover fell significantly for the three-month period after launching their individualized online Total Rewards Statements.[15]

Similarly, Watson Wyatt found that how well a company communicates the value of its health benefits can impact employee retention more than the benefits themselves. Among employers that offered rich benefits but communicated them poorly, the average turnover rate of high-performing employees was 17%. Employers that offered less costly benefits but communicated them effectively lost only 12% of their high performers. And those that combined rich benefits with effective communications lost only 8% of their top performers.[16]

Flexible scheduling improves retention and productivity

Best Buy offers its headquarters' employees complete freedom to schedule their work and attendance at all meetings is optional. Employees are encouraged to not judge colleagues on how they spend their time. To increase flexibility, employees are offered cell phones and BlackBerry smartphones, and most desktop computers have been replaced with laptops. Productivity has increased 35% and turnover has dropped from 52% to 90% in divisions offering this flexibility.

More than 42% of IBM's global workforce operates from outside IBM locations. The company offers part-time, compressed workweeks, flextime, and job-sharing arrangements. Employees have indicated in surveys that "flexible work options" is their top reason for staying with IBM.

Sun Microsystems' Open Work program saved the company $67.8 million in real estate costs for one year and eliminated an average of two hours of commuting time for each employee. More than 40% of Sun's employees participate in Open Work, where they work from home or other locations. On average, participating employees contribute 34% more work.[17]

Call centers offer work-from-home options

Alpine Access, LiveOps, JetBlue, and PHH Arval all enable agents to work from home. Annual turnover for these agents is 10% to 25% for Alpine Access, less than 10% for LiveOps, and 4% for JetBlue—all enviable rates for the call center industry. PHH Arval has lost only one at-home agent since the at-home program began 12 years ago.

Because turnover is so low, JetBlue opens their online application process for one 24-hour period *each year.*[18]

Putting Mojo behind flexible schedules

This is a story about *extreme* employee input that led to a terrific outcome.

Mojo Interactive is an Internet-based marketing company that connects patients to physicians, and the founders pride themselves in retaining their 32 talented employees. One way they invite their input is by providing an online employee suggestion program. Unlike traditional programs, Mojo employees see all suggestions online and then add comments to them. In other words, all ideas and discussions are public rather than conducted behind closed doors.

One employee posted a suggestion that the company provide alternative schedules so employees could live better lives and also save money on gas. After eighteen employees posted supportive comments, the founders appointed a cross-functional committee to identify flexible options. After several meetings, the committee recommended that each employee be given the option to either retain their current schedule, work four ten-hour days each week, or work one day each week from home. The founders then invited the committee to offer the options to the full team and each employee made an individual choice.

Said Senior Vice President Ron Fischer, "This was easy. We invited employee input and responded to it, and as a result our team will stay longer and be more productive. Small businesses must keep their productive workers to survive."[19]

ESOP + daily communications = lower turnover

American Door & Millwork has 200 employees and 5 manufacturing plants, with headquarters in Sanford, Florida. In the past two years annual turnover has dropped from 87% to 42%, and CFO John Bartley believes implementing an ESOP is the main reason why.

Owners Chad Barton and Bob DelloRusso wanted to share ownership with their employees, and the resulting numbers are impressive. To date, American Door has saved $4 million in reduced turnover compared to total ESOP costs of $2 million. Because the $2 million investment includes significant startup costs, this 2-to-1 ratio should improve each year going forward. Other post-ESOP improvements include fewer injuries, less overtime and sick time, less property and vehicle damage, and higher profitability.

Giving stock to employees is only part of the story. Workers are greeted daily with "employee-owned" signs on the front doors of all plants, on employee uniforms, and on company trucks. In the shipping areas where damage can easily occur, a sign overhead proclaims "Treat it like you own it, because you do." Bartley is especially pleased that his employees will have "real retirements" rather than worry their savings will fall short when they reach retirement age.[20]

Bartley and his team began preparing for the ESOP a full two years before implementation, working closely with the ESOP Association, a nonprofit support group.[21]

Cafeteria benefits plan helps startup

A *startup* in the business community usually refers to an entrepreneur who employs others to help chase her dream. Imagine the challenge of starting up a university.

Harrisburg University of Science and Technology opened its doors in 2005. Early on, Provost Eric Darr and HR executive Linda Wright looked for ways to pull established professionals from other universities into both faculty and staff positions. Darr recognized that his targeted group was age-diverse, so providing choices in employee benefits might aid recruitment.

Darr believes their success at both hiring and retaining was bolstered by their cafeteria benefits plan. He and Wright successfully recruited faculty and administrators from high-tradition organizations such as Penn State, the University of Virginia, and William and Mary. Many were tenured or on track for tenure.

The plan permits employees to choose all, some, or none of the benefits, and receive cash for any benefits they forgo. In its first three years, total turnover was five staff members from a base of 58 full-time employees. No faculty members have left, nor have any of those who have come from more established universities. Darr believes the cafeteria benefits plan is one of several tactics that have contributed to their retention success.[22]

 ## Closing Thoughts on Policies, Practices, and Retention

The following are three major conclusions for rethinking retention based on the ideas presented in this chapter regarding policies and practices.

Traditional Thinking	Rethinking Retention
Employees perform best when they work in the office.	Flexible schedules and work locations increase productivity and retention.
Pay is driven by centralized policies.	Supervisors leverage policies to differentiate pay for performance and retention.
Career growth means promotions.	Careers are enhanced by learning new skills and doing different work.

Cutting your turnover might require changing long-revered policies and practices in areas such as pay, benefits, schedule flexibility, and maybe others. Top executives must approve change, managers and supervisors must implement it, HR must support it, and employees must embrace it. Some executives will shiver when hearing additional money should be allocated to compensation or that hotshot applicants will choose between your company and a competitor that permits them to design their own schedules.

To assist with these decisions, use the comprehensive cost of turnover as your guide to demonstrate the resulting ROI. Highlight the examples in this chapter of productivity improvement that resulted from lower turnover. Emphasize that productivity gains lead to more revenue, and well-targeted investments in retention move organizations from their current levels of growth to a higher place.

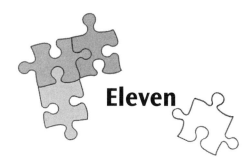

Calculate Turnover's Cost to Galvanize Retention as a Business Issue

P utting a cost on turnover makes cutting it more important, as expressing results in dollars stimulates much more urgency than numbers and percents.

The CFO and finance department must own all aspects of costing turnover, including the original cost studies and the monthly reporting of turnover because:

1. Finance is best qualified to perform a complex analysis that involves your company's money.
2. Finance brings necessary credibility that will influence executives to push retention initiatives.
3. Finance likely reports your company's important numbers to the management team and the board, and retention is now one of those important numbers.

Whereas most retention initiatives take place in human resources and operations, finance becomes the linchpin between the two. Managers who have failed to accept the mantra that retention matters will now get an extra boost from the CFO in the form of reports that are driven from on high. All finance personnel will gain increased interest in retention as they tie turnover to dollars and see patterns of success and failure among supervisors. Involving finance in retention makes achieving retention goals more important, top to bottom.

The first role for finance is to develop turnover cost figures that executives believe are real. This is a time when conviction is more important than accuracy, so turnover cost studies must be detailed and withstand the scrutiny of any high-level doubters. On the one hand, real turnover costs can be a hard sell, especially when they reach six or seven figures for salespeople, technology gurus, knowledge specialists, and similar workers. On the other hand, nearly any mutually agreed upon amount will spur action when multiplied by the number of leavers in a year.

The best solution is to be thorough in analysis rather than compromise. Use the information in this chapter to build a compelling case to ensure that the methodology and outcome of your cost study is right.

This chapter covers the following topics:

- **Top categories of turnover's cost,** so you include the essentials
- **Top free turnover cost calculators** to give you models for costing turnover
- **Top cost ideas to expand your thinking,** so your results change behaviors

The True Stories section discusses examples of turnover's costs in three traditionally high-turnover industries: Healthcare, fast food, and call centers.

 ## Top Categories of Turnover's Cost

Turnover's cost is usually calculated within five categories—lost productivity, separation, vacancy, hiring, and onboarding—although cost calculators sometimes refer to them with different names. The following sections discuss these categories and include measurement areas for you to consider for each one.

Lost productivity

Most calculators list lost productivity last after other costs that are easier to measure. It is listed first here because it is usually the greatest cost and requires the most creativity to measure correctly.

Lost productivity includes everything that doesn't happen from when an employee leaves until a replacement is fully proficient. Typical areas for consideration are:

- **Incomplete work.** How many widgets don't get made? Mortgage packages that are completed late that delay closings? Missed product development deadlines that push back launches? Technology upgrades that are put on hold? Checkout lines that make customers wait longer? Calls with increased hold times? Patients who get medications off schedule? Buildings that get finished past deadlines that result in financial penalties? Teams that produce less work because their leader is gone?
- **Poor quality.** How many items are returned? Parts that don't meet specifications? Customers who complain? Calls that get escalated? Supervisors who must solve problems rather than do more important work? Colleagues who must redo work for others? Or who make errors because they must take on more work?
- **Lost customers.** How many customers leave lines rather than make a purchase? Switch to a competitor because of repeated mistakes? Hang up rather than wait on hold? Leave your company because their favorite employee is no longer there? Or worse, follow your ex-salesperson to your competitor?

"Lost productivity" will never capture all elements of impacted work. Some areas such as lower team morale and turnover that leads to more turnover are hard to account for. But creative thinkers can usually quantify a high percentage of the actual lost productivity that results from losing an employee.

In the cost calculators described later in this chapter, the first model that is on our website www.TheRetentionFirm.com provides a comprehensive way to put a cost on lost productivity. Additionally, the Wyoming Department of Workforce model offers a good list of lost productivity considerations. The Trincom model for truck drivers and TopMark LLC model for salespeople both provide very good structures for estimating the lost work when one of these employees leaves.

Separation

Separation covers the work required when an employee resigns or leaves to close them out from your company. Typical activities include:

- Exit interviews or surveys
- Transition meetings so work continues
- Team announcements
- Separation pay
- Collection of all equipment, such as laptops, cell phones, tools, and uniforms
- Payroll processing to remove them from the payroll
- Administrative tasks, such as calculating unused vacation and advising them of COBRA procedures

Vacancy

This item covers hard costs for getting work done before the replacement is fully proficient. These costs might include:

- Consultants and contractors
- "Renting" workers from other departments
- Temporary help
- Outsourcing work
- Overtime

Hiring

Hiring covers all costs for bringing a replacement onto your payroll. These costs vary greatly depending on the level of the job and might include:

- Advertising and online postings
- Search and recruiting agency fees
- Relocation

- Travel for interviews
- Hiring bonuses
- Employee referral bonuses
- Interviewing
- Reference checks
- Assessments including any type of preemployment tests
- Background checks
- Drug tests
- Physical examinations

Onboarding

These costs cover all activities from when a new hire starts until they are ready to work and might include:

- Administrative work to distribute information, gather signatures, and process the employee on the payroll
- New equipment, such as uniforms, vehicles, laptops, and cell phones
- New employee orientation
- Initial training
- Supplies and material required for the job

 ## Top Free Turnover Cost Calculators

Organizations need to know the cost of turnover for all jobs or key jobs in order to garner the command and energy required to fix it. To help, many vendors and professional associations have developed turnover cost calculators to measure this cost. These are usually based on Excel spreadsheets, so you can enter data and the calculator does the math.

I searched the web and my own experience for turnover cost calculators. To make this list, calculators had to:

- Avoid easily challengeable assumptions, such as "turnover costs 50% of annual salary and benefits." Estimates such as these are stated repeatedly in the literature but are far too broad to be convincing.

- Include specific calculations for lost productivity, as this is often the greatest turnover cost. Inferior calculators might include a line for this amount but give no guidance on how to calculate it. Only the teacher model failed to meet this standard, but it merited inclusion for other reasons.
- Avoid terms such as "soft costs" to cover other turnover costs that are not easily quantified; such terms invite dart-throw estimates that won't survive close scrutiny.
- Be free and easily available, although some of these require registration.

These criteria screened out the majority of available calculators. The calculator on our site and the Wyoming Department of Workforce Services calculator can be used generically across all jobs, while the others are designed for particular jobs or industries. If your industry is not represented, ask your professional associations if they have a calculator you can use, but make sure it meets the preceding criteria.

Use these as tools to build your own turnover cost rather than rely on one particular calculator for your answer. You might review several and take the best parts of each.

TheRetentionFirm.com calculator

This calculator on our website divides costs in direct and indirect, and the indirect piece results in a dollar figure for lost productivity. This method begins with identifying the lost productivity by employee for each day and then helps the user apply those costs to the days the job is open and the days required for ramping up to full productivity. This model is available at www.TheRetentionFirm.com.

Wyoming Department of Workforce Services model

The Wyoming model adds some new twists and can be used for public or private jobs. Color-coded, it groups together the easily measurable costs as "green money" and other costs as "blue money." Green costs are the usual ones for the notice, vacancy, and hiring/orientation periods. The blue costs help the user identify lost productivity by offering the following "hidden costs":

- Missed deadlines and shipments
- Loss of organizational knowledge
- Lower morale due to overwork
- Learning curve
- Client issues due to turnover
- Loss of client relationships
- Disrupted department operations
- Chain reaction turnover

No specific formulas are offered for these categories, but the list will stimulate good thinking to help calculate lost productivity costs for your particular job. The Wyoming model is available at *www.wyomingworkforce.org/resources/tools_turnover.aspx.*

TopMark LLC sales calculator

Calculating turnover's cost for lost salespeople is easier than for other jobs because the sales job is easily quantifiable. This calculator leverages that advantage by asking for information such as:

- Percentage of revenue that will continue to flow from the territory while the position is vacant
- Weeks to reach full sales productivity
- Number of lost customers and resulting lost revenue from each exit
- Search firm expenses
- Relocation expenses
- Hourly pay and time commitments from key personnel during the search

The result is a highly defensible cost that quickly leaps to six and seven figures. The TopMark LLC model is available at *www.top-mark.com/turnover_cost_calculator.htm.*

Cornell University's School of Hotel Administration turnover tool

This calculator measures turnover's cost for many jobs in the hospitality industry. The "Five Costs of Turnover" are labeled as pre-departure, recruiting, selection, orientation and training, and productivity loss.

Productivity loss is then measured across four categories: Diminished productivity of the departing employee, learning curve for the new employee, disruption to peers and supervisors, and opportunity costs that result from lost revenues or sales.

This is an easy tool to use. The professors who developed it ask for fundamental data but shield the users from seeing the mathematical calculations that are included in the software. Add some numbers, choose one or more jobs from drop-down boxes, click on the summary tab at the top, and your turnover cost numbers will display.

Once they developed the calculator, these same professors gave it a test run by calculating the cost of losing a front desk person. Entering data from different markets, they found the comprehensive cost was 30% of annual salary, reaching an average cost per exit of $5,864.[1]

This tool can be accessed at *www.hotelschool.cornell.edu/research/chr/*. Click the "Cornell Hospitality Tools" link, then under the list of tools published in 2005 click "Turnover Cost Evaluator." You need to register, but it's free.

National Commission on Teaching and America's Future teacher turnover cost model

The teacher calculator is also easy to use. Costs are segmented into recruitment, hiring incentives, administrative processing, induction, and professional development. Predetermined estimate amounts are available for each category for either urban or nonurban locations. The authors caution that the calculator excludes "district-level costs, the costs of student learning, and many other hidden costs that are the result of teacher turnover."

The calculator concludes with a "Now What?" button that leads to recommended retention solutions.

I used the urban estimates and the resulting cost for losing one teacher was $8,400. Presuming the all-in costs of losing an effective teacher are significantly higher, this calculator might be best used as a starting point for costing your actual teacher turnover. These costs might be the ones that are easy to measure but, as the authors note, the far greater costs are likely to be reduced student learning, failure to obtain or keep grant money, and all that comes with worse school performance.

You can access this tool at *www.nctaf.org/resources/teacher_cost_ calculator/school_calc_sdp.asp*.

Trincon Group turnover cost worksheet

This calculator is for quantifying the cost of losing truck drivers, with a heavy focus on lost productivity based on the number of trucks that are still in the parking lot. Specific data it requests include:

- Operating truck count
- Number of idle trucks
- Weekly revenue per truck
- Gross profit margin
- Days needed to reseat a truck

Like salespeople, the truck driver job is highly quantifiable because empty trucks produce no revenue. All who are searching for ways to put an accurate cost on turnover for any job should review this model to stimulate new thinking. This tool is available at *trincon.com/resources/cost-calculator*.

 ## Top Cost Ideas to Expand Your Thinking

Now that you have the essential ingredients for your cost study and the models that can help, here are creative ideas to help make your study change behaviors and gain long-term traction. These ideas cover two categories: (1) hidden costs that traditional models miss and (2) creative ways to position turnover's costs and savings.

Some organizations will feed their data into one of the calculators referenced in the previous section, provide a one-time report to the top team, and move on to other projects. However, the following ideas take your thinking further and increase the likelihood that your study will become a real retention tool.

Consider lost customers

The good work of Professors Robert Hurley and Hooman Estelami makes clear that employee turnover can be used as a predictor of customer satisfaction. As they say, "When people depart, their intelligence regarding processes, methods, and customers also leaves."[2]

Here's one example: A new supermarket checkout clerk will likely be slower than an experienced one. The resulting long lines can cause a weekly shopper to take her $200 cartful of business across the road. Losing $200 a week for 10 years results in a total revenue loss of over $100,000.

Coca-Cola studied supermarket turnover and found the cost of turnover across the industry actually exceeded the total industry's profits. Since profit equals revenue minus expense, the actual cost of turnover was higher than the resulting profit once all expenses, including those associated with turnover, were subtracted from total revenue. As the report summarized, "This cost is hard to imagine, in part because—unlike other supermarket costs—it does not show on the P&L statement."[3]

Loyalty expert Frederick Reichheld gives us a second example of the impact of turnover on lost customers. Reichheld has contributed much to costing the value of loyalty, and one of his studies found that more than half of brokerage clients who changed companies did so to follow their brokers who switched first.[4] What does this tell us about the cost of losing a good broker?

Check for added headcount

What is the likelihood that high-turnover organizations add to their headcount to offset open positions due to turnover? Or said another way, how many positions can you cut when turnover goes down? This is a built-in turnover cost that won't appear in traditional cost models.

Check for higher pay

For professional positions, new hires often make more money than the person they replace. For low-skill jobs, finding replacements can drive up starting pay and lead to across-the-board increases to facilitate internal equity. So another cost of turnover might be added salary dollars in addition to all other replacement and productivity costs.

Some peers cost more to replace

Some employees contribute more than others, so should outstanding individual performance be considered in your cost model? Should you increase your cost-per-exit for a salesperson who consistently exceeds goals by 20%? Are nurses with ten years of experience more valuable than those with one? Are science teachers more expensive to replace than English teachers?

Can your model address all jobs in your company?

Group together jobs that have similar replacement costs and do one study for each group. For example, you might find that all administrative positions across your company have a similar cost when an employee leaves, including their contribution to productivity. Then consider separate groups for middle managers, salespeople, individual contributors, executives, and any other group that would likely have a similar turnover cost.

The result will be that every job fits into one of your cost study categories, so you can apply a specific cost to any employee who leaves, regardless of which job they left.

Communicate potential mega-savings

Once you've placed a cost on turnover for some or all of your jobs, put that data to work. Measure the turnover cost for the previous year and announce the financial outcome when this year's goal is achieved. Then apply those savings to the numbers that matter most in your company, such as decreased costs, increased sales, or returns to shareholders. The following are examples of actual projections.

- A major hotel chain was spending $350 million each year on turnover, which is equal to 45% of their pretax income. They projected that by cutting turnover in half, the company's stock price would increase by nearly 25%. If they reduced turnover to 15%, the stock price would rise nearly 50%.[5]

- Frederick Reichheld reports that customer retention is directly influenced by employee retention. A 5% increase in customer retention can result in a 25% or more increase in profits in some industries.[6]
- An organization with 10,000 employees found that each percentage point of turnover led to $366,000 of additional costs to search for and hire replacements.[7]
- A study for a retail store found they would have to sell 3,000 additional pairs of khaki pants at $35 each to make up for the loss of one employee.[8]
- Another study found that turnover costs represent more than 12% of pretax income for the average company. But for those in the 75th percentile for turnover—those with higher turnover than most others—those costs are nearly 40% of earnings.[9]

 ## True Stories

Healthcare: Some losses are immeasurable

Chapter 3 discussed the challenges healthcare administrators face to retain nurses. To add further pressure, a report in the *Journal of the American Medical Association* put the cost of turnover in grim perspective:

> In hospitals with high patient-to-nurse ratios, surgical patients experience higher risk-adjusted 30-day mortality and failure-to-rescue rates, and nurses are more likely to experience burnout and job dissatisfaction.[10]

Housekeeping turnover is also costly. When rooms can't be cleaned, hospitals are forced to keep patients in critical care areas for more days than insurance companies will reimburse, so the hospital must absorb the extra costs.

In another study, hospitals with low turnover outperformed high-turnover hospitals by providing lower per-patient charges, shorter stays, lower risk-adjusted mortality rates, and higher profits.[11]

These studies support the importance of measuring turnover's impact on metrics that are specific and critical to your industry.

Fast food: How much does turnover impact sales?

When Taco Bell wondered why sales were higher in some stores than others, they found turnover was the answer. In fact, the top 20% stores for employee retention had double the sales and were 55% more profitable than the bottom 20% stores for retention.[12]

So what does this tell us about the impact of turnover on profitability, and ultimately on cost? Applying a traditional costing model to fast food turnover would probably result in a conclusion like this:

> The cost of employee turnover is largely driven by recruiting, training, and uniform costs. We're pleased if the employee stays with us a year, and then the total replacement cost is $2,000.

But Taco Bell found that the costs of turnover are far greater because they chew into sales. Common sense might have suggested the opposite: That consumers choose fast food because of taste or location. However, Taco Bell's internal study confirms that fast food consumers choose because of service. If the lines are too long, tables are dirty, or customers find the food in the bag is not what they ordered, they don't go back.

Consider, too, that only about 1 in 10 fast food employees ever talk to customers. The rest are backroom operators who prepare food and other tasks.

So what is the cost of losing employees who don't touch customers directly but impact them in other ways? And once more, what is the cost of customers you lose because of turnover?

Call centers: lost productivity far exceeds direct costs

An outbound call center with high turnover conducted a cost study and learned its annual cost of turnover was $5.7 million. More alarming was the proportion of cost associated with lost productivity. Of the total cost, only $1.3 million was for direct costs versus $4.4 million for "lost productivity, operating under capacity, and lost accounts."[13]

Generalizing from this example, lost productivity comprises 77% of all turnover costs for outbound call centers. Whereas one might think the direct costs of hiring and training make up most of the total costs, those costs should be multiplied by 4.4 to calculate the total turnover cost for this industry.

Closing Thoughts on Calculating Turnover's Cost

The following are three major conclusions for rethinking retention based on the ideas presented in this chapter regarding identifying and leveraging turnover's cost.

Traditional Thinking	Rethinking Retention
Our executives know turnover is expensive.	Putting a dollar amount on each exit focuses management's attention on solutions.
Turnover's greatest costs are hiring and training.	Turnover's greatest costs are the productivity and customers we lose.
Announcing turnover's cost will encourage retention actions.	Turnover's cost must be integrated forever into all strategic planning and management reports.

Research has found that 33% of U.S. organizations put a cost on turnover,[14] but only 18% of organizations globally do the same.[15] These studies do not tell us how diligently the companies measured that cost or how much they use it in reports and meetings to change behaviors.

So identifying and leveraging turnover's cost presents another potential competitive advantage. Imagine how much more retention-focused your company would be if the following regularly occurred:

- Supervisors view a resignation with the same feeling of loss that comes from losing a major customer or missing a crucial project deadline

- Your CFO reports turnover trends and includes the cost of turnover for each department, so high-turnover areas are identified and addressed
- Financial analysts project the impact of increased retention on earnings over the next five years so your CEO can report this to your board

Our experience is that if only 33% of companies put a cost on turnover, only a handful of them leverage those costs in ways that make them a weapon against turnover. Make your company one that does.

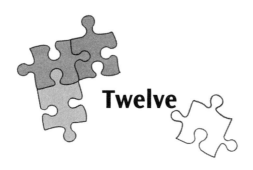

Twelve

Drive Retention from the Top

L ike all major strategic initiatives, retention must be driven from the top. For your organization, this might be the CEO or any other top manager of a division, plant, or center who strives to improve retention. Before moving forward, specific duties must be in place and assigned to the right people.

One way to visualize your organization's retention responsibilities is to spotlight your company's sales responsibilities for comparison. Think of those who set sales goals, design sales strategies, provide marketing for sales, track sales results, report sales results, manage those who sell, train those who sell, and, of course, those who actually sell. Imagine those employees who impact sales in any way as red and all other employees as green. You will likely find large splotches of red in departments that are totally dedicated to sales, as well as smaller patches of it throughout other departments because sales-related duties tend to "spider" their way into most employees' jobs.

Let's now apply this same type of thinking to retention. This chapter includes specific roles for executives, human resources, finance, and marketing. Each of these areas report to the chief executive, so it is there that the buck stops and full responsibility must reside—as it does for sales, service, quality, and safety.

Included in this chapter are:

- **Top executive roles for retention,** because executive push is required to create change
- **Top human resources roles for retention**, as HR drives hiring and many other people-management processes
- **Top finance roles for retention,** because retention won't get the top push it needs unless everyone understands its true cost
- **Top marketing roles for retention**, as marketing's role is to influence, and retention requires influencing people to stay

The True Stories section presents organizations that have tied executive compensation to retention. It also profiles one executive who put into place unique ways to hold his top managers accountable.

 ## Top Executive Roles for Retention

Top executives drive retention, whether their organization is a Fortune 500 corporation, a manufacturing plant, or a local nonprofit. Executives must direct this initiative by positioning retention as a top-five priority, identifying who does what to improve it, and motivating those below them to do their assignments.

Most of the following ideas can apply to any type of executive, regardless of the organization's size or industry, or whether that executive leads the total company or a major unit.

Make achieving retention goals a requirement for your C-suites's executive compensation—and for your own

Your executive compensation criteria might include only measurable results like stock price or profits, or others such as sales and quality. Regardless, adding retention to this level drives focus from the top down and underscores its importance as a pathway to achieving top-level goals.

Report retention results vs. goals to owners and directors

True accountability equals tying retention to pay and job security. Those at the highest levels must commit to keeping retention in the forefront of their daily priorities.

Report retention results to employees to reinforce your strong efforts to keep them

Telling employees you care about retention is like telling them you care about *them*. Old-school executives might believe saying "turnover" out loud will make employees think about quitting. This, of course, is like believing teenagers won't think about sex or drugs if we don't mention them. Most employees are savvy about other employment opportunities within their markets, but they also understand that your organization can only give them so much. Executives who lead trustworthy organizations should feel proud to disclose retention strategies and results.

I once worked with a CEO who was brazenly open with his employees. When a focus group suggested he approve a childcare allowance, he told them he had considered doing so but hesitated because only half of the current workforce would benefit from this investment versus other potential benefits that would impact all. Employees responded positively because they believed he really considered the childcare allowance and was looking out for the greater good.

Executives should highlight retention as an essential company goal in all written and spoken communications with employees, and provide periodic or annual updates on retention success.

Set retention goals and establish proper consequences for all levels of leadership

Executives must oversee that retention goals are set at each organizational level from top to bottom. This requires that the executive has a retention goal not just for the entire organization but also for her direct report team. Likewise, first-level supervisors must have goals that are established, measured against, and rewarded. Some organizations might need to build tracking systems to get data at this level, and executives must see that this gets done.

Remove all supervisors from supervisory roles who cannot retain talent, including those who report directly to you

Supervisors who fail to achieve their retention goals once or even twice might have valid excuses. But those who continuously miss this important goal are sending a clear signal they are in the wrong role. Why would any CEO want to keep a supervisor in a supervisory role when good workers choose to leave him?

Executives must vigilantly oversee the removal of supervisors who drive good workers away. These supervisors might be able to contribute in other nonsupervisory ways or might need to leave. The gritty work for executives is to hold those who report one or two levels down from the top to the same standard. Presuming that the cost of an individual leaving is higher at the top of the organization chart, those near the top who drive workers away produce your greatest turnover costs.

Drive creation of new ideas that will improve retention

Retention-driven executives invite HR and other top team members to recommend new retention tools. All understand that improving schedules, pay, or other ideas can be expensive, yet the clear message should be that all reasonable ideas should be spoken and heard. Finance can then weigh the cost benefit of any idea and report it to the executive for a decision.

Role-model trust behaviors

Employees smell distrust, both locally and at the top. Executives, therefore, must speak and act in trustworthy ways so they send the right messages, as well as role-model the right behaviors for managers and supervisors. Employees hear and circulate stories about executives, and sometimes these stories are all they know. Care must be taken that these stories reflect trustworthy intent and behavior, and the best way to make this happen is for executives to always think and act in trustworthy ways.

Conduct focus groups with employees to learn why they stay and leave

Fortune 500 CEOs should do this, as should all other top executives for smaller organizations. The purpose is to know firsthand how employees think by observing and listening to them. Smart CEOs schedule groups while doing onsite visits and minimize the formality to enhance openness.

Opening comments should invite employees to look beyond pay and benefits, as these are often their default responses. One broadening example is, "Let's consider the things that make working with us good or not so good for you day to day. What things do you look forward to on your way to work? What things turn you off?" Follow-up questions might include, "On a scale of 1 to 10, with 10 being high, what's the likelihood that you will still be with us in 2 years?" This invites everyone to speak, with a response that invites further discussion, such as, "John, your answer was 6. What must we do to make it a 10?"

 ## Top Human Resources Roles for Retention

HR's retention roles fall into two categories:

* Ensure new hires are likely to stay by designing and implementing hiring and onboarding processes. It is right, then, that HR share accountability for early turnover of up to 90 days.
* Support the operations group to achieve its retention goals by providing information, implementing support tools, and coaching supervisors on using these tools.

The following sections describe the retention activities for a human resources department, with the top HR executive assuming responsibility for seeing that these things get done. Many organizations are now appointing a retention manager who focuses entirely on employee retention. Should you appoint someone to that role, this list is a solid start toward a job description.

Make certain all who are hired are likely to stay long-term

In most organizations, HR has first look at each applicant and decides which will continue on as potential hires. So if each new hire in your company must be initially screened in by HR, then HR shares responsibility for all new hires. As a result, HR is then accountable for designing and executing tactics to screen out those who are likely to be short-timers. These tactics are described in Chapter 8.

Strengthen 90-day retention

HR and operations typically share the influence on new hires during their first 90 days. HR or a separate training department designs and delivers new-hire orientation and group training, and operations then delivers subsequent onboarding processes once employees move into their jobs. HR's role during employees' first 90 days is to ensure initial group activities are designed and administered so employees learn the company's strengths and are positioned to succeed in their jobs. HR's responsibilities continue once employees have moved into their jobs by codesigning additional onboarding processes and ensuring that operations and coaching supervisors use them.

Track retention achievement vs. goals

Reducing turnover requires setting retention goals and tracking their achievement for the organization, departments, and individual supervisors. Automated payroll systems usually contain methods for tracking turnover, and HR typically owns these systems. HR can then add retention goals and variances, and it can produce reports each month or even each week. But whereas HR produces the report, distribution should be handled by finance or whichever department reports important productivity numbers so retention doesn't become pigeonholed as "an HR measure" and therefore an HR project.

Organizations that lack a sophisticated tracking system or are putting off tracking turnover until a new system arrives should track turnover by hand. The improvement gained from setting and achieving retention goals will by far offset the extra work or extra person required to track it.

Stay current regarding retention best practices as well as retention-related data in the marketplace

Savvy HR managers stay current by reading industry and HR publications, attending conferences, and networking to know hot retention ideas and trends. Then they recommend new ideas to implement, some of which may challenge long-held beliefs.

Likewise, HR must keep all key hiring managers apprised of talent shortages, days to fill positions, planned recruiting methods, future outlooks, and any other data that connects HR and operations managers into partnerships for recruiting and retention.

Build trust skills into all leadership selection, development, and coaching processes

Earlier discussions in this book described how building trust with teams is the most important retention skill for leaders on all levels. HR must take the lead to retool processes to measure trust-building and develop it (see Chapter 7 for techniques).

Support supervisors who need retention help, and if necessary support their removal

Supervisors who fail to develop retention skills need help, and usually only their managers have the authority to assist them. HR's role is to coach the manager as needed to help the supervisor. HR might join in the coaching, but only at the request of the manager and with the manager participating. Retention coaching should be like other forms of performance coaching, with the operations manager owning responsibility for the coaching and the outcome.

Supervisors who cannot achieve healthy levels of retention must be removed from their supervisory roles and perhaps completely from the organization. HR can lead by counseling the supervisor's manager on the proper steps for giving feedback and performance coaching, as well as documenting the file so fair and essential steps can be taken in timely ways. Top HR professionals help managers identify facts, provide clear feedback, describe potential consequences, give timelines for improvement, and ultimately manage subordinate supervisors to improve or move out.

Report to the CEO any person, policy, or issue that blocks retention

The top HR executive must have a straight line to the CEO to report any major obstacle to retention that cannot be addressed through other channels. Old-time locomotives had cowcatchers on the front for throwing obstacles off the track. The top HR executive must have "cowcatcher" responsibilities.

 ## Top Finance Roles for Retention

CFOs and their finance departments wield tremendous influence regarding what becomes important in their organizations. Ultimately they are in charge of deciding what to measure, how to measure it, and how to report it. As a result, finance can become a power player in your efforts to improve retention. Most important, finance brings credibility that usually cannot be replaced by HR or any other support department.

The following sections present five roles finance can play to contribute mightily to your retention initiatives. These must be hardwired into their strategic plans, annual project planning, job descriptions—all documents that ultimately become the finance department's to-do list.

Conduct a comprehensive turnover cost study

Finance must conduct a full turnover cost study and distribute the results so all know that the turnover cost data have been approved by the CFO and ultimately the CEO. After fully investing themselves in the study, the finance team is then more likely to proactively discuss retention's dollar impact and include it in all presentations and informal discussions.

Report retention results to executive and management teams at the same time as other key metrics

If finance reports the key metrics—such as profitability, sales, quality, and safety—then turnover can only be a major number if finance reports it. In contrast, bringing HR to the front of the room to report turnover contributes to the perception that turnover is an HR issue, to be resolved entirely by the HR team.

Report consequences of increased or decreased turnover on other key metrics

Should you have any remaining doubters regarding turnover's drain on productivity, finance can convert them by linking decreased turnover to increases in key productivity metrics. Likewise, turnover spikes should be reported next to decreases in sales and other key metrics: Retail stores will correlate reduced turnover to increased sales; manufacturing will correlate to increased quality; and call centers will correlate to higher customer satisfaction and lower handle times.

Utilize turnover's costs to project savings or risks of proposed benefits or policies

One advantage to knowing turnover's cost is you can estimate the dollar impact of major management decisions. Run a model to compare the potential savings of reducing incentive payouts to a possible resulting turnover increase of 5% or 10%. Or weigh the investment of permitting employees to work from home against a potential retention increase of 10% or higher. Applying the costs of turnover and projected savings from retention brings clarity and velocity to make better people-management decisions

Leverage major vendors to provide employee benefits and discounts where appropriate

One smart person sparked the idea that Las Vegas cabbies could sell rooms and shows while driving their cabs, as described in Chapter 4. Consider any advantage your vendors can offer your employees and propose a mutually beneficial arrangement, even if the vendor's only benefit is to retain your business.

Top Marketing Roles for Retention

Marketing's job is to influence customers to buy your products. Why not recruit them to help influence your employees to stay?

Traditionally, marketing's sole focus has been external, with little participation in employee programs. The worst-case scenario is HR won't ask marketing to help and marketing won't volunteer, and the result is wasted talent. Marketing brings a research orientation, big-picture thinking, on-message communications, a targeted approach, and pizzazz. HR sometimes buys these services for recruitment advertising but operates on an island for other critical employee activities.

Marketing departments in high-retention organizations place the following roles in their required duties rather than consider them as "extras," and prioritize them on the same level as services they provide for customers.

Develop branding that leverages glues for prospective and current employees

The overall retention strategy is based on answering, "What glues do we offer that employees cannot get elsewhere?" and clues come from asking, "Why do our employees stay?" Direct your marketing team to help find these answers and then build a branding campaign to attract and keep employees.

Design the realistic job previews

HR and operations are expert at everything about your jobs, and marketing's specialty is communicating and persuading. Working together, they can design a realistic job preview that will attract the right applicants and repel the rest. Marketing can especially contribute by designing a preview that reaches applicants' senses: How do you communicate sitting for long periods? Being enclosed in a small room? Listening to disgruntled customers? Working in a cold building with a wet floor? Hearing the constant sound of machinery?

Participate in the development of onboarding programs

Onboarding is all about informing, engaging, motivating, and persuading. Help marketing understand your onboarding program's objectives and turn them loose to build a program from a clean slate.

Develop communications and rewards for the employee referral program

Recall the principle of "marketing more than money" discussed in Chapter 8: High-powered referral programs require targeting the right applicants, identifying the most motivating and affordable rewards, introducing the program, and then keeping it fresh. Marketing can help with all of these aspects.

 ## True Stories

Connecting executive compensation to retention is increasing

In a 2007 study, Hay Group reported that 8.2% of respondents used turnover as a performance measure in executive compensation plans, more than three times the 2.3% who said the same in 2005.

According to a recent proxy statement, car retailer Penske Automotive Group tied 8% of CEO Roger Penske's bonus to achieving an employee retention goal. The resulting turnover across 300 stores was just below 31%, down from 80% when Penske Corp. first acquired a controlling stake. Mr. Penske earned a $240,000 bonus for leading his organization to achieve its retention goal. Senior vice president Tony Pordon explained that managing retention is crucial for customer satisfaction: "Our business is one that is based on people. There has to be a tone at the top."

Pep Boys links 10% of three executives' bonuses to turnover of middle managers.

Technology vendor Extreme Networks based up to 20% of several executives' bonuses on "undesirable attrition."[1]

Managing retention from the top, weekly

Years ago, the president of a client company taught me a lesson worth repeating.

Doug Samuels is the top executive of Space Coast Credit Union, headquartered in Melbourne, Florida. Frustrated by high turnover, Samuels board tied his annual bonus to retention, and Samuels then did the same for his management team.

At the start of the project, annual teller turnover was 65%. Using many of the ideas presented in this book, turnover dropped at the end of year one to 32%, decreasing by more than half. Samuels then set the next year's goal at 25%.

Midway through the next year, turnover had crept above the goal. After discussing several alternatives to fix it, Samuels decided on a strong, simple approach: He told his management team that the first agenda item at every Monday morning executive meeting would be that each would report the names of employees who left the previous week and lessons learned from their departures.

Samuels understood that preparing these reports would require his top team to dig deeper into real turnover reasons and solutions. The one downside Samuels saw to his plan was that subordinate supervisors would scramble every Friday to provide information for their managers, distracting them from other work. But Samuels decided this was a good thing—that spreading the turnover pain would unite all to reduce it.

Samuels made his retention goal, and his story underscores the importance that executives drive retention as a top-five priority.

 ## Closing Thoughts on Driving Retention from the Top

The following are three major conclusions for rethinking retention based on the ideas presented in this chapter regarding retention roles and driving retention from the top.

Traditional Thinking	Rethinking Retention
Human resources is responsible for retention.	Driving retention is an executive duty, just like sales, service, quality, and safety.
Finance and marketing can contribute to retention efforts.	Finance and marketing should include specific retention activities in their annual strategic plans.
Retention progress should be shared with the management team.	Retention progress should be reported to the board of directors or owners, as well as employees.

Responsibilities for retention must be clear. HR develops and carries out many retention-related processes, especially regarding hiring and onboarding. But once employees are doing their jobs, operations is the retention point of attack. Finance and marketing contribute with specific roles, and all must be held accountable by those at the top.

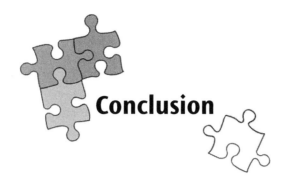

Conclusion

What's Next?

So—three principles, seven strategies, and over three hundred ideas later, where do you start?

Implementing the Retention Model

Start at the beginning, of course. Based on the three principles of the Rethinking Retention model—(1) employees quit jobs because they can, (2) employees stay for things they get uniquely from you, and (3) supervisors build unique relations that drive retention—work on the strategies themselves.

Hold supervisors accountable

Start by adapting the tactics to your organization and establish a company-wide retention goal that resonates down to leaders on all levels. Target annual turnover or turnover for the first 90 days, one job or every job, to be achieved next quarter or next year, but set a goal and announce it throughout your management team. Supervisors on all levels will learn quickly that retention is everyone's job—just like sales, service, quality, and safety.

Develop supervisors to build trust

HR and training should work together to rethink processes and ask the following questions.

- How can we measure trust skills among supervisor candidates before we place them in this critical retention position?
- How can we develop trust training that details behaviors that build and break trust and add it to our supervisor curriculum?
- How can we teach managers on all levels to observe and coach supervisors to build trust with their teams? And teach the same to the managers themselves?
- How can we measure supervisors' trust effectiveness with their teams?
- What corrective steps should be taken with supervisors who cannot build trust, before they are moved out of their positions?

Operations should support and implement these practices by:

- Contributing real-life examples and experiences to these processes
- Supporting the overall trust emphasis with their supervisors
- Having big eyes for trust breakdowns and coaching supervisors accordingly
- Being great role models, always

Narrow the front door

While the operations side implements retention goals, the HR team should lead on hiring applicants who stay. Begin developing your employee value proposition and employment branding as described in Chapter 4, with strong input from marketing and your executive team. Then move rapidly to put the processes into place from Chapter 9, to narrow the front door. Marketing can help design the realistic job preview, employee referral program, and any other piece that requires communications.

Operations has responsibilities for improving hiring, too, as they must be drivers of the referral program and bulldogs about not accepting any new hire who they don't believe will stay.

The remaining strategies can happen concurrently, so prioritize them according to which will give the quickest improvement. HR will be in the forefront for those that require new processes, and operations will implement putting those processes to work.

Script employees' first 90 days

HR, training, and operations must work together to build these plans as all must execute them. Marketing can contribute significantly to traditional new employee orientation design and any other early "program" to make them glue-building and engaging.

Challenge all people-management policies and practices

While HR will likely speak first on these issues, the top management team must own the company's policies and practices. All must study trends, think creatively, make bold suggestions, and weigh costs versus outcomes.

Likewise, managers and supervisors must become local thought leaders for retaining their teams, thinking for example, "Can I restructure schedules for this job to give more flexibility?" "Am I willing to give no merit increases to average performers to reward high performers with more money?" Some of the best retention ideas will come from the bottom of your operations chart.

Calculate turnover's cost to galvanize retention

Finance owns the important numbers and reports, so they shine here as turnover's chief cost-assigner and communicator. Tie cost savings to your newly announced retention goals and supervisors' attention will multiply exponentially.

Drive retention from the top

Executives must agree that all parts of your employee retention initiative are right, and ensure that they are executed according to the roles assigned to HR, operations, marketing, and finance.

As important, they must talk retention constantly in board meetings, management meetings, employee meetings, and individual meetings, top to bottom throughout the organization, because people do what executives instruct them to do.

 ## The Time Is Yesterday

Taking firm steps to improve retention is new to many companies, so you must move quickly to get ahead of the curve. So let's look further out at the curve. What trends will likely impact retention in the next five to ten years? Here's the final list, the top future trends that will impact retention.

The SEC will require retention data in annual reports

This idea was first introduced about ten years ago, so those who regulate the types of information publicly owned companies must release have been considering it for some time. The recent pattern of CEOs being accountable for turnover will lead to the SEC requiring turnover data in annual reports so traders know this important information before deciding to invest. Directors might anticipate the SEC requiring this data and therefore require it from their CEOs before the SEC mandates making it known to all.

Baby boomers will age themselves out of the workforce

This valuable block of employees will tuck away its strong work ethic as it finally retires. The replacement generations will be smaller in numbers and likely not have the same high standards, making turnover more costly and creating an even stronger demand for good workers.

Health insurance costs will continue to rise

Unless the U.S. government finds ways to slow the growing cost of healthcare, employers will struggle with how much to pass on to employees. Job seekers, in turn, might place more weight on insurance when choosing jobs than they do now. Those companies that pony up with more insurance dollars might have to offset those costs by becoming less competitive on other types of rewards.

Technology will enable more employees to work remotely

Technology that we cannot envision will make working from our homes and even our cars as common as working from an office today. This is the time to gain a competitive advantage on telecommuting and other forms of remote work, because technology advances and the fierce competition for workers will turn remote work into a commodity rather than the special benefit that it is today.

Fuel costs and other factors will drive employee-preferred schedules

Fuel costs will continue to fluctuate, and employees will change jobs for four-day workweeks and other conditions that create more time and save fuel. Additional staff might be required to meet employee-demanded scheduling requirements to get the same amount of work done. Employees also might choose to work close to home to save on time and transportation. Look for more company-sponsored transportation methods.

Emerging economies cost the United States more talent

The U.S. and other Western economies will suffer from the pattern of Indian and Chinese workers returning to their homelands. Mix in the creation of more professional jobs from emerging economies in Asia, Europe, and even South America, and the United States's shortcomings in science will become much more expensive.

Unions gain strength

If proposed U.S. legislation takes place, employees will more easily form unions and organizations will pay a price. The potential outcome for employees is more tangible benefits and maybe better work schedules, but management and supervisory relationships might suffer as a result.

Green is good

Keying in on the concerns of the defense industry that is challenged to find young engineers, employees will migrate toward companies that care—about the environment and the overall good of the universe. Employment branding will emphasize how working for companies will equate with helping the earth and those who inhabit it.

Some executives, managers, and supervisors will have strong retention skills—and some will not

This is a constant, but just maybe the emphasis on retention goals, developing trust, and other innovations not mentioned here will raise the skill levels for everyone.

 # Employee Retention Is a Really Good Thing

Throughout this book, the emphasis has been that retention leads to more productivity, lower costs, and thus to more profits. But retention does other good things, too.

The Container Store and Whole Foods Market are regulars on the Fortune 100 Best Companies to Work For list, with the Container Store making the list each of the past nine years and Whole Foods making it *every year.* As retailers, they face obstacles that some other industries avoid such as schedules based on customer needs and a high percentage of low-skill jobs with corresponding pay. So how do these companies gain their edge?

CEOs Kip Tindell of the Container Store and John Mackey of Whole Foods recently participated in an interview to describe their philosophies. Coincidentally, they were once college roommates. Among their common beliefs is that pleasing employees as stakeholders is essential as is doing the same for customers and shareholders. As Tindell states:

> We actually say that we put the employee first and then the customer...I think if you're fortunate enough to be somebody's

employer, you have a huge moral obligation really to make sure that the person really looks forward to coming to work in the morning.

There's a harmonic effort that takes place, like a chorus is so much more beautiful than a single voice. These people are all interconnected. And it not only provides a higher return to each of them—compensation for employees, return for the shareholders, this creative crafting of a mutually beneficial relationship from the vendors—but it enriches the lives of those people, too, as crazy as that sounds.[1]

Mackey also describes the beauty of synergy:

The purpose of business is not primarily to maximize shareholder value, that's a myth . . . you manage the business on behalf of all of these interconnected stakeholders—the customers, the team members/employees, the suppliers, the investors, the greater community, the environment . . . you create value for all of them, they're all interdependent. And that will create the most successful business.[2]

Cued by these CEOs' perspectives, let's imagine our lives—yours, mine, and our neighbors'—when companies manage employees with full knowledge of the scarcity of talent and with the same top-to-bottom zeal they dedicate to sales and other critical outcomes. The following would be possible:

- Our lives would be more stable. Companies would still cut jobs, but voluntary turnover would be lower and we would be leaving a good job for a better one rather than to escape.
- More stability would mean more peace in our families, at our dinner tables, and in our hearts—and maybe better physical and mental health, too.
- Companies would improve our lives by offering better lifestyle benefits like concierge services, housing support, language training, and others that lower our stress levels and make living easier.

- Technology and schedule flexibility would enable us to be better parents, relatives, and friends.
- Companies would make more money, create more jobs, and make better products and services. This would enable more training, more promotions, and more interesting jobs.

Reaching these ideals requires a great deal of trickle-down, that executives will do the right things and all will win, top to bottom. I predict success and look forward to being part of it.

To end our rethinking retention journey on a high note, think of your children and grandchildren as you reread Chapter 3 on "because they can." History reflects that we spend many more years in strong economies than weak ones, so our loved ones should have plenty of great jobs to choose from in their futures.

Good luck, everyone!

Appendix A

Case Studies: Hilton's Call Centers and Curley & Pynn

This appendix includes two case studies of very different organizations that applied the rethinking retention principles and strategies to significantly reduce their turnover. Their company missions, sizes, and employees have little in common, and the retention paths they took were equally diverse. But all tactics they employed were based on the model presented in this book, and their results are worth millions of dollars.

 Hilton's Call Centers: Putting the Strategies and Tactics to Work in a Large Company

Company: Hilton Reservations and Customer Care (HRCC), headquartered in Dallas, Texas, with locations there and in Tampa, Florida; Hazleton, Pennsylvania; and Hemet, California

Employees: 2,500, whose primary job is to receive inbound calls from Hilton customers to reserve hotel rooms and related services

Main players: Top executive Russ Olivier; HR manager Bryan Thomason

Retention challenge

Facing annual turnover of 55%, Olivier and Thomason recognized that doing the same traditional retention tactics would lead to the same results. They were pleased with their overall performance against aggressive business goals but wondered how much better their centers could perform if turnover was lower and they retained more veteran agents. So they asked our company to conduct a retention review at each of their four centers and then implement solutions.

Retention solutions

Whereas HRCC had been tracking annual and monthly turnover, we found that half of all new hires failed to reach 90 days. As a result, we recommended three new metrics for center directors: (1) 75% of new hires reach 90 days, (2) 50% of all new hires come from employee referrals, and (3) applicant-to-hire ratio goals be established that varied by location. Center directors were told they had six months to achieve each goal, as new tools would be introduced month-to-month, but tracking would start immediately. They were also told that the first goal was most important: 75% of new hires reaching 90 days. Achieving that goal but missing on the others would be okay, but any who missed that goal had best achieve the others as an indication of effort.

Over the next five months, we reviewed each process that agents experienced in their first 90 days and recommended revisions to Olivier, Thomason, and the executive team. With their smart feedback and endorsement, we proceeded to install the following tactics.

- **Why they stay.** Built our retention strategy around why workers stay by leveraging the Hilton brand, employee travel benefits, and the opportunity for some applicants to work from home.
- **Skills for success.** Identified core job skills to develop a structured interview with special focus on retention, then trained interviewers to conduct these interviews effectively.

- **Employee referrals.** Designed employee referral programs by center, including forming center-wide committees comprised of top performers who were in their thirties or older to attract middle-aged and older workers.
- **Technology skills.** Removed technology experience as a job requirement and instead relied on trainers to teach the level of skills required for the job. This enabled the company to attract older workers who had all the other core job skills.
- **RJP.** Developed a facilitated realistic job preview that was conducted by trained experts that led to several candidates opting out.
- **Retention supervisors.** Assigned the best supervisor in each center to take teams immediately after training. These supervisors understood their performance standard included retaining their teams until the end of their 13th week, which comprised the first 90 days.
- **Focused on retention coaching.** From weeks 2 through 13, trainers and then supervisors coded each employee red, yellow, or green in a confidential database to indicate which were likely to stay or leave based on either their performance or their preference. The trainer or supervisor then met with her manager weekly to review the coding and decide who to coach and who to terminate based on performance.
- **Welcomes from all.** Provided all new hires with a color-coded identification badge to encourage all others in the centers to greet and welcome them, and also lay groundwork for a celebration when they progressed to a regular identification badge after they completed 90 days.
- **360° accountability.** To ensure all who interacted with new hires accepted their roles for retention, center directors conducted a meeting 91 days after each class began and invited HR, training, the new-hire supervisor(s), and their managers. That team reviewed the status of all who had joined 90 days ago. The key focus areas were whether the 75% retention goal had been achieved, the week each leaver left, and the coding for each leaver. Discussions included whether HR should have

seen prehire signs that a particular agent would leave in week 2, or why a supervisor continuously coded an agent green who surprised everyone by leaving in week 12.

* **Executive report.** The center director completed a weekly report for Russ Olivier that tracked the 30-, 60-, and 90-day retention results along with progress on applicant-to-hire ratios and employee referrals. Olivier designed the report himself, and center directors originally referred to it as the "Russ Report" until Olivier modestly asked that they not refer to it by that name. Instead, they colored the report purple and gold to reflect Louisiana State University, Olivier's alma mater, so directors continued to remember who would read the report.

Retention results

Total company retention improved rapidly with this plan, as turnover declined at least 20% each month for the first four months compared to the same months of the previous year. Business metrics also improved as quality measures reached an all-time high, and cost per call and average handle time improved. With these new processes in place, HRCC executives are optimistic that retention improvements will continue.

 ## Curley & Pynn: A Customized Retention Plan for Small Business

Company: Curley & Pynn, which provides public relations services with one location in Orlando, Florida

Employees: A total of 11, mostly degreed professionals with a minimum of three years public relations experience

Main players: Founder Roger Pynn, partners Dan Ward and Kim Taylor

Retention challenge

Roger Pynn's "because they can" moment came on a Monday morning when he greeted Tom, a two-year employee.

Roger: How was your weekend?

Tom: It was great, Roger; we sold our house.

Roger: I didn't know you were selling your house.

Tom: We've had it on the market for a year but didn't think it would sell but somebody gave us our number.

Roger: Congratulations. So where will you move to now?

Tom: New Hampshire. My wife wants to move there for the kids and I'm going to start an independent consulting business. So I guess I'm giving you my two-week notice.

Roger Pynn and his team provide public relations services to clients on retainer, so he depends on having the right number of professionals on board each month to provide and bill for the agreed-upon services. Turnover cuts right to the bottom line because empty chairs result in lower billings. The price of turnover is easy to calculate based on the number of days to fill jobs and the days required until new hires can provide full services. For Curley & Pynn, losing and replacing a public relations professional costs $70,000.

Curley & Pynn employees already enjoyed competitive pay, benefits, bonuses, and feel-good social events. Pynn had even given all employees a permanent week of extra vacation to keep his organization ahead of the market. But to ensure full billing every month, he took two strong steps to improve retention by (1) customizing retention plans for each employee and (2) stating an expected number of years he wanted each new hire to stay.

Retention solutions

Large organizations offer a fixed set of benefits and other retention tools and match them as best they can to employees' needs. But whereas most large organizations lock into one retention approach, employees are idiosyncratic and bring with them individual wants and needs. After much flip-charting and debate, we worked with Pynn and his partners Dan Ward and Kim Taylor to develop a retention plan that reached out to each employee individually. Our goals were to narrow the front door, provide a unique retention plan for each employee, and ensure all employees felt a strong emotional connection that made working for Curley & Pynn an honor.

- **Owner's retention interview.** For hiring, Ward or Taylor screen candidates and tell Pynn when they have found a winner. Pynn then conducts an "owner's retention interview" in which he explains his all-in stake in the business and asks six structured questions regarding the candidate's reasons for joining, staying, and leaving past jobs.

- **A three-year expectation.** Pynn concludes the interview by telling the potential hire that she should not join unless she intends to stay at least three years, and shares the dollar amount he will invest in her success as a way to frame his three-year expectation. To protect himself legally, Pynn makes it clear that the three-year commitment is based on continued good performance and the need for her position. He then asks the candidate to call or visit with him the next day and lay out the conditions that Pynn and his team have to meet for the candidate to stay at least that long.

- **The individual "stay list."** The next day, Pynn and Ward or Taylor meet with the potential hire to hear and negotiate the "stay list." Requests might include pay, benefits, types of customers, schedules, training, corner office—all is on the table and all can be negotiated. An offer is made if the parties reach agreement, and not made if they do not.

- **A personalized stay-list journal.** On their first day, Pynn presents employees with a blank journal with his own inscription encouraging them to record their experiences with Curley & Pynn, with special emphasis on what they learn and contribute. Then every six months he and Ward or Taylor meet with the employee to review the negotiated "stay list" and ask the employee to score management on a 1–10 scale for each item. Any score below 10 is discussed and an action plan presented for improvement. It is most important to Pynn that his team uphold all agreements he and the employee made prehire, and that any misunderstandings are presented and resolved.

- **A three-year bonus—the IUE.** Once the new hire completes the 90-day probationary period, Pynn, Ward, and Taylor congratulate her on making the team and offer this unique benefit: On the employee's three-year anniversary, Pynn and his partners will award an extra week's vacation and present $1,000, tax free, that the employee has to immediately use for an "Irreplaceable, Unmatchable Experience" (IUE). This might be a visit to a foreign country, an extreme outdoor activity, violin lessons, some type of spiritual experience, or whatever. The only requirement is that the employee take along the digital camera she will also receive and conduct a presentation for the entire team when she returns. During the presentation she must explain how she will turn her learnings from her IUE into new ideas for clients.

Of course, existing employees also participate in all of the new retention plans.

Roger Pynn saw his financial investment in the plan as a win-win proposition: By providing IUEs every three years, he was investing $333 per employee per year in order to retain the employees who contribute to his company's success.

Results

All employees have made minimum three-year commitments to Curley & Pynn, and none have left since the inception of the retention program.

Appendix B

Top Sections of the Bureau of Labor Statistics' Website

The BLS website is a gold mine of data for savvy retention experts and a deep source of data for organizations that strive to reduce turnover and seek comparisons for various types of workforce data. The government has done a very good job of collecting, analyzing, and presenting data to help organizations manage people effectively. The data is derived from statistically significant samples across organizations, and the total amount presented is massive and much of it unique. These data will help you align your workforce issues with national, regional, and local data so you can execute better in both the present and future.

This appendix is an attempt at a "guided tour" of the site and points out pages and reports that might be most helpful to you. Take the BLS for a spin and make your own decision if the data you find is worth a return trip. URLs are provided for direct access, but you can also take the scenic tour by starting at the homepage and using the tabs to locate each recommended report. You'll encounter much helpful additional information along the way.

Homepage: *www.bls.gov/*

The recently improved homepage provides a helpful guide to assist users through the maze of workforce data. A detailed index is on the left, "Latest Numbers" on the right, and "Latest from BLS" in the middle. Tabs on top will take you to databases, publications, and economic releases, and the bottom contains featured publications to pique your interest.

Most notable are the right and center portions, Latest Numbers and Latest from BLS. Latest Numbers is a shortcut to the most recent findings, including unemployment rates, consumer price index, and productivity. Latest from BLS contains new data with explanations and charts. On a recent look, a report on older workers provided the following new information:

- From 1977 to 2007, the employment of workers age 65 and older increased by 101% versus an increase of 59% for total employment.
- This increase is due to choice rather than volume, as the baby boomers had not reached 65 during this period and were not included in the data.
- More than half of older workers, 56%, work full time.
- The graying of the workforce will definitely continue. From 2006 to 2016, the number of workers age 65 and older will soar by 80% and will comprise more than 6% of the total workforce versus the 3.6% they comprised back in 2006.

 Job Openings and Labor Turnover Survey (JOLTS): *www.bls.gov/jlt/*

The centerpiece of the JOLTS data is the monthly report, which contains information by nation, region, and industry on the following topics:

- *Job openings*, which includes those jobs that were open on the last day of the month.

- *Hires,* which includes the net changes in the number of employees from month to month or period to period.
- *Separations,* which are reported as a group and also separately for quits, layoffs, and discharges.

The workforce information provided in Chapter 1 as well as the data in Appendix C was taken from the JOLTS report. For those seeking turnover benchmarks, the Separations area presents *quits,* which is comparable to voluntary turnover. The total separations data also includes discharges and layoffs.

JOLTS reports industry findings from the following industries, and some of these have sub-groups as well:

- Construction
- Manufacturing
- Trade, transportation, and utilities
- Retail trade
- Professional and business services
- Education and health services
- Leisure and hospitality
- Accommodation and food services
- Government
- State and local government

The JOLTS section also provides related reports and publications. It can be accessed by clicking "Employment" on the homepage index and then "Job openings and labor turnover."

 ## Local Area Unemployment Statistics: *www.bls.gov/lau/*

This section provides tables and analyses of unemployment trends and is updated monthly. This data can help when comparing recruiting issues for multiple locations, analyzing degrees of difficulty for one location, or planning an expansion or relocation to another area. Research studies and databases are also available.

Employment Projections: *www.bls.gov/emp/*

This section includes all information regarding job growth and includes the annual *Occupational Outlook Handbook*. This data is very helpful for workforce planning as it projects job growth and pay for individual job categories. For example, by looking up *physical therapists* we can learn many details including the following:

- **Employment change.** Employment of physical therapists is expected to grow 27% from 2006 to 2016, "much faster than the average" for all occupations. The impact of proposed federal legislation imposing limits on reimbursement for therapy services may adversely affect the short-term job outlook for physical therapists. However, the long-run demand for physical therapists should continue to rise as new treatments and techniques expand the scope of physical therapy practices. Moreover, demand will be spurred by the increasing numbers of individuals with disabilities or limited function.

- **Job prospects.** "Job opportunities will be good" for licensed physical therapists in all settings. Job opportunities should be particularly good in acute hospital, rehabilitation, and orthopedic settings, where the elderly are most often treated. Physical therapists with specialized knowledge of particular types of treatment also will have excellent job prospects.

- **Earnings.** Median annual earnings of physical therapists were $66,200 in May 2006. The middle 50% earned between $55,030 and $78,080. The lowest 10% earned less than $46,510, and the highest 10% earned more than $94,810.

The Employment Projections area of the BLS site also provides future information for jobs and industries projected out to 2016. Whereas the BLS information provided in the JOLTS section detailed changes by industry, this area lists information for specific jobs. For example:

- Fastest growing occupations by percent of jobs added are network systems and data communications analysts, personal and home care aides, and home health aides

- Most new jobs by number are registered nurses, retail sales-persons, and customer service representatives
- Largest job declines will come from stock clerks and order fillers, cashiers except those in gaming, and packers and packagers who work by hand

You can use this information to know the challenges you face when recruiting and retaining the people you need. Instructions for using the *Occupational Outlook Handbook* are in the center of the page and reports referenced here and more are at the bottom.

 ## Wages by Area and Occupations:
www.bls.gov/oes/current/oes_nat.htm#b00-0000

This is like hiring a compensation consultant for free. Included here is comparative pay information for over 800 occupations based on national, regional, state, and metropolitan area surveys. Clicking on any individual job gives you additional detailed information.

 ## National Benefits Comparisons:
www.bls.gov/news.release/pdf/ebs2.pdf

This link will take you to a brief summary report of benefits trends for private employers. Instructions are provided near the end of the report for obtaining a full copy, which contains common and not-so-common benefits comparisons. A study is available for government workers as well.

 ## Resources for Business Leaders:
www.bls.gov/audience/business.htm

This section provides information for top-level business planning. Included is helpful data to negotiate contracts, identify employment costs, determine new markets for products, and compare your business to others in your industry.

2007 vs 2008 Voluntary Quits and Job Openings by Private Industry[1] (in 000s, low to high for quits by major industry group)

Industry Group	Voluntary Quits[2]			Job Openings[3]		
	2007	2008	% Decline	2007	2008	% Decline
Other services	25.5	25.1	1.6	2,352	1,889	19.7
Mining and logging	25.3	24.2	4.3	175	232	32.6[4]
Construction	24.9	23.1	7.3	2,188	1,352	38.2
Education and Health Services	20.4	8.71	8.3	9,132	8,647	5.3
Educational services	14.1	12.7	10	820	782	4.6
Healthcare and social assistance	21.6	19.9	7.9	8,313	7,868	5.4
Trade, Transportation, and Utilities	28.7	25.9	9.8	9,520	7,540	20.8
Wholesale trade	19.5	16.8	13.8	2,542	1,660	34.7
Retail trade	35.8	31.7	11.4	5,004	4,489	10.3
Transportation, warehousing, and utilities	18.2	19.1	5.0[5]	1,974	1,390	29.6
Leisure and Hospitality	55.4	49.7	10.3	7,239	5,725	20.9
Arts, entertainment, and recreation	32.1	28.9	10	849	653	23.1
Accommodation and food services	59.4	53.2	10.4	6,387	5,075	20.5
Professional and Business Services	32.3	28.9	10.5	9,282	8,127	12.4

Financial activities	22.8	18.8	17.5	3,460	2,849	17.7
Finance and insurance	22.8	17.4	23.7	2,696	1,870	30.6
Real estate and rental and leasing	23.1	22.6	2.2	766	771	.7[6]
Information	19.2	15.5	19.3	1,770	1,025	42.1
Manufacturing	18.1	14.4	20	4,206	3,050	27.5
Durable goods	16.2	12.6	22	2,581	1,768	31.5
Nondurable goods	21.5	17.3	19.5	1,625	1,285	20.9
Total	28.7	25.6	10.80%	49,328	40,435	18%

[1] All data extracted from BLS JOLTS information, not seasonally adjusted

[2] Quits are presented as a rate, based on the number of quits as a percent of total employment; this controls for fluctuations in the overall employment within each group

[3] Openings are presented as actual job openings for each industry group on the last day of the month

[4] Mining and logging showed a 32.6% increase rather than a decline in job openings between 2007 and 2008

[5] Transportation, warehousing, and utilities showed a 5% increase rather than a decline of voluntary quits between 2007 and 2008

[6] Real estate and rental and leasing showed a .7% increase rather than a decline in job openings between 2007 and 2008

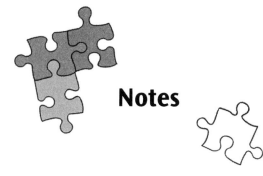

Notes

CHAPTER 1

1. In the report titled "The Job Openings and Labor Turnover Survey: What Initial Data Show," in *Monthly Labor Review*, November 2004, Kelly A. Clark indicates quits tend to increase during recessions, and also that nearly 50 million hires and separations occurred during any 12-month period in the previous 3 years.
2. Ibid
3. The BLS reference to the highest turnover industries is from "Job Openings and Labor Turnover," August, 2008; these are the industries with the highest percentage of employees who voluntarily quit.
4. The reference to 82% of U.S. jobs being in the service sector is from "Increasing Human and Social Capital by Applying Job Embeddedness Theory" by Brooks C. Holtom, et al., *Organizational Dynamics*, Volume 36, Issue 4, 2006.
5. The reference to two-thirds of all college graduates moving back home is from "2006 College Grads Flock Back Home," Collegegrad.com, September 28, 2006.
6. The reference to 8% percent of the U.S. workforce working for themselves is from "Occupational Employment Projections to 2016" by Arlene Dohm and Lynn Shniper, *Monthly Labor Review*, November, 2007.
7. The reference to job embeddedness research is from "Why People Stay: Using Job Embeddedness to Predict Voluntary Turnover" by Mitchell, Holtom, Lee, Sablynski, Erez, *Academy of Management Journal*, 2001, 44, 1102–22.
8. Buckingham, Marcus, and Curt Coffman. 1999. *First, Break All the Rules*. New York: Simon & Schuster.
9. The reference to supervisor fit is from "The Role of Person–Supervisor Fit on Employee Attitudes and Retention" by Tiffany M. Greene-Shortridge and Lisa Wager, *Kenexa HR Newsletter*, Volume 7, Issue 1.

10. The reference to the Society for Industrial and Organizational Psychology (SIOP) panel discussion is from "Collect, Use Employee Data to Drive Retention Practices" by Pamela Babcock, SHRM HR Measurements Library, May 1, 2007.

11. The reference to the top HR professional trend is from "Workplace Trends: An Overview of the Findings of the Latest SHRM Workplace Forecast," published in *Workplace Visions*, a publication of SHRM, No. 3, 2008.

12. The reference to 14% of organizations setting retention goals at the first-line leader level is from "Employee Turnover Trends 2007" by TalentKeepers, 2007.

13. The reference to TalentKeepers surveying employees regarding trust skills is from "Retention Corner" by Richard P. Finnegan, published in *Recruiting Trends*, July 31, 2007.

14. The reference to Leadership IQ finding that 32% of employees' decisions regarding staying with their companies involve trust is from "Research Shows Five Ways to Gain Workers' Trust" by Kathy Gurchiek, *www.shrm.org/hrnews*, April 11, 2007.

15. The reference to the Sirota survey is from "Boomers, Gen-Yers Agree: It's All About Respect" by Wallace Immen, *www.theglobeandmail.com*, January 24, 2007.

16. Branham, Leigh. 2005. *The 7 Hidden Reasons Why Employees Leave.* New York: Amacom.

17. Employee referral research is from "Social Networks and Employee Performance in a Call Center" by Emilio Castilla, *AJS*, Volume 110, Number 5 (March 2005), and "A Note of Recruiting Sources and Job Survival Rates" by Decker, Cornelius, et al., *Journal of Applied Psychology*, August, 1979, Vol. 64, Issue 4.

18. Realistic job preview research is from "The Effects of Realistic Job Previews on Applicant Self-Selection and Employee Turnover, Satisfaction, and Coping Ability" by Mary Suszko and James Breaugh, *Journal of Management*, Vol. 12, No. 4, (1986), and "Reduce Turnover with Realistic Job Reviews" by P. G. and P. L. Roth, *The CPA Journal*, September 1995.

19. The reference to older workers being more loyal is from Spherion's Emerging Workforce Study, 2007.

20. The reference to older workers being most satisfied is from a study by Leadership IQ, December 5, 2007.

21. The reference to length of service increasing with the age of the employee when starting a job is from "Number of Jobs Held, Labor Market Activ-

ity, and Earnings Growth Among the Youngest Baby Boomers: Results from a Longitudinal Survey" by the Bureau of Labor Statistics, August 25, 2006.

22. The reference to Wal-Mart being the United State's largest private employer is from "Global 500: The Top 25," *www.CNNMoney.com*, accessed March 30, 2008.
23. The reference to Wal-Mart's high early turnover is from "Employee Retention: The Secrets Behind Wal-Mart's Successful Hiring Policies," by Coleman H. Peterson, Human Resource Management, Spring, 2005
24. The University of Florida study is "Employee's First Month on the Job Can Predict Turnover," *University of Florida News*, November 18, 2004.
25. The Aberdeen study is from "All Aboard: Effective Onboarding Techniques and Strategies," January 2008.
26. The Salary.com study is "Employee Job Satisfaction & Retention Survey 2006/2007."
27. Sirota, David, Louis Mischkind, and Michael Meltzer. 2005. *The Enthusiastic Employee: How Companies Profit by Giving Employees What They Want.* Upper Saddle River, NJ: Wharton School Publishing. Note: The data presented is from their website, which they say is from this book.
28. The reference to TalentKeepers' research is from "The Tides of Talent" by Craig R. Taylor, *T & D Magazine,* April 2003.
29. The reference to "health care cost containment" is from "2007 Benefits: A Survey by the Society for Human Resources Management," June 2007.
30. The reference to the Bureau of Labor Statistics research is "Employee Benefits in Private Industry, 2007," August 22, 2007.
31. The reference to the CareerBuilder.com and Robert Half survey is from "Negotiating Power Continues to Shift to Job Candidates" by Kathy Gurchiek, *www.shrm.org/hrnews,* September 13, 2007.
32. The Corporate Voices for Working Families study is titled "Business Impacts of Flexibility: An Imperative for Expansion," November 2005.
33. The WorldatWork study is titled "Attraction and Retention, *The Impact and Prevalence of Work-Life and Benefit* Programs," published in October, 2007.
34. The reference to flexible options availability for some jobs more than others is from "A Time to Work: Recent Trends in Shift Work and Flexible Schedules," *Monthly Labor Review,* December 2007.

CHAPTER 2

1. The National Bureau of Economic Research announced this recession in their paper titled "Determination of the December 2007 Peak in Economic Activity" on December 11th, 2008.
2. Historical prices from the Dow Jones Industrial Average are from finance.yahoo.com.
3. Inflation rate derived from calculator at InflationData.com.
4. Price of gas is based on Energy Information Administration, www.eia.doe.gov.
5. Consumer confidence comparison information based on an e-mail provided by Lynn Franco, Director of The Conference Board Consumer Research Center, on July 24th, 2008.
6. Layoff information is based on data presented by the Bureau of Labor Statistics' Mass Layoffs Summary, June 2008.
7. Government bailout information is provided by "History of U.S. Gov't Bailouts" by ProPublica, December 22nd, 2008.
8. The quote from President-elect Obama is from "Obama: 'Millions of jobs' in danger next year." MSNBC.com, November 22nd, 2008.
9. Information regarding layoffs and unemployment are from the Bureau of Labor Statistics.
10. Ibid
11. Ibid
12. Ibid
13. The data regarding increase in applicants is from "Even in a recession, some companies are hiring," msnbc.msn.com, March 10th, 2009.
14. The survey of executives regarding staffing issues is titled "To Have and To Hold," with a headline of "Even in the current economy, employee retention still top concern, survey shows"; conducted by Robert Half International, December, 2008.
15. Marino, Ruggero. 2005. *Christopher Columbus, The Last Templar.* Rochester, VT: Destiny Books; "Christopher Columbus Discovers America, 1492," *www.eyewitnesstohistory.com,* accessed September 29, 2008; and "Christopher Columbus: The Facts vs. the Myth," *www.geocities.com/mutmainaa/history/columbus2.html,* accessed September 29, 2008.
16. Data presented from PricewaterhouseCooper's Saratoga Institute is from their report titled "Driving the Bottom Line: Improving Retention," 2006.

17. The reference to $25 billion to train replacements due to turnover is from "The Real Cost of Turnover" by Rudy Karsan, *Kenexa Connection* newsletter, Volume 6, Issue 3.
18. The reference to turnover reducing U.S. corporate earnings and stock prices by 38% is from research by Sibson & Company as reported in "Employee Turnover Rates & Employee Retention Statistics," *www.morebusiness.com*, October 12, 2000.

CHAPTER 3

1. Number of Americans turning 60 is from "Oldest Baby Boomers Turn 60!," U.S. Census Bureau, January 3, 2006.
2. Data regarding the aging workforce is from the BLS as quoted in SHRM's 2009 HR Trendbook.
3. 2007 birthrate information is from "U.S. births break baby boom record, topping 4.3 million; 40 pct of babies born out-of-wedlock," by Mike Stobbe, *AP Medical Writer*, March 19th, 2009.
4. 2006 birthrate information is from "A Second Baby Boom," *Time Magazine*, February 4, 2008.
5. Jobfox Top 25 Most Recession-Proof U.S. Job Candidates: October 2008.
6. The careerbuilder information is from "10 Recession-Proof Jobs" by Rachel Zupek, posted on careerbuilder.com, sourced April 8th, 2009; information clarified in a phone call with the author on April 8th, 2009.
7. The Laurence Shatkin interview appeared in "Where the Recession-Proof Jobs Are," by Barbara Kiviat, time.com, November 13th, 2008.
8. The jobs that will increase due to the stimulus plan is from "15 Jobs the Stimulus Plan May Boost" by Selena Dehne, careerbuilder.com, sourced April 8th, 2009.
9. BLS Unemployed persons by industry, class of worker, and sex, 2007 vs. 2008.
10. BLS 10-year projections are from Eric B. Figueroa and Rose A. Woods, "Industry Output and Employment Projections to 2016," *Monthly Labor Review*, November, 2007.
11. Healthcare job increase information is from "Health-care jobs brighten bleak labor-market picture" by Kristen gerencher, marketwatch, January 20th, 2009.
12. Healthcare concerns are from "Nursefinders Survey Identifies Top Challenges, Business Objectives for Healthcare Executives in 2007," *Nursefinders*, March 8, 2007.

13. Data regarding future nursing jobs and the number of nursing school graduates is from "Nursing industry desperate to find new hires," *Associated Press*, January 5th, 2009.

14. The data regarding nurse turnover is from the American Association of Colleges of Nursing Fact Sheet on Nursing Shortages, April 2008.

15. Nurse satisfaction data is from "Hospital Check-Up Report 2007," Press Ganey.

16. Study conducted by Peter Buerhaus as published in "Amid Nation's Recession, More Than 200,000 Nursing Jobs Go Unfilled," *Reuters*, March 9th, 2009.

17. Physician data is from "2007 Physician Retention Survey," supplemental edition, by AMGA and Cejka Search.

18. Pharmacist data is from "The Next Generation of Pharmacists," *Recruiting Trends*, February 20, 2008.

19. Stimulus Bill funds for healthcare are from "Amid Nation's Recession, More Than 200,000 Nursing Jobs Go Unfilled," *Reuters*, March 9th, 2009.

20. Information regarding most needed skills is from "Are They Really Ready to Work?", Society for Human Resources Management, the Conference Board, Partnership for 21st Century Skills, *Corporate Voices for Working Families*, 2006.

21. Ibid

22. Reading information is from "To Read or Not to Read," National Endowment for the Arts, November 19, 2007.

23. Comparative science scores are from "Pisa 2006 Results", OECD Programme for International Student Assessment; also reported in "Workforce Readiness and the New Essential Skills," Workplace Visions, Society for Human Resource Management, No. 2, 2008.

24. Information regarding more Americans attending school is from "America's Dynamic Workforce," U.S. Department of Labor, August, 2007.

25. Information regarding high-school dropouts is from Christopher B. Swanson, "Cities in Crisis, A Special Analytic Report on High School Graduation," research by Editorial Projects in Education, supported by America's Promise Alliance and the Bill & Melinda Gates Foundation.

26. College major information is from Digest of Education Statistics, U.S. Department of Education, sourced August 9, 2008.

27. Ibid #10

28. The "Why the gap?" quote and conclusion is from "Workforce Readiness and the New Essential Skills," Workplace Visions, Society for Human Resource Management, No. 2, 2008.

29. Post-layoff turnover information is from "Halting the Exodus After a Layoff," harvardbusiness.org, May, 2008.
30. The information regarding number of job boards is from "What Job Seekers Want From Job Boards," www.collegerecruiter.com, sourced October 13, 2008.
31. The information regarding personal videos and the information above it regarding social networks were sourced from "Creative Ways to Recruit," *Recruiting Trends*, February 11, 2008.
32. The information regarding earning referral awards from job boards is from "Tapping the Pool of Quality Candidates," *Recruiting Trends*, October 11, 2007.
33. The typical online job seeker profile is from WEDDLE'S Annual Source of Employment Survey, March 27, 2008.
34. The information regarding AT&T trying to return jobs to the United States is from "AT&T CEO Says Hard to Find Skilled U.S. Workers," www.reuters.com, March 26, 2008.
35. Information regarding young engineer work preferences is from "WANTED: Next generation of defense, space engineers" by Richard Burnett, OrlandoSentinel.com, August 21st, 2008.
36. The declining populations information is from "Incredible Shrinking Countries," The Economist, January 7, 2006.
37. Japan's declining population is noted in "The Downturn," *The Economist*, January 7, 2006.
38. Information regarding the doubling number of retirees is from Testimony of NCPA President John C. Goodman before the House Ways and Means Committee, RetirementReform.org, sourced August 2, 2008.
39. The information regarding Alberta, Canada is from "Opportunity Knocks in Canada," *USA Today*, September 17, 2008.
40. The Saskatchewan information is from "Sask. Sees recession as opportunity to lure workers," ctv.ca, March 1st, 2009.
41. The quote from Canada Prime Minister Stephen Harper is from "Canada will face labour shortage after recession: Harper," The Canadian Press, March 13th, 2009.
42. The information regarding Canada's declining workforce is from "Despite recession, looming labour shortage big threat," *Canwest News Service*, February 16th, 2009.
43. The information from Indians returning home to work is from "Indian Professionals Return Home as Economy Booms," www.voanews.com, October 8, 2007.

44. The information regarding the Chinese government's effort to bring workers home is from "National Foundation to Help Overseas-Educated Chinese Return Home," China.org.cn, April 10, 2007.

45. The data regarding the number of Chinese who wish to return home is from "Most Chinese Students Abroad Wish to Return Home to Work," *People's Daily Online*, December 17, 2004.

46. The data regarding the impact of the U.S. dollar on manufacturing is from "Weak Dollar Adds Twist to 'Made in America,'" *Marketwatch*, December 17, 2007.

47. The data regarding transport costs is from "Transport Costs Could Alter World Trade," *USA Today*, August 12, 2008.

48. The information regarding states re-hiring reitrees is from "States Eye Cycle of Retiring, Rehiring," *USA Today*, July 17, 2008.

49. The travel nursing information is from "Travel Nursing Moves Mainstream," *Recruiting Trends*, sourced October 11, 2007.

50. The retention ideas of Sam Panarella were obtained during a phone interview with, July 29 2008.

CHAPTER 4

1. The data regarding employee value propositions is from the Corporate Leadership Council's Employment Value Proposition Survey, quoted in "Employment Branding: The Candidate Experience," in the Human Capital Institute's white paper, August 6, 2007.

2. The data regarding the most important three attributes is from the Corporate Leadership Council's Employment Value Proposition Survey, quoted in "Becoming an Employer of Choice" by Kathy Haake, APPA National Conference, June 25, 2007.

3. The small business advantages information is from "The Top Five Retention Strategies for Small Businesses," Salary.com, 2006.

4. You can access the Texas Instruments homepage at *www.ti.com*.

5. You can access the Herman Miller homepage at *www.hermanmiller.com*.

6. You can access the General Mills homepage at *www.generalmills.com/corporate/index.aspx*.

7. You can access the eBay homepage at *www.ebay.com*.

8. You can access the Children's Healthcare of Atlanta homepage at *www.choa.org*.

9. You can access Stew Leonard's homepage at *www.stewleonards.com*.

10. You can access Southwest Airline's homepage at *www.southwest.com*.

11. You can access the Quicken Loans' homepage at *www.quickenloans.com*.

12. You can access Macy's homepage at *www.macys.com.*
13. You can access Delta's homepage at *www.delta.com.*
14. You can access Publix's homepage at *www.publix.com.*
15. You can access Barnes & Noble's homepage at *www.barnesand noble.com.*
16. You can access Borders' homepage at *www.borders.com/online/store/ Home.*
17. I learned this originally by talking with a cab driver in Las Vegas in November 2007, and confirmed benefit details in a phone interview with Brent Bell, executive with Whittlesea Blue Cab and Henderson Taxi, on August 21, 2008.
18. PETCO information is from a phone interview with Charlie Piscitello, PETCO senior vice president and chief people officer, August 29, 2008.
19. HealthONE information is from a phone interview with Roger Smith, vice president of human resources for HCA-HealthOne, August 26, 2008.
20. Data regarding concierge services is from "Employee Perks That Pamper," Associated Press, published in the *Orlando Sentinel,* November 21, 2007.
21. Information regarding the New York City Department of Education is from *Staffing Management News,* Society for Human Resources Management, August 2007.
22. Information regarding repaying college loans is from "College Loan Payments Boost Recruitment, Retention," SHRM online, accessed May 18, 2007.
23. Language training information is from "I Say Potato, You Say Patata," *HR Magazine,* January 2004.
24. Information regarding the Fortune Top 100 application number is from *money.cnn.com/magazines/fortune/bestcompanies/2008/full_list/index .html.*
25. Information regarding the SHRM application number is from "Nation's Best Employers Revealed" in the press release "Society for Human Resource Management 50 Best Small & Medium Companies to Work for in America," June 23, 2008.
26. Southern Progress information is from a phone interview with Carole Cain, Southern Progress Corporation, July 29, 2008.
27. Hard Rock information is from a phone interview with Jim Knight, Hard Rock, August 28, 2008. Additional information was gathered on a visit to their headquarters.
28. Phone meeting with Mary Deatrick representing Rosen Hotels, August 27, 2008.

29. Magellan International information is from a phone interview with Jonathan Phillips, July 16, 2008.

CHAPTER 5

1. The Yahoo reference is from "What Managers Want for 2008: A New Boss!" Yahoo! HotJobs, accessed August 25, 2008.
2. The Florida State University research is from "Who's Afraid of the Big Bad Boss? Plenty of Us, New FSU Study Shows," *Florida State University News*, August 25, 2008.
3. The information on retention in China is from "Employee Retention in China 2006–2007—The Flight of Human Talent," published by SHRM and DDI, January 1, 2008.
4. The Salary.com study is "Employee Job Satisfaction & Retention Survey 2006–2007."
5. The information regarding why employees join versus stay is from "The Tides of Talent" by Craig R. Taylor, *T & D Magazine*, April 2003.
6. The information on the power of employees staying for their supervisors is from "Retention Corner" by Richard P. Finnegan, *Recruiting Trends*, May 22, 2007.
7. The Saratoga Institute study is from "Hint: If You're a New Manager, It's Not All About You," *www.shrm.org*, accessed February 11, 2008.
8. The information regarding teacher retention is from "Study: School Systems Testing New Teacher Retention Strategies," *SHRM Staffing Management News*, August 2007.
9. The Kenexa research is from "Should I Stay or Should I Go?" *Kenexa Research Institute Employee Insight Report, No. 16.*
10. The Maslow reference is from "Maslow Hierarchy of Needs," *www.abraham-maslow.com*, accessed August 28, 2008.
11. The supermarket information is from "New Ideas for Retaining Store-Level Employees," Coca-Cola Retailing Research Council, 2000.
12. The data regarding states proposing anti-bully legislation is from the Workplace Bullying Institute, *www.bullyinginstitute.org*, accessed August 31, 2008.
13. The data regarding the prevalence of bullies is from "Bullies Beware: Employees Have More Options—Including Court—to Confront Bad Bosses," *Boston Business Journal*, August 15, 2008.
14. The NIOSH study is from "While Some Employers Address Bullying Few Work Policies, No Laws Currently Exist," Workplace Bullying Institute, *www.bullyinginstitute.org*, accessed August 25 2008.

CHAPTER 6

1. The reference to Professor Edward Lorenz is from *http://crossgroup. caltech.edu/chaos_new/Lorenz.html.*
2. The Monster.com study that recommends supervisors be held accountable for retention is from "Retention Strategies for 2006 and Beyond," Monster Intelligence, Winter 2006.
3. The data regarding the prevalence and cost of teacher turnover is from "Study: School Systems Testing New Teacher Retention Strategies," *SHRM Staffing Management News*, August 2007.
4. The recommendation to amend NCLB is from "The Cost of Teacher Turnover in Five School Districts," National Commission on Teaching and America's Future.
5. The recommendation to hold nurse managers accountable for retention is from "Hardwiring Right Retention," The Advisory Board, 2001.
6. The Wegmans information is from a phone interview with Karen Shadders, Wegmans, June 18, 2008.
7. The information from Chuck Moore is from a phone interview on July 14, 2008.

CHAPTER 7

1. The information from the Florida State University study is from "Bad Bosses—More Than Bad Salaries—Drive Workers Away," *http://shrm. org/hrnews*, accessed January 11 2007.
2. The loyalty information is from "Loyalty in the Workplace," Walker Information, September 2007.
3. The trust study is from "Trust Factors at Work," Pennington Performance Group, 2004.
4. The reference to the trust index is from "The Trust Index," Great Place to Work Institute, *www.greatplacetowork.com/best/trust-index.php.*
5. The information from DaVita is from "Execs Who Build Truth-Telling Cultures Learn Fast," *The Wall Street Journal*, June 12, 2006.
6. The quote from the Great Place to Work Institute can be accessed at *www.greatplacetowork.com/great/model.php.*

CHAPTER 8

1. This data comes via two sources: the information regarding $11 billion spending and half using the Internet is from a study conducted by

Research and Markets as quoted in *Workforce Management*, April 29, 2008, and the reference to Fortune 500 companies is from "Driving Job Seekers to Your Corporate Web Site," *http://shrm.org*, accessed on July 29, 2008.

2. The data regarding Googling candidates is from "Online Networks Can Enhance Job Searches," *http://shrm.org*, accessed July 29, 2008.

3. The PetSmart reference is from "Realistic Job Preview: A Review of the Literature and Recommendations for Michigan Family Independence Agency," CPS Human Resource Services, June 17, 2004.

4. The Sheetz information is based on a phone interview with Earl Springer of Sheetz conducted on September 11, 2008.

5. The note about the 2012 workforce is from "Labor Force Projections to 2012: The Graying of the U.S. Workforce," *Monthly Labor Review* (online), February 2004.

6. Two studies that indicate older workers will continue to work are "Courting Senior Workers," Staffing Management, *http://shrm.org*, July 9, 2005, which references "Staying Ahead of the Curve: The AARP Working and Retirement Study," and "Successfully Leveraging Older Workers," SHRM white paper, June 2007.

7. The information from older workers delaying retirement is from "Six-in-Ten Workers Over the Age of Sixty Postponing Retirement Due to Economic Downturn, Finds CareerBuilder Survey," careerbuilder.com, March 17th, 2009

8. References to nurses and nuclear power workers are from "Companies Optimistic on Retaining Older Workers," *http://shrm.org*, May 15, 2006.

9. The National Council on Aging reference is from "Attracting and Retaining the Mature Workforce," *http://shrm.org*, accessed October 15, 2008.

10. The *BusinessWeek* reference is taken from "Old. Smart. Productive." *www.businessweek.com*, June 27, 2005.

11. The study regarding the slight increase in employing older workers is from "The Business Case for Workers Age 50 + ," a report for AARP prepared by Towers Perrin, December 2005.

12. The reference to refugees is from "Refugees to the Rescue," *HR Magazine*, November 2000.

13. The reference to structured interviews is from "Using Structured Interviews to Increase Your Organization's Hiring Investments," *SHRM Research*, October 2006.

14. The reference to Houston employers using employee referrals is from "Do Employee Referral Programs Really Work?" SHRM white paper, September 2000, reviewed again June 2002.

15. The reference to AmeriCredit's employee referral program is from "Referral Programs That Result in Great Hiring and Retention," SHRM Staffing Management Library, accessed January 16, 2008.
16. The reference to Coffee Bean & Tea Leaf is from "Coffee Bean & Tea Leaf Finds Fun Is the Key to Retention," *Nation's Restaurant News*, October 9, 2006.
17. The reference to Badger Mining is from "The Top 25 Best Small Companies to Work for in America," *HR Magazine*, July 2008.
18. The reference to the Greater Rochester YMCA is from "Nonprofits Urged to Hire Older Workers, Boost Talent," *http://shrm.org*, June 6, 2007.
19. The reference to Borders is from "Courting Senior Workers," *Staffing Magazine*, July–September 2005.
20. The information presented from Destination Hotels & Resorts was gathered from a phone interview with Robert Mellwig on August 6, 2008.
21. The information from OIX Trucking was gathered from a phone interview with Jeff Lamble on July 25, 2008.
22. The information presented regarding MITRE was gathered from phone interviews and e-mails with Gary Cluff completed on July 30, 2008.
23. "The Business Case for Workers Age 50 + ," a report for AARP prepared by Towers Perrin, December 2005.

CHAPTER 9

1. The Walker reference is from "Loyalty Report," executive summary, Walker Information, September 2007.
2. The Sirota reference is from "Boomers, Gen-Yers Agree: It's All About Respect," *www.theglobeandmail.com*, January 24, 2007.
3. Watkins, Michael. 2003. *The First 90 Days: Critical Success Strategies for New Leaders at All Levels.* Boston: Harvard Business School Press.
4. The reference to spouses is from "In Sickness, Health, or Job Change," *www.accountemps.com*, January 8, 2008.
5. The references to Corning Glass and other organizations is from "How to Avoid the Four Deadliest Onboarding Mistakes," *www.ere.net*, November 22, 2005.
6. The reference to Intel is from "Virtual Mentoring," *HR Magazine*, March 2006.
7. The Whole Foods Market reference is based on a phone interview with Paula Labian on September 11, 2008.
8. The Wyndham Vacation Ownership reference is based on a phone interview with Barry Ogle on August 29, 2008.

CHAPTER 10

1. The reference to the small amount of merit increases that are actually based on merit is from "2006–2007 WorldatWork Salary Budget Survey," as quoted in "Role of Base Pay in Employee Retention," *http://vurv.com.*

2. The reference to aligning pay for performance is from "Out of Touch: Towers Perrin Survey Shows Rewards Seldom Aligned with Business Strategy," *www.proxy.library.upenn.edu,* accessed March 10, 2008.

3. The reference to stock ownership increasing longevity is from "Effects of ESOP Adoption and Employee Ownership: Thirty Years of Research and Experience," Organizational Dynamics Working Papers, Penn Libraries.

4. The reference to nonprofit pay is from "Is Mission Attachment an Effective Management Tool for Employee Retention?" *Review of Public Personnel Administration,* September 2007, as cited in EBSCO Host research databases.

5. The reference to employees preferring additional health care coverage versus taxable income is from "2007 Health Confidence Survey: Rising Health Care Costs Are Changing the Ways Americans Use the Health Care System," EBRI Notes, *www.ebri.org,* November 2007.

6. The statistics regarding flexible scheduling are from the 2007 SHRM Benefits Survey.

7. The reference to the need for work–life balance for all is from "The New Workforce Reality," a study by the Simmons School of Management and Bright Horizons Family Solutions, Inc., referenced in "Executive Briefing, Young Boomer Executives May Need Financial Education; Men Want Work/Life Balance, Too."

8. The reference regarding perceived favorable treatment for employees with families is from "Are You Too Family Friendly?" *HR Magazine,* October 2007.

9. The reference to Bureau of Labor Statistics research for part-time employees is from "Employee Benefits in Private Industry, 2007," August 22, 2007.

10. The reference to part-time pay is from "Compensation in Part-Time Jobs Versus Full-Time Jobs: What If the Job Is the Same?" BLS Working Papers, December 1994.

11. The reference to in-office workers having potentially higher turnover is from "Telecommuting May Harm Workers Left Behind in the Office," Rensselaer Polytechnic Institute, January 9, 2008.

12. The reference to ways employees learn is from Michael Lombardo and Robert Eichinger, *For Your Improvement: A Developmental Coaching Guide* (Lominger Limited, 1996).

13. The information regarding Pacific Service Credit Union was first published in "Money Talks," *HR Magazine*, July 2005. This information was later confirmed via an e-mail from a Pacific Service Credit Union executive on October 8, 2008.

14. The references to McDonald's and Costco are both from "Red-Carpet Treatment," *Staffing Management*, October–December 2007.

15. The reference to Yahoo is from "Attracting and Retaining Employees with Total Reward Statements: The Yahoo Way," *Workspan*, October 2006.

16. The Watson Wyatt study is referenced in "Communication Plays Critical Role in Improving Retention Power of Health Benefits," *www.world atwork.org*, February 23, 2005.

17. The references to Best Buy, IBM, and Sun Microsystems are from "Clocking Out," *HR Magazine*, June 2007.

18. The references to Alpine Access, LiveOps, JetBlue, and PHH Arval are from "Call Centers Come Home," *HR Magazine*, January 2007.

19. The reference to Mojo Interactive is from a phone interview with Ron Fischer on August 29, 2008.

20. The reference to American Door & Millwork is from an onsite visit there hosted by John Bartley on March 24, 2008.

21. The ESOP Association can be reached at *www.esopassociation.org*.

22. The reference to Harrisburg University of Science and Technology is from a phone interview with Eric Darr on March 25, 2008.

CHAPTER 11

1. The hotel cost figure came from the model presented in "Development and Use of a Web-Based Tool to Measure the Costs of Employee Turnover" by Timothy R. Hinkin and J. Bruce Tracey, The Center for Hospitality Research, Cornell University, *CHR Reports*, May 2006.

2. The quote from Professors Robert Hurley and Hooman Estelami is from their article "An Exploratory Study of Employee Turnover Indicators as Predictors of Customer Satisfaction," *Journal of Services Marketing*, Volume 21, Number 3, 2007.

3. The supermarket information is from "New Ideas for Retaining Store-Level Employees," Coca-Cola Retailing Research Council, 2000.

4. The reference to brokerage turnover is from Frederick F. Reichheld, *The Loyalty Effect* (Boston: Harvard Business School Press, 1996).

5. The example of a major hotel chain is from "Sitting on a Gold Mine" by Jude T. Rich, *WorldatWork Journal*, Second quarter, 2002.

6. The reference to a 5% increase in employee retention is from "Greener Pastures," *Training*, November 2001.

7. The reference to the organization with 10,000 employees is from "Lessons from the Selection Forecast: You Can Attract and Retain the Best Candidates (Part 2 of 4)," *DDI Directions*, January 19, 2005.

8. The retail store reference is from "Sitting on a Gold Mine" by Jude T. Rich, *WorldatWork Journal*, Second quarter, 2002.

9. The reference regarding turnover costing 12% of pretax income is from "Driving the Bottom Line: Improving Retention," Saratoga Institute, PricewaterhouseCoopers, 2006.

10. The reference regarding 30-day mortality rates is from *The Journal of the American Medical Association* as referenced in *Workforce Week*, October 27–November 2, 2002.

11. The study regarding hospitals with low turnover is from "Health Care at the Crossroads," published by the Joint Commission on Accreditation of Healthcare Organizations.

12. The reference to Taco Bell is from Frederick F. Reichheld, *The Loyalty Effect* (Boston: Harvard Business School Press, 1996).

13. The reference to call center turnover's cost is from "Manage Turnover to Boost Retention," *Contact Professional*, January/February 2003.

14. The reference to 33% of U.S. organizations placing a cost on turnover is from Monster.com's "Retention Strategies for 2006 and Beyond," as referenced in "Many Executives Don't Share HR Concerns on Retention," *http://shrm.org*, February 1, 2006.

15. The reference to 18% of organizations globally that place a cost on turnover is from "Playing to Win in a Global Economy," published by Watson Wyatt and WorldatWork, 2007/2008.

CHAPTER 12

1. All data in "Connecting Executive Compensation to Retention Is Increasing" is from "Keeping Workers Earns a Bonus in Some Offices," *www.wsj.com*, accessed June 30, 2008.

CONCLUSION

1. "Former Housemates John Mackey and Kip Tindell Talk about Poker, Retailing, and the Limitations of Shareholder Capitalism," *www.time.com/time/blogs*, June 26, 2008.

2. Ibid.

Index

supervisor(s): accountability for retention goals, 13, 26–29, 113–125, 230–231, 241; brand support by, 80; bullying by, 109; company examples of, 108–110; connecting with employees, 105–106; critical knowledge sharing by, 107; dislike of, 101, 127–128; employee referral goals for, 148; employee's self-assessments, 35; feedback solicitation by, 180; guidance by, 107; human resources' support for, 233–234; ineffective, 127–128, 233; language training for, 92–93; as leave reasons, 102–103; new hires assigned to, 173; nontrusted, 136–138; personal support from, 105; promotion of, 122; questioning of new hires by, 178–180; relationship building by, 13, 23–25, 99–111; removal of, 233; retention power of, 25, 100–104; rewarding of, 122; selection tools for, 159; self-assessments, 111; skills for retention, 104–108; stay decisions of employees affected by, 101–102; strategies used by, 28; studies regarding, 101–102; tracking of new hires by, 173; training by, 204; trust building with teams, 14, 29–31, 127–141; turnover caused by, 103; unconditional personal support from, 105
Suszko, Mary, 33
symbols, 95–96

T
Taco Bell, 223
teacher turnover, 103–104, 114

teams: new hire involvement in, 169; nontraditional-schedule employees' participation in, 196; telecommuters, 201; trust building with, 14, 29–31, 127–141
technology, 201–202, 245
telecommuters, 38, 200–202
termination, 205
Texas Instruments, 81
TheRetentionFirm.com, 216
Thiry, Ken, 139–140
Tindell, Kip, 246–247
top-down support, 14–15, 42–44, 121, 227–239, 243–244
TopMark LLC sales calculator, 217
top-performing employees: applicant meeting with, 153; recognition of, 59; retention of, 22, 57–65
training: of new hires, 198; of part-time employees, 199; of telecommuters, 201
travel, 196
travel nurses, 69
Trevor, Charlie, 57
Trincon Group, 219
trust: behaviors and, 31, 129–132, 141, 230–231; company examples of, 139–140; personal, 30; reflection on, 133–134; surveys about, 138; turnover affected by level of, 138
trust building: character and, 131; communication and, 129; competence and, 130; consistency and, 130–131; courage and, 131–132; employee value propositions and, 133; importance of, 29–30, 38, 233; opportunities for, 134; promotion of, 242; retention through, 104; skills for, 132–135; summary of, 140–141; by supervisors, 14, 29–31; with